HN   HICKEN, VICTOR
65   The World is Coming
H47   to an End!

THE WORLD IS COMING TO AN END!

"Well, he certainly __eats__ like there's no tomorrow."

THE WORLD IS COMING TO AN END !

An Irreverent Look at Modern Doomsayers

Victor Hicken

ARLINGTON HOUSE PUBLISHERS   New Rochelle, N.Y.

Library of Congress Cataloging in Publication Data

Hicken, Victor, 1921-
    The world is coming to an end!

    Bibliography: p. 208-212
    Includes index.
    1. United States—Social conditions—1960-
2. Radicalism—United States. 3. Conflict of generations. I. Title.
HN65.H47   309.1'73'092   74-28181
ISBN 0-87000-303-8

To those dedicated university instructors who taught what they were employed to teach during the 1960s—individuals who, because of their dedication to principles and scholarship, remained as apolitical as it was possible for them to be.

Contents

Foreword 11
1 Roots Far and Wide 14
2 The Ancient and Modern Art of Doomsaying 40
3 Rhetoric on the Campus 64
4 The Education of the University Establishment 87
5 The Intellectual-Media Establishment 103
6 The Underground Press and Days of Doom 125
7 Two Presidents and Middle America 145
8 Rhetoric and Causes in the Sixties 163
Epilogue 188
Notes 191
Bibliography 208
Index 213

THE WORLD IS COMING TO AN END !

THE WORLD IS COMING TO AN END !

Foreword

Nations do not grope toward a known destiny. As in the case of most humans, they merely struggle to achieve the only really attainable goal, which is survival. In the instance of the United States, the most favorable conditions in which the country has prospered and grown have also allowed for the establishment of two secondary benefits—a great material prosperity and the ultimate in personal freedom.

The struggle for survival, as well as the attempt to achieve these secondary goals, has been the basis for the emergence and existence of America's two major political parties. It does very little good here to describe one of the parties as liberal or the other as conservative in their approach to issues. The very words "liberal" and "conservative" lose their meaning when measured against the milestones of history. Some Republicans say, for example, that it is wrong to place the power to manage society so much in the hands of the federal government. Yet, over a hundred years ago, it was the Republican Party which managed the Northern effort in the Civil War; a conflict which, as Carl Sandburg used to say, determined whether we should use the phrase "the United States is" rather than "the United States are." Democrats on the other hand sometimes espouse the principle of using federal power to end what they consider to be the wrongs of society. About 180 years ago, when the Jeffersonian party was being organized, the philosophy of its founders was in direct antithesis to the present tenets of "liberalism."

In a sense then, what happens is that principles and philosophies become obscured. Political parties in the United States, as in any other democratic nation in the world, become caught up in the much less noble goal of achieving and keeping power. And since, as Gilbert and Sullivan once implied, every little girl and boy born alive is either a liberal or a conservative, then virtually every American, one way or another, is caught up in that struggle for power.

This is a long way from the principal aim of surviving from one decade to the next. And since it involves more elemental passions, it also evokes instincts among men which are among the least admirable and yet most human symptoms of the human condition. Among these are rhetoric and paranoia.

In the sense that it is used here, rhetoric might be defined as exaggeration in all forms of oral and written communication. Paranoia, as it is used here, may be defined as a kind of popular psychosis most characterized by delusions of grandeur and persecution. Both rhetoric and paranoia, in a political sense, tend to walk together as companions—each attempting to express itself with logic and reason, and each failing to do so.

Both are stimulated by the stress of traumatic events. For the United States in the 1960s there was a multitude of these, some of which, like the assassinations of the two Kennedys and Martin Luther King, were of dramatic immediate significance. Two other developments of a more evolutionary progression were the Vietnam War and the extension of the age of affluence. The last two, products of an attempt by the nation to provide both guns and butter, were probably most responsible for the stimulation of rhetoric and paranoia in the 1960s.

From 1972 to 1974, which years really represent the ending of the decade of the Sixties, the months were marked with milestones of surpassing significance. President Nixon all but annihilated his Democratic opponent in the 1972 election, which event was followed with the breaking of the so-called Watergate scandal. The newly reelected President seemed to lose his popular majority almost immediately, and there was an avalanche of stories involving electronic eavesdropping, political dirty tricks and sabotage, and alleged administration-directed burglaries.

It is of little service now to argue that all of these have probably been done in previous years—by Democrats as well as Republicans. Perhaps it would be far better to look at the 1960s and early 1970s to see what was happening then in terms of rhetoric and paranoia, and to try to comprehend whether Watergate and related events were parts of a long chain of circumstances. After all, from the time of its inauguration in 1969, the Nixon administration was forced to contend with agency and department leaks of major significance. Washington is basically a Democratic city, and the electronic copier made such leaks not only inevitable but easy. But most of all, President Nixon, in winding down but not breaking the line of American policy, was the object of an incredible torrent of radical and liberal rhetoric and paranoia.

President Nixon will stand permanently flawed in the annals of history. Yet it is interesting to attempt to imagine another individual in the presidency during the years from 1969 to 1973. Would any other individual operating in the same milieu and political environment have reacted any differently? Was President Nixon very simply a human being who responded in a most elemental manner to the paranoia and rhetoric of his times?

1
Roots Far and Wide

Long before the last minute of the last day of the 1960s had ticked away, the people of America knew that this decade had provided among the best of times and the worst of times. Few other eras had so sorely tried that nation's will and spirit. Few periods in the national past had seen such an apparent exhaustion of the American well-spring of optimism.

For one who might have evaded the violence and accomplishments of the decade, and there were both, it would have been difficult for him to distinguish clearly what had happened to America over that span of time. Some ten-year space traveler, or an Enoch Arden lost in some remote island paradise, might actually have seen little obvious change in the life of the people. Returning American prisoners from Vietnam in 1972, some of whom were imprisoned for as long as eight years, saw no profound changed upon their return; excepting, of course, those having to do with modes and styles among the young.[1]

It all depended upon where one was in 1973 or 1974. Relaxing in the golden circumambience of a Michigan summer or fishing in the clear lakes of the Gunflint Trail in Minnesota offered little in the way of insights into the 1960s. Brilliant spinnakers bursting forth any summer's day on New York's Finger Lakes gave no contrast to a picture of what the country had been like ten years before. Throughout the land, the same unrevealing vistas could be seen. Bayou towns of the Louisiana Delta, lazing away the hours in the fragrant dank of the Spring highwater, provided no insights. On Cape Cod, the playground of New England exurbanites, one could still find remembrances of Henry David Thoreau in the salt marshes—even if he was forced to motor to them past increasing numbers of hamburger stands and "leaning towers of Pizza." And, far out in the Grand Tetons, the tourist could watch the mountains emerge at dawn in a kind of pink and white auroral splendor.

In fact, in 1973 it was possible to witness a kind of renaissance. It was a proving out of the old French adage: *"Le plus ça change, le plus c'est la même chose!"*[2] Some suburban schools in the New York City area were once again teaching middle-class white students the intricacies of the Charleston and the Lindy Hop. Nostalgia was in vogue: the past in full blossom. One television program, "The Waltons," had managed to drive a successful black comedian from his usual time slot. Despite some rather frantic protestations from *New Yorker* critic Pauline Kael, this family show—with its emphasis upon grace under pressure, homely virtues, and the Protestant Ethic—seemed to be successful because it was emphasizing all that had been derided in the previous ten years. At least, it was some considerable distance from one of the more popular television shows of 1963, "The Beverly Hillbillies," which mocked the same mountain folk idealized by "The Waltons."[3]

In truth, however, what had happened during the thirteen years from 1960 to 1973 was almost too difficult to comprehend. There had been brushes with atomic warfare, the assassinations of one president and one candidate for the presidency, and the grievous wounding of another candidate. A noted civil rights leader had been murdered, and there had been a long conventional war which had stretched the nation beyond the sacrifices needed for the winning of it. There had been, between 1963 and 1968, some 369 civil rights disturbances, 104 antiwar demonstrations, 91 student protests on campus issues, 239 Negro riots and disturbances, 213 incidents of white terrorism against Negroes and rights workers, an uncounted number of attacks by blacks against whites, and hundreds of other types of evidence of unrest. And those figures only included five years in the middle of the decade. What was to happen in 1970 alone would stretch even beyond these figures.[4]

Although, as historian William E. Leuchtenburg has pointed out, the violence in the United States in the 1960s never approached the levels of Stalinist Russia, it was all very disturbing and seemed at times to threaten the very future of the great republic.[5] Looking back from the comfort and security of 1974, it might be said that the events of the decade were peripheral to the sentiments of the nation as a whole. The avalanche of votes for Richard Nixon in 1972 was in part a rejection en masse of the tactics of the revolutionaries, their wild rhetoric, and their philosophies. That election may not have proved the popularity of the incumbent President, but it certainly proved that the nation was not ready for the changes offered up by the American radical left.

The revolution of the radicals, or the *movement* as it will henceforth be termed, had so many facets to it that even now it is difficult to dissect and analyze. Perhaps it can best be considered as analogous to a flood, rushing across the countryside here and forming little cul de sacs there; moving into areas of little opposition on one hand, and quickly creating fronts in sections of the nation in which opposition did hold fast. The movement was contradictory, evanescent, willful, predictable, and unpredictable. It rushed to support one leader after another, only to desert each upon finding another with more palpable possibilities of success.

It was anti-Vietnam War, though some of its more admired heroes showed a strong pro-Israeli bias during the Yom Kippur War of 1973.[6] It was theoretically pro-ecology, though in 1973 members of the movement who were still active were to blame American oil companies for not having drilled more wells and pumped more oil in order to meet the gasoline shortage. It was antiauthoritarian; yet, it sought to gather power unto itself. It was anticapitalism, but more than a few members of the movement were quick to seize upon business opportunities created by the drug, trinket, and underground newspaper mania.

What were the circumstances which gave impetus to the movement? What caused the revolt against authority, so vicious at times that faculty members at some universities were afraid for the lives of themselves and of their families? Not a few historians, psychiatrists, and others have made studied guesses concerning the enigma. Historian David Potter has stressed the relationship between the economy of abundance in American life and the cultivation of a system of education which defers maturity among the young. University of Chicago psychiatrist Bruno Bettelheim has convincingly argued that the rebelliousness of the 1960s came from American society's persistence in keeping the young too long in dependence. William Leuchtenburg seems to lay the causes of the movement to affluence, the Vietnam War, and a host of other factors. A more recent article in the *Manchester Guardian*, which applauded almost every demonstration of the movement in America while it viewed similar acts in Britain proper with mild alarm, stated that the protests against authority were hatched in the "optimistic age" of contemporary alienation. For whatever that judgment implies, the *Guardian* ploughs on to contend that such issues as the Vietnam War and other stresses of the "youth culture" spurred the impetus of that alienation.[7]

It almost goes without saying that books, theses, doctoral dissertations, and articles upon the subject of the movement will in time overlay the current decade like an avalanche. No one disputation may be wholly right: few will be wholly wrong. One can, for instance, draw a logical and appropriate comparison between the movement of the 1960s and the *Burschenschaften* crusades of the post-Napoleonic era. Then, German student groups pressed for the creation of a new society in which morality and devotion to intellectual concerns were theoretically to parallel devotion to the nation. There was, in truth, a maudlin sentimentality among the Burschenschaften which is easily identifiable to the sickening sentimentality of the 1960s. Goethe's Werther, a fictionalized romantic, became the ideal of the post-Napoleonic period, and there is indeed some similarity between his behavior and some student protesters of the 1960s. Werther travels freely, he dresses as he pleases, and in the end he kills himself over hopeless love. But most of all, Werther was an exemplification of Goethe's notion that "feeling is everything"—a concept that is easily noted in the 1960s, even in beer commercials which advised youth that "you only go around once. . . ."

In considering the 1960s, it is important to remember that most history textbooks are written by individuals whose inclinations are politically liberal. Not a few such literary efforts handle the Johnson-Goldwater election of 1964, for instance, as one colored by "dirty-tricks" activities of such supposedly right-wing groups as the Ku Klux Klan and the John Birch Society. Little if any reference is made to those scurrilous television commercials which were produced by the Democratic campaign organization, and which exploited the national fear of atomic warfare. Another incident which receives interesting treatment by many of these historians is the My Lai massacre. Few, if any of the newer histories properly establish the date of the event as 1968—a full year before Richard M. Nixon was inaugurated as President of the United States.

Yet in the covering of isolated issues relating to the student unrest and the counterculture of the 1960s, the new history produces some startling coincidences. Even the most liberal historians approach the development of the movement with a sort of vengeance. William Leuchtenburg's presentation of a rationale for the movement, for instance, is not too far removed from that of Bettelheim, who, when he first voiced his opinions in the 1960s, was considered as conservative. Leuchtenburg treats the subject of the "greening of America" with all of the finesse of a man who has been close to the fire and has

17

found it to be hot. He recognizes that the movement rejected "systematized knowledge," that it was based upon the curious flaw of "radical truth," and that there was a broad streak of irrationality seemingly inherent in the crusade. Furthermore, he appears to recognize that much of the "nobility" of the movement was a product of self-description, and that there were dangers present which seemed to transcend one's capacity to speak openly about them in the 1960s. In other words, one senses that a significant part of the movement had very little at all to do with the extension of democracy.[8]

Just as the Napoleonic era was the ultimate result of the overstatement of the enlightenment, so was the movement the product of the liberalism of the 1960s. Therein lies the great dilemma of the contemporary liberal historian—the conflict between his instinctive loyalty to the liberal credo, and the sure knowledge that if the movement had succeeded, he would have been among the first to go to the wall. The movement, which was born from the womb of twentieth-century American liberalism, was not really liberal in the accepted meaning of the word. And, in the end, it was the realization of this flaw which tore fundamental and orthodox liberalism from the movement, and which caused the movement in turn to attack liberals. It wasn't difficult for the liberal college history teacher to catch up on the ABC's of revolution—once his classroom was invaded or a bomb was placed in the proximity of his family. And, it must be hastily added, the fatal flaw in academic liberalism was too often exposed to the light of day by those aspects of teaching dearest to an instructor's heart —the effect of the movement upon his paycheck, and the unforeseen invasions of his classroom privacy brought on by the movement.

In the end it was the knowledgable classroom instructor who realized that the left did not merely mean to change the system; it meant to destroy the true essence of liberalism. This possibility appeared, at least for a moment in the 1960s, as one of the real achievements of the movement. True liberals are, after all, quite vulnerable—especially in the philosophic protection of radicalism even to the point of their own extinction. This, one supposes, is what brought about a recanting of the movement by such men as Paul Goodman. Even though Brigitte and Paul Berger had offered assurances that the rhetoric of the movement was "Rousseauean rather than Jacobin," and that the children of the revolution were "but naked children of nature dancing to the tune of primitive drums," the intuitive liberal could see that beneath it all was the remainder of the iceberg.[9]

After all, there was an implicit and explicit violence to be found in every aspect of the revolution. From January 1969 to October 1970, a period which marks the high tide of the movement, there were over 370 bombings in New York City alone. This element in the greening of America amounted to one explosion every other day in Fun City.[10] These acts were part of the culmination of the violence of the 1960s and, in this respect, it must be pointed out that too few of the "new" histories point this out. One example of this is *The National Experience*, a text edited by such prominent historians as Arthur M. Schlesinger, Jr., and C. Vann Woodward.* After reading their presentation of violence in the 1960s one could be given the impression that it began on the day of President Nixon's first inauguration.[11]

The evolution of the liberal interpretation of events during the Sixties is startling when one truly comprehends the mutations which really occurred. Eugene McCarthy, writing on the conscience of an American liberal in 1960, was actually describing the parameters of what was soon to become an old-fashioned early twentieth-century New Deal philosophy of society. To McCarthy, the liberal of 1960 was a person given to "more subtle or sophisticated explanations. . . ." The true liberal in McCarthy's eyes was characteristically an optimist— "not blindly so as one who fails to understand . . . but rather as one . . . who remains hopefully confident that improvement and progress can be accomplished."[12]

McCarthy's definition of liberalism was soon to be outdated. In fact, McCarthy as a candidate in 1968 did not always exude optimism, nor did he always offer "subtle or sophisticated explanations. . . ." Before the decade was finished, his type of liberalism had been forced into a most unenviable position, primarily because of its position on the civil rights issue in the early 1960s, and later because of argumentation upon the propriety of the Vietnam War. The change was a vital one, and it came with the acceptance of the notion that one could safely defy the law if he felt that it violated his own personal interpretation of morality. Once acceded to, even if only in part by the liberals, it took but one giant step to move into the great urban riots of the 1960s and into antiestablishment violence of the same period. It meant that any minority, no matter how small, had an exclusive privilege of violating the law, or of defying the law, if it could draw upon any moral grounds for doing so.

There was, to play upon the words of Eugene McCarthy, hardly anything sophisticated about the attempts to blow up the Statue of Liberty, the Liberty Bell, the Capitol in Washington, or hundreds of university structures throughout the land. There was hardly anything subtle about the rhetoric of the movement during these years. That weapon alone was to reach the limits of vulgarity, libel, slander, misdirection, and just plain untruth during the decade. The only optimism which was visible about the urban riots of the 1960s was in the faces

*There are numerous contributors to this volume.

19

of looters emerging from stores, their arms loaded with whatever they could carry. These were acts never contemplated by the liberal of 1960. They were acts which were in actuality antithetical to his doctrine and which, eventually, caused him to shift temporarily to the right or to join the legions of doomsayers who were predicting the decline of American society.[13]

Where the liberals seem to have failed in the 1960s was at the point which they had always argued primacy—a true understanding of historical context. During the decade, either through willfulness or stupidity, time and time again they ignored the facts of the recent past. Violence of a political nature had been abuilding in the world's democracies for years prior to the main events of America in the 1960s. The Zengakuren, the leftist student organization of Japan, had taken to the streets to forestall a visit by President Eisenhower in the last years of his presidency—and many American liberals had either applauded or had been pleasantly beguiled by the development. Latin America had seen numerous student riots, especially during Vice President Nixon's visit to South America in the 1950s. And once again, in this instance, American liberals seemed quietly amused. By 1960 such activism had reached America. It was reported that students had engaged in "sit-in" demonstrations on certain campuses and that in San Francisco the police were forced to swing clubs during a student riot in that city.

One of the more acceptable adages of the 1960s was that, to understand the United States, one must look to events in California. In the case of the San Francisco confrontation this was most certainly proved out. Here could be found the accepted identification marks of the decade to come. Student riot leaders were distinguishable by long hair and beards. There was a good deal of clever organizing of the proceedings by individuals who were well into their middle years and theoretically past the classroom stage of life. There was the violent antipolice attitude of the crowd; the law men were not yet "pigs" but they were fascist enforcers of immoral laws. And, last but not least, there was an incipience of that polarized rhetoric of later days —signs which called upon humanity to "protect our teachers from intimidation."

It is essentially wrong, of course, to write of this era as beginning in January 1960 and ending in December 1970. Historical eras do not come and go in such a precise pattern. The depression decade, for example, was longer than ten years; it began in 1929 and ended in 1941. The era which is erroneously called the "apathetic 1950s" really began before 1950: it was to end around 1958.

Furthermore, in respect to the latter period, it is historically inaccurate to argue that America was adrift during those Eisenhower years.

It should be obvious to anyone who observes the American political scene that both the partisan left and the partisan right have their political ploys. Conservatives, at least in more recent years, have argued that liberal administrations in Washington do too much, interfere too much, and simply go too far in regimenting local government. President Eisenhower's admonition to the country in 1952, for instance, was that it could expect a period in which it would be allowed to catch its breath. Liberals, as a rule, have contended during Republican administrations that the country is adrift; that the "outs" should be allowed in so that the tiller might better be directed.

The myth that the 1950s was a decade of inaction persists only because liberal historians contend that it was so. Yet, in terms of real achievements, the Eisenhower years stand up well in comparison with the Kennedy-Johnson years in most categories, and a great deal better in some. In almost every area of American society during the 1950s, there were significant advances. As far as the whole period from Eisenhower to Nixon is concerned the progress in the whole of America has been immense—all of which tends to deny the wild rhetoric of the radical movement of the 1960s.

An examination of a statistical comparison between 1950 and 1970 suggests some pleasing revelations. In 1950 the typical American family had three *young* children: twenty years later the typical family had two, usually in the fifteen- to nineteen-year-old range. Middle-American family income in 1970 approximated $9,870, which in terms of purchasing power was twice as much as that of the middle family of 1950. A great many more women were working in 1970 than twenty years previously, a development which probably added some leverage to a growing women's liberation movement. Both parents in 1970 were likely to have finished high school, but two decades previously the average years of schooling was about nine grades. Typical American families in 1970 lived in houses worth approximately $17,000. For a good many in 1950 there was no adequate housing.[14]

Beyond these changes were those advances having to do with a broadening of American affluence. There was infinitely more central heating and cooling in the housing picture, there were more automobiles, and more television. Much of America had moved to the suburbs and, in general, the advance in affluence had extended itself to a rapidly growing black middle class. During the early 1970s there was to be an energy shortage, especially with gasoline. This last development probably needed some apt rhetorical twisting. Perhaps, due to the burgeoning of American affluence, the problem lay less in an oil shortage than in an automobile glut.

There were in all of these statistical developments some signs and portents of things to come. There was a kind of time bomb in the unloading of vast numbers of children into the educational pipeline; a pipeline which the so-called American Dream had extended beyond the chasm separating high school from college. There was a tremendous dislocation of the white middle class and its persistent seeking of suburban green. There was an equally significant dislocation of poor black families from south to north: rural blacks of the South in search of housing and jobs in the city. To mirror all of these changes was the most revolutionary medium of entertainment and news ever developed by man. That was television, of course.

By 1960 there were some sixty million television sets in American homes and the number was increasing by giant steps in each succeeding month. At no time, as writer John Brooks was to state, was television a "plaything of the rich." American families began to arrange their evening meal around the news broadcasts, and new industries were created in order to feed those people who remained glued to their sets throughout the evening. Statistics could soon prove that many Americans were watching television almost as long as they were working. The big eye was, as some people were to describe it, a "hot" medium—one which cleaved to action rather than logic; emotion rather than reason. It could destroy the public image of any personality in one instant; it could create a public figure from whole cloth. Though the Republicans were the first to perceive this in 1952, it was the Democrats and in particular John Fitzgerald Kennedy who foresaw the total value of television upon political campaigning.

Kennedy's 1960 campaign for the presidency took full advantage of the hot appeal of television by following the line that the country had floated upon a Sargasso Sea of stagnation for some eight years. He argued, wrongly, that Russia had overtaken the United States in a military sense and that President Eisenhower had lost control of the international situation. Kennedy took his key to the campaign from such men as Arthur M. Schlesinger, Jr., the historian who, in 1959, had argued that the country was ready for a "bold new advance."[15] Others, in turn, took their cues from the candidate. There would be a new era, a new "frontier," exciting rather than dull, progressive rather than moderate, and adventuresome rather than timorous. Norman Mailer, later a Vietnam dove, saw it all in a grand and heroic framework:

I knew that if he [Kennedy] became President, it would be an existential event: he would touch depths in American life which were uncharted. . . . America's tortured psychotic search for security would finally be torn loose from the feverish ghosts of its old generals . . . , we as a nation would finally be loose again on the historic seas of a national psyche which was willy-nilly and at last, again, adventurous.[16]

The temper of the eastern intellectual class was to take on an emotional tone during the Kennedy-Johnson era. On both the east and west coasts the rhetoric of exaggeration, accusation, and activism pervaded the more important university communities. Poet Robert Lowell became an instant hero because he flamboyantly refused to read his poetry in LBJ's White House. Norman Mailer likely assured himself a full season of one-night university lectures because he stated that President Johnson inspired nothing but "nausea" in himself. These and others were to carry their activism into every issue of the times—Vietnam, unblinking support for possible violators of civil law, appeals for clemency for convicted Russian spies, protests for clemency for the scatalogical comedian Lenny Bruce, and even into demands that Adlai Stevenson resign as the American ambassador to the United Nations.[17]

Years later, Theodore White was to conjecture that the 1960s was a "decade of simple thought—that enough goodwill, enough money, enough brains, and we could do anything." Truly there was a sense of this during the Kennedy administration, and a veritable flood of similar logic in the Johnson period. But there were pitfalls. In time, as some were to argue, it was a philosophy which led the nation into Vietnam. Even more importantly, perhaps, was the total effect which such visionary illusions was to have upon human expectations.

Despite the claims of candidate Kennedy in 1960, the varying impulses which television added to the national psyche and the effective carping from the intellectual left, the nation had plenty to point to in the way of progress. In no other nation, as Jean Revel the French socialist was to argue, was human progress so measurable. During those dark days of the 1960s when it did seem momentarily that the movement was to sweep all before it, great advances were taking place. Americans not only hurtled other Americans around the earth by means of rockets, but they walked in space and trod on the moon. Infant mortality continued to drop during the 1960s, and by 1968 it was half of what it had been in 1930. Heart disease, cancer, kidney failure, and other killers were being attacked with increasing success. By the end of 1970 there had been such medical innovations as transplants, arterial inserts and bypasses, blood pressure treatments, and cardiac pacemakers—all partly developed in a period which leftish rhetoric often described as one plagued with insensitivity to "the people."

In these same Sixties there were developments of a different sort as well. The racial problems of the nation had come into the cusp, so to speak. They were not solved by 1970, but the changes had been phenomenal. Washington had "tipped," and its city government became black-directed. Newark and Gary had black mayors. Detroit was in the process of tipping, and would elect a black mayor in the 1970s. Los Angeles, essentially a white city, would soon elect a black mayor. In the heart of the old South, Atlanta would elect a black mayor in the 1970s, and throughout Dixie there were more and more black legislators. The trend was altogether a new frontier.

Equally important in the broad sense was another revolution in American life, and one which may have equalled the so-called "black revolution" in importance. Suburbia was likewise a new frontier and its rapid expansion, though noted in passing by most intellectuals, was generally ignored in terms of significance. But suburbia's growth tended to parallel the black revolution and, though each represented a frontier, each was as divergent from each other as the sources of the Mississippi and Ohio Rivers are. And each, like those two great rivers, was to meet eventually and provide both turbulence and sustenance to the radical revolution of the 1960s.

The expansion of suburbia was an obvious physical phenomenon, so obvious that it seems surprising that much of the importance of the change was momentarily overlooked. New York City, for instance, thrust itself by a kind of proxy deep into the heart of Connecticut. Los Angeles seemed boundless, and edged farther into California's hills and valleys. White Detroit was transplanted almost overnight, it seemed. Chicago, in many ways America's most vital and virile city, inched its way toward the Wisconsin border. Everywhere and anywhere it was the same. Between two distant worlds of white affluent suburbia and the black inner city was a third world—blue-collar America.

In March 1971, *Time*, with the help of pollster Louis Harris, attempted to develop a new typology relating to the new and broader ranges of American society. There were the "affluent bedroom" suburbs; plush and exclusive towns such as New Canaan, Connecticut, or Winnetka, Illinois. Here the highest paid professionals and executives built their homes. Closer in toward the cities were the "affluent settled" towns, the "low-income growing" areas, and the "low-income stagnant" suburbs. Property values between each division in the new typology differ enormously, and so did the relative racial frictions between blacks and whites. There is, for instance, little racial friction in affluent Birmingham, Michigan, simply because contacts between blacks and whites are either rare or noncompetitive.[18]

In consequence there arose during the 1960s a kind of paper-moon liberalism in more affluent suburbs—especially upon the racial issue. Down the economic ladder and in toward the inner city—in towns like Cicero, Illinois—that type of liberalism disappeared. Wherever it existed, however, it was a patronizing liberalism to say the least and considerably removed from the reality of rasping contact. In a sense it was the kind of liberalism so often found in states such as Minnesota, which has a very small percentage of blacks. It was, as well, part of what Tom Wolfe has described as "radical chic"—a combination of racial stargazing at long range and a surfeit of sneering at those whites who struggled between wealth and poverty. Those caught between the two poles were accorded hues and tints by the intellectual elite; they were the "red necks" of the South and the "blue collars" of the North.

It does not require much in the way of memory to recall the stereotypes foisted upon the public by the television or movie screens of the 1960s. Archie Bunker is still around, of course: a bigoted WASP who lives in the city and who speaks with variations of a Brooklyn accent. But then there were also quick visions of loutish truckdrivers, fat (always fat) southern sheriffs, thin and terribly perverted poor white killers, and oafish day laborers.

Out of the more affluent suburbs came a new breed of children. Just as they were to be far removed from the reality of the inner city, so were they removed from the reality of life. The world of supermarkets and drive-ins offered up no teleological insights into the meaning of life. The father of any suburban white child had very likely seen someone die; a relative perhaps, or in a war fast disappearing into the past. The grandparents of the same white child had not only witnessed the truth of death but the miracle of life. America in 1915 or even 1920 was a land in which infants first saw the light of day in the family home. The two most essential facts of humanity had been erased from the curriculum of the young.

Beyond this, there was the undeniably caustic factor of numbers. The peak year of the post-World War II baby boom was 1947, when 3,834,000 children were born. Coupled with the increased desire of parents to send their children to college, the sheer volume of young people to be placed in university communities was to affect American life profoundly. By 1954 there were an estimated 2,500,000 college students in the United States; half way through the 1960s the number passed 6,500,000. The crush to enter college became so great that special college admissions centers were established. The herd instinct for a college education became so great that some "colleges" were established openly as profit-making ventures. Students unable to survive their freshman or sophomore years at established institutions found ready acceptance at these institutions of "higher education."

The entire business of catering to the young attained an almost incredible significance in its effect on the nation. It would, before the end of the Sixties, create a youth cult in American society, and the extent to which American prosperity as well as American morality became dependent upon the affluent young tended to create an ever expanding bubble of financial speculation. It was estimated in the early part of the decade that teenagers in America were spending $11 billion a year on such assorted goods as sports equipment, phonographs, cameras, cosmetics, and automobiles. Estimates of future expenditures in the same market went as high as $21 billion—only a few billion short of the 1964 American defense budget.[19]

These astronomical figures only partly told the story of the growth of the new culture. Almost every state in the Union launched into vast programs of educational construction which, in many instances, were found to be wasteful and frivolous. The "upgrading of the American educational system," a euphemistic phrase which could have provoked considerable discussion ten years later, cost the American taxpayer billions of dollars. Indeed, he is still spending his monies on the educational construction of the 1960s, since the original expenditures were met with expensive and overpriced bond issues. An almost immediate result of the first expansion of facilities for higher education in the early 1960s was an extension of the concept that every American boy and girl, plus a great many foreign students as well, were entitled to a college degree. Hence, more and more state expenditures were demanded, more and more buildings constructed. Private colleges added their own expenditures to the wave of building in a frantic attempt to survive the decade.

It was inevitable that the twin jolts of the Vietnam War and educational expansion would cause certain disruptions in American society. Then too, the specific pressure of the military draft spurred students into the protective sanctuary of the campus where, unable to get out, unwilling to stay in, and deprived of none of the affluence which marked the whole of American society, many of them fell into a kind of directionless existence.[20]

Also true of the decade was the emergence of forced growth universities. These institutions, backed by economic interests and regional loyalties within certain states, seemed to grow without planning or rationale. In many instances standards were questionable, both on the student and on the faculty levels. Expansion was the theme of these institutions and that being the case, many of them became havens for individuals who sought either to avoid the draft or to avoid responsibility. The 1960s saw deep troubles at some of these schools— institutions such as Southern Illinois University or Kent State—and they represented the high price paid by policies calling for too many students and too few standards.

Naturally, these developments were only part of the entire picture. The increasing urgency placed upon families to send their children into higher education quite often added financial burdens which, when added to other costs brought on by an age of affluence, caused further problems. The guilt syndrome which so afflicted parents during the decade, either through the Vietnam War or by custom of the time, made it obligatory for many middle class families to opt for two incomes rather than one. But it was true even before the war that wives and mothers were entering into the labor market. Some 30 percent of mothers with children under eighteen were working outside the home in 1960. These "second car" jobs represented, according to one judge, a kind of "brinksmanship with delinquency."[21] Hundreds of thousands of teenagers, raised in highly mobile and transient suburban society, lectured by their teachers that they should reject the "apathetic Fifties," bored with having discovered too much too soon, and claiming an alienation from one or both parents, were not about to respond willingly to President Johnson's call for the defense of far off Vietnam.

To examine this war as a causal factor in the unrest of the 1960s is to risk the exposure of a persistent myth. The war did undoubtedly serve to exacerbate the strains of the time, but it was only one of many sources of youth discontent. Vietnam was a long way from San Francisco, and it was even farther from Harvard. But so was Korea in 1950. Furthermore, Korea was as cold as Vietnam was tropical; it was subject to as much wartime corruption as Vietnam; and the general aims of the Korean War were as fuzzy as any war participated in by the United States. But the real difference in the two conflicts lay in the presence of the movement, with all of its ancillary threads of antimilitarism, antinationalism, antiestablishment sentiment, ecology, and the so-called generation gap.

All of these variegated tendencies had been knocking about in the last years of the Eisenhower period. Driven underground sometime earlier by the intensity of right-wing vigilantism in the early Fifties, they emerged approximately in 1958. Left-wing and socialist groups began to draw new strength from the civil rights movement and from frightening visions of atomic warfare. The evidence of the rebirth of the far left lies principally in the writings of the so-called underground press, which, as writer Arnold Beichman has pointed out in his *Nine Lies About America,* was neither clandestine nor underground.[22]

This aspect of the movement began its expansion between 1958 and 1963. It is repetitive, but necessarily so, to point out that these dates precede both the Vietnam War and the turbulent racial problems of the mid-1960s. One excellent example of the new journalism was the Canadian publication *Sanity,* which crossed the border in terms of circulation and content and which provides excellent examples for a case study in pre-Vietnam left-wing activities.

Sanity was violently anti-American. In the early 1960s it never hesitated to attack President Kennedy either directly or by innuendo, thus giving lie to the maudlin sentimentality about the murdered

President expressed in later issues of the paper. *Sanity's* rhetoric was typical of that of later underground publications; it was highly charged, emotional, and exaggerated. It could switch positions in an instant, as shown in the issues following the death of President Kennedy. Almost immediately after November 1963, *Sanity* began to proclaim that the assassination was sponsored by fascistic elements in the United States. Like many underground publications of later years, *Sanity* was extremely pro-Castro, and strongly supported demonstrations both in the United States and Canada on the Cuban issue.[23]

The phraseology of the movement, as it came to infect so many college-sponsored publications in the 1960s, was present in early issues of *Sanity*. And so were some of the names of figures who were to attain a greater prominence in the following years. In 1963, *Sanity* provided the following quotes:

I think that the men who function without conscience as far as the Negro people are concerned—the men who believe in segregationist conduct— are generally the same people who embrace the idea of nuclear testing and nuclear weapons.

—Harry Belafonte

The deep acceptance of the fact that we . . . are not interested in preserving society as it is, and that we are seeking to create another way of life, will also help to solve one of our internal problems, viz. "What to do between demonstrations."

—A. J. Muste, Committee for Non-Violent Action

The peace movement has penetrated the establishment. . . .

—Theodore Olsen, World Peace Brigade

The peace movement can attain legitimacy and can influence the power elite provided it offers new ideas. The civil rights movement has this great importance today. . . . There is a growing opportunity to influence faculty members with the fruits of peace research and hence, to get universities to give seminars, and indeed undergraduate credit, on disarmament.

—Tom Hayden, Students for a Democratic Society

Without pressing the point too far at this juncture, one may quickly spot evidences of the activist cant of later years. The notion of turning society over, the realization of the importance of faculties and college campuses, and the clever knotting together of disparate issues are all present. In the latter case, it is interesting to note that the "nuclear threat" is tied to the civil rights issue—almost in the same manner in which in 1968 racism, the Vietnam War and a multitude of other fronts were entwined by the New Left.

Sanity offers other insights as well concerning the movement. Long before the full scale commitment to Vietnam the publication was to argue that "peace is a radical proposition," and that it could not be achieved "without profound social change." One Sanity writer, tired of "stuffing envelopes," contended that the movement needed to adopt a position which was more violently anti-established religion. After all, he argued, religion "forces you to do something" which might be wrong for society as a whole. The world needed more active socialist cohorts, concluded the writer, and a much more vigorous campaign against all university military training programs.

A later issue of Sanity provided a call for a crusade to carry "radical analysis-understanding" to others. Crying the need for a "new consciousness," the writer recorded:

> A revolution (this is what world peace means when one thinks of abolishing the thousand year old institutions of war and exploitation) does not travel directly to its announced goal . . . , but the transformations it effects are more fundamental and permanent than those achieved at smaller cost under the leadership of moderates. . . .[24]

That is a revealing statement indeed. Long before the 1970 call on the part of many to "turn over the system," the seedling of that aim was planted. Long before there was a movement to kiss off the liberals in 1970, so to speak, this early activist was pointing up the uselessness of accepting the goals of moderation.

By 1964 the organized aspects of the movement, such as those demonstrated in the writings of Sanity, had penetrated into specific university communities of the United States. The University of California at Berkeley was already faced with problems caused by "beatniks," as they were then called. On this and other campuses there were growing numbers of individuals who were not only affecting the Werther pose, but who were promoting "uncompromisable" social causes as well. Some university administrators found themselves hard put to explain the new developments, and were forced into assumptions that the unrest was rooted partly in the activities of outside agitators. Dr. Eric Walker of Pennsylvania State University, in March 1964, admitted for instance to having received some ominous warnings from the Federal Bureau of Investigation. There was, according to the bureau, the possibility of "an organized attempt by foreign money to disrupt the universities of America through the use of 'bogus students and bogus faculty members.'"[25]

There had been organized campus demonstrations prior to 1964, but the first one of significance occurred in that year. It lasted three months and consisted of class boycotts, sit-in confrontations, and other generally disruptive activities. The goal of these campus activists at the University of California at Berkeley was to force the university to permit the solicitation of funds and volunteers for what had been previously considered off-campus activities. By quickly tying the goal of the demonstrations to the larger and more acceptable principle of free speech, the strikers quickly exploited the mood of an already ripened generation. After all, it all seemed to be heroic in nature and the leaders of the rebellion appeared as romantic offspring of a Werther generation. As Mario Savio, one of the more prominent figures in the "free speech" crusade, put it: "I'm tired of reading history. Now I want to make it."[26]

It is in error to insist that such movements sprang from the Vietnam War. It is equally in error to insist that organized and institutional radicalism could have promoted the unrest of the 1960s by itself. The roots of the movement were many—but one, hitherto only lightly touched upon, gave a special flavor and distinction to the decade. The element here was an essential difference between this period, and those of the Jacksonian and Depression eras. It was a new hedonism based partly upon the general affluence of the nation.

The explosion of material wealth in the 1960s was almost beyond previously established bounds of imagination. Much of the new wealth was a result of a reckless borrowing upon the future; defense-stimulated expansion, the erosion of natural resources, widespread American investment abroad, the issuance of long range debentures, and a tremendous expansion of national and private credit. The affluence penetrated almost all levels of American society, and even the poor seemed less poor than those of the past. By 1965 the affluence had reached some astounding limits. Youngsters of high school and college age thought no more of going to Europe for the summer than their parents had considered a trip to Coney Island. *Readers' Digest* was to advertise in 1970 that its readers were the first buyers of new cars, and that some 60 percent of Lincoln Continental purchasers were also *Digest* subscribers. And, as late as 1973, the *New York Times Magazine* was to boast that its reading public was the most affluent in the nation.

What all of this did to the newest American generation is still unmeasurable. Some observers, early on in the 1960s, foresaw a new kind of youth culture. One commentator in a national magazine was to argue in 1960 that the new materialism "shrinks a child's knowledge of the world around him" in such a manner as to cause a loss of perspective. Margaret Mead, whose views throughout the 1960s seemed to have peregrinated from one extreme to another, stated at the beginning of the period that the United States had created a "more, more, more" generation.

The new hedonism, once in the making, could well afford an elasticity in morality, values, dress, and standards. The revolution in behavior extended into drugs and other forms of aberrant behavior.

Less affluent nations, such as France, Canada, Britain, and West Germany, saw the new hedonism move only to the limits to which their own national economies developed. Hedonism, after all, may only develop within a certain personal or national prosperity. A previous American generation in the 1930s had sought desperately to shed its overalls and blue work shirts. Its children, at least those white children maturing in the 1960s, not only wore overalls but they bleached them when new or deliberately rubbed them through in order to necessitate patching. Incredible as it seems, the classroom shuffles at any large university in the 1960s were suggestive of the People's Republic of China—lines of solid blue which interlaced one building to the next. What ought to be added is that the fad seldom filtered into the black university community; and perhaps that had something to say about the economic circumstances of the backgrounds of these less privileged Americans.

By 1964 the new affluence was already having an enormous effect upon the youth of the nation. Fort Lauderdale in Florida had become a kind of Eastertime mecca to thousands of college students. Rock or music festivals were becoming a new fad, indicative of what was later to come. One New England town in 1964 found itself a temporary host to three or four thousand students. The behavior of these youngsters became so riotous that the national guard was called in to bring an end to the resultant vandalism. One police expert was to point out that such gatherings had become a "feature of the Labor Day week-end along the Eastern seaboard."[27]

One aspect of the growing affluence among college students was to be seen in the broad campus power attained by more activist students. These individuals were quick to perceive two possibilities emerging from the rapid growth of the educational system. First of all, it was increasingly easy for them to force university presidents to cede ground on important issues. After all, the older type of university executive—the kind who appreciated respect rather than popularity—had long since disappeared. His place had been taken by a new breed; men who were essentially politicians or corporate types, or gentler types who were hobbled by academic views of freedom.

A second possibility for an appreciation of power by activist students lay in the control of student "activity" funds. These monies, collected as part of each term's tuition, amounted to considerable sums. By controlling this source of power one could also control the campus newspaper. Most of all, however, the control of such funds allowed for the natural manipulation of the college lectureship and entertainment programs. This latter activity was big business by the 1960s, offering thousands of dollars to those nationally known revolutionaries or activist comedians for single night appearances. The university lectureship and entertainment circuit was far more lucrative than many other phases of the general entertainment business. Even politicians were not beyond its call, and some such individuals drew in considerable yearly incomes from this work. All one had to do to qualify was to pronounce one's self to be an activist, and to remember to grace each lecture with a paean of praise to the now generation—something on the order of "this is the most knowledgeable, the most sensitive, indeed, the very best generation to grace this planet since the beginning of time."

Unfortunately, for these young people and for the nation as a whole, there were too few politicians and educators brave enough to face the task of informing college audiences that Isaac Newton and Copernicus were not born yesterday. No one dared to point out that encomiums expressing claims of generational superiority were without validity. One survey conducted by the National Assessment of Education Progress did belatedly discover that such prostitutions of the truth were just that. It was found that adults from twenty-six to thirty-five years of age managed to better seventeen-year-olds in awareness concerning government officials. It should be pointed out that the survey failed to identify the younger subjects as college students, but it should also be added that the adults in the survey were also randomly selected.[28]

One of the most revealing sets of statistics concerning educational change was that provided by the Educational Testing Service of Princeton, New Jersey. By 1973 it was revealed that, for the tenth straight year, both verbal and mathematical scores continued to fall in the highly regarded and nationally administered Scholastic Aptitude Test. In 1962, a date which would mark the general expansion of the national university educational system, the S.A.T. mean scores were 478 (verbal) and 502 (mathematical). The steady downward trend which occurred through the Sixties and down to 1973 saw the scores reach the levels of 445 (verbal) and 481 (mathematical). While there may well be appropriate explanations for part of the drop, the downward swoop of mean scores does indicate that the college generation of the 1960s was *possibly not* the best ever.

Among the major culprits who failed to face up to the twin issues of lowered standards and weakened curricula were the nation's college and university presidents. So committed to growth at any cost were they that it may have been constitutionally impossible for them to tackle such issues. Some college presidents did, among them the administrators of Rockford College in Illinois and Beloit College in Wisconsin. The same was true of Dr. David Mathews of the University of Alabama, a place not previously noted for academic excellence. Yet Mathews pointed out that he was not extending the point of view that the generation of the Sixties was any less intelligent or any less responsible; he simply meant to point out that there was no real value in "romanticizing the young . . ." As Mathews put it:

From what students have told me, there is nothing so unsettling as praise apart from any deep personal sense of having done something that they, themselves, recognize as important. And nothing convinces them so much of the superficiality of the older generation as its willingness to praise for superficial reasons.[29]

But Mathews and the few other exceptional college administrators were small voices in the crowd. Grading standards at Harvard and other supposedly elite institutions continued to decline until, even to members of those faculties, it seemed as if the "gentleman's C" had been forgotten. Television, radio, and the cinema continued to promote the theme of generational superiority to the point of reductio ad absurdum—how could there ever be any generation better than the perfect one? On the other hand the same media continued to reinforce the notion that corruption and evil were associated with older generations. It was the base "Mrs. Robinson" who seduced the clean-cut youngster of *The Graduate*. It was the older generation which had concocted, through some undefined processes, the various assassinations, war, racism, poverty, and the "rape" of the ecological system. Yet, how strange it was that few commentators braved the contradictions of it all. President Kennedy, the idol of the young, was well past the movement's deadline of thirty years and his and Robert Kennedy's assassins were under the deadline.

It became almost obligatory for some pillars of intellectual America to iterate the popular cant that the young were destined to do what the older generation couldn't. Margaret Mead, who had begun the 1960s with some choice words on the "more, more, more" generation, now saw the light. As she put it:

They [the young] are ready to make way for something new by a kind of social bulldozing—like the bulldozing in which every tree and feature of the landscape is destroyed to make way for a new community.[30]

Down in the trenches, however, where some earnest professors continued to fight battles for classroom standards, strong degree requirements and self-discipline, the change in the university scene was observed in a different light. Professor Martin Trow of Berkeley was to write in 1970 that universities were threatened by a kind of structural disintegration. The younger professors, he argued, "do not accept the proposition that the freedom and autonomy of the university is built on the assumption that it will not engage in political activity and that the classroom will not be the locus for partisan recruitment and persuasion." As Trow saw it, there had been too much coercion by special power entities within the university structure, too many political criteria in faculty recruiting, and too much reduction in academic quality.[31]

What Trow was arguing was evident on almost every major university campus in America in 1970. The History Department of the City College of New York, once prestigious, was riddled with dissension and conservative professors on the staff were claiming that they had been objects of economic discrimination. Members of the faculties of Ivy League schools were beginning to complain that too many high grades were being handed out. Elsewhere there were minor revolts against the presence of activist students on what had been academic committees. And by 1973 there were even some complaints among blacks that the United States needed far fewer black studies experts than it did black doctors, black dentists, and black lawyers.

Why had the entire university structure weakened so drastically before the onslaught of the 1960s? How and why had college faculties and college presidents so quickly accepted the peculiar notion that inexperience and activism represented the most important bases of natural insight among students?[32] The answers lay in the myriad of causes which have been discussed previously, but they also existed in the academic encouragement of student activism. If one was to inveigh heavily upon the faults of the "apathetic Fifties," he was perforce required to reward the idealistic concept of revolutionary activism. Activism then was "good," and what better way to be active than to be an activist, as Bruno Bettelheim expressed it.[33]

But activism among the young could only flourish in its healthy state by feeding upon causes and victories. If it were to be once, twice, or three times denied, then activism could quite well become something else indeed. And, since activism needed ever bigger and bigger triumphs, the time would approach when there was to be a denial of victory. An activist deprived of the prize is soon awash with paranoia. It is a condition which George Santayana recognized over sixty years ago. "Fanaticism," he wrote, "consists in redoubling your efforts when you have forgotten your aim."

There were, of course, a great many overworked words and phrases during the 1960s—among them such gems as *relevancy, committed, paradigm, cognition,* and *participatory*. But two—paranoia and rhetoric—have a special application to the troubles of that decade. The first as a mental state and the second as the chief weapon of paranoia existed at both ends of the political spectrum between 1960 and 1973. But, in all truth, it was the radical left which most fell victim to the excesses generally found in both states.

By far and away the most brilliant exposition on the implications of paranoia in America are to be found in Richard Hofstadter's essay, "The Paranoid Style in American Politics." The statement was composed as a kind of background analysis of McCarthyism in the 1950s, and it was first delivered at Oxford in November 1963, the month of the Kennedy assassination. An abridged text appeared in *Harper's Magazine* in November 1964.[34]

What is the paranoid style, according to Hofstadter? The definition is broad, but it includes the "absence of verifiable facts" in argumentation, in some cases the actual manufacturing of facts, a "curious leap in imagination" when presenting argumentation, and the continued presence of the notion that there is, somewhere, an evil and malignant power which manipulates events and people. Furthermore, as Hofstadter pointed out, history never assumes the mantle of truth unless it strikes agreement with the paranoic himself.

Evidence of these facets of political paranoia abound in the rhetoric of the movement of the 1960s. At one moment during the decade, Bertrand Russell, a movement hero of the time, announced that the United States was "giving" Canada a liberal supply of atomic bombs. Because Russell had said it, and because he was the grey eminence of British radicalism, the statement was passed throughout the underground press as fact—even though, to this day, there is no verifiable evidence to support the assertion.[35]

One of the major aspects of paranoia is its persistence in seeing events as part of one giant plot, a manipulation of circumstances by someone or something usually designated as "they." "They" is the giant octopode which must be defeated immediately, for the fate of mankind is at stake. Hofstadter defined the characteristic as a sense of conspiracy set in motion by "demonic forces" which require defeat by an all-out crusade. "The paranoid spokesman sees the fate of the conspiracy in apocalyptic terms . . . ," wrote Hofstadter, "Time is running out . . . , and he is sometimes disposed to set the date for the apocalypse."[36]

The conspiratorial concept as a part of history obtained a level of expression among leftist activists during the 1960s which boggles the mind. The world was doomed, and appropriate dates were limned out. *Candle*, an Ann Arbor, Michigan, publication saw history as guided by sinister and corrupt forces. One of its contributors wrote:

> The dying generation is "dead." Before they wasted away they gave us 2 World Wars, the Korean War. They [sic] Viet Nam War and left "us" with a world full of phoney lies, a world full of TV bullshit, a world full of discrimination, a world full of Power Structure, a world that's on the edge of complete destruction. . . .[37]

Although the "enemy" in Hofstadter's paranoid style rarely attains a consistent form, he or it is the "perfect model of malice, a kind of amoral superman, sinister, ubiquitous, powerful, cruel. . . ." Only the paranoic himself has the insight to clearly perceive the conspiracy woven by the enemy, and the battle lines are clearly formed. Evil and corruption are on one side; goodness, innocence, and truth are on the other.[38]

A writer for *East Village Other*, an eastern underground paper, had no difficulty in describing the unending conflict of the 1960s. The "enemies" were many and were listed thusly:

> Politicians, the state, the total body politic, the repressive and corecive [sic] forces, the lackeys of the bourgeoisie, the big and the petty bureaucrats, the bad teachers, sadistic cops, soldiers, trained to kill, mechanistic physicians, miserable inhuman designers of "bureaucratic" anti human things, the unanswerable foremen, the dictator-bosses, the autocratic parents determined their children shall grow up as miserable as they are. . . .[39]

As the above might indicate, the 1960s proved to be a test of endurance for the more scholarly and moderate college instructor. The "successful" teacher was one who was willing to accept a reclassification of life, an appropriate sense of doom and guilt, and the principle that the United States was guilty on all counts. One was not constrained to be an optimist, and should he fail in that regard, he was doomed to turn off the receptive apparatus of a substantial number of his students.

Paranoia allows for little in the way of a sense of humor. Life is real and it is earnest, the enemy is at hand, and an air of lightness is not appropriate. So it was in the 1960s. The movement was not to be cozened into laughter not of its own making. Those instructors who might be part of the "enemy" were to be met with straight face and penetrating gaze.[40] *Connections*, a Madison, Wisconsin, paper offered a perfect insight into this type of behavior. Describing a legislative hearing a correspondent wrote admiringly of "several bears, one or two chics [sic] with long black hair and fleshy stockings who sat right up front, never changing their focus except to light a cigarette." As for the enemy, "the rest of the listeners," as the writer saw them, they were your "typical American 'boojhwa-zy', i.e. brown business suit with boring rhymed ties, viscidly lipstuck females with broad asses and smiles."[41]

In general the rhetoric of the movement was oppressive in nature and depressing in spirit. After all, whether younger or older, the adherents of the faith had the only true vision of the past, the present, and the future. Even the most ordinary campus revolutionary or activist was bound and tied by his suspicions to viewpoints which were "overheated . . . , grandiose, and apocalyptic in expression."[42] No fact set forth by the enemy was ever too difficult to destroy. No evidence offered up by the foe was indisputable. One young instructor of the Sixties, attempting to moderate a radical classroom attack upon American WASPs, was almost rendered mute by the logic of his antagonists. WASPs, so said the students, were responsible for virtually everything which was wrong in American society. Grasping for a straw the instructor cried out: "But what about John Kennedy? He wasn't a WASP." "Perhaps not outwardly," was the reply, "but he thought like one."

It is true, of course, that Hofstadter's great essay on the paranoid style was an attempt to delineate the so-called McCarthy "witch-hunt" of the 1950s. What better yardstick could be used to measure the paranoia and rhetoric of the American left in the 1960s? Hofstadter's paranoic amasses "evidence" to prove his case and it matters not whether the facts are wisely or injudiciously chosen. Once the mass of evidence is assembled the paranoic then shuts his "receptive apparatus" down and he denies any other argumentation which does not support his case. As Hofstadter defines it, one who operates in the paranoid style knows exactly at which point he becomes a "transmitter" of ideas rather than a "receiver."[43]

In a broad sense some of the better evidence of paranoid rhetoric during the 1960s is to be found in the underground newspapers of the time. More will be written later about these amazing publications, but it can be added now that their editors usually *knew* exactly what was right. They were transmitters of ideas, and they amassed great quantities of indiscriminate information to prove their cases. Once having done this, they could in their own imaginations demolish and confound their opponents. *East Village Other*, in September 1967, ingeniously illustrates this characteristic. Those within the movement, claims the writer, always destroy those who are less intelligent. An example is called up. Dick Gregory, the black activist comedian, is described as eradicating the opposition offered by country bumpkins with "telling karate satire. . . ." One woman, with "preposterous breasts and a womb which smelled of corruption," was left "bare and ridiculous" by Gregory. Abbie Hoffman, one of the gurus of the movement, destroys a radio interviewer during a broadcast. "The tyranny of the faceless voice turned back on itself," and Hoffman leaves the questioner "helpless amid a mass of truth mirage. . . ."[44]

Just as certain religions given to revelations from divinity are inclined toward a claimed monopoly on truth, so it is with movements afflicted with paranoia. The insights claimed by the movement of the Sixties denied all restriction. Each true follower lived in his exis-

37

tentialist world; only the corrupt society on the outside sought to deny him that privilege. Truth—his version of the truth—was to be free, and those restricting that freedom were oppressors. *Free Student,* an underground paper of Los Angeles, spelled out what that freedom meant. It was a world in which individuals were tired of being told that Communists and Timothy Leary were bad. Police were never trusted, and teachers were the handservants of oppression. That oppression was defined:

> We, as students are shackled—denied our rights, responsibilities and, indeed, place in American Society. We are imprisoned by autocrats who, under a thin sham of legality, fraudulently claim mastery over ourselves. I refer, of course, to a small clique of dictatorial ogres who wield insolent reign as "administrators" in several though assuredly not all, public high schools.[45]

This was all part and parcel of the movement. Its adherents saw themselves as part of a romantic vision of tomorrow. Their self-portraits were stylized and heroic; they were all Goethe's Werthers. But most of all, they were the "tribe"; self-portrayed alienated intellectuals who were the "social misfits" of the world. Always, during the 1960s, they considered themselves to be the wreckage of war, even though the draft and combat were separated from themselves by college deferments. They were members of a mystic communion who recognized each other by "certain minute signals."

But most of all, it was they and only they who had the true vision of life. The logic of history was revealed to them alone. As one writer of the movement explained the breadth of their knowledge, they had progressed step by step to the inner light. Diligent study had shown communism to hold no dangers, and from that effort they had passed to research among the "other major civilizations—India and China...." It was but one giant step from the dialectic of Marx and Hegel "to an interest in the dialectic of early Taoism."[46]

What makes the 1960s a most difficult period to explain is the symbiosis of factors and issues in the decade. The guilt syndrome of the older generation, which fed upon the Vietnam War, was exploited to the last by the movement. Television, the civil rights struggle, the deprived past and the affluent present, and the multitudes of the young all combined to interact upon each other. It mattered not about the hardships of the past; that London had been decimated by plagues or a fire during the time of Charles II. It held no water that for hardships the Vietnam War could not compare to World War II. This was the moment, and the movement saw youth as suffering more than any generation in the past. The movement's maudlin sentimentality told the story. "In this vast city of Detroit," spoke one of the anointed,

"I see everyone washing themselves in the blood echoes of their soul, in the beneficial and harmful karma they created in the blood and sweat and laughter and tears and orgasms and hysteria of their past decade."[47] Incidentally the very word *blood* found great usage during the period.

The movement, then, saw the truth as it wanted the truth to be. An underground writer describing the Washington demonstrations of 1967 was moved to write of the real excitement brought on by "the romantic vision of this beautiful revolutionary army occupying the lawn of the Pentagon." The simple gesture of a soldier taking off his gas mask in order to wipe his brow was reinterpreted: the soldier really wished to "suffer with the demonstrators." Once in a while, of course, there was the heretic: the young individual who simply rode the movement for his own personal pleasure. "I went to Washington to have a good time . . . ," wrote one such young man. "I did."[48]

The 1960s, then, was a decade of overblown rhetoric, of paranoia, of occasional doomsaying, and of maudlin sentimentality, especially on the radical left. Fortunately the great mass of the country held firm, which might lead one to conclude that the Missouri instinct in America is stronger than had been supposed. That aspect of contemporary American society may have been the most understressed characteristic of the country, a historical deficiency which needs to be corrected.

2
The Ancient and Modern Art of Doomsaying

Predictions of doom and the exaggerated rhetoric which accompany them are as old as literate history and, one may assume, a good deal older than that. The word doomsay has specific reference to the Biblical day of the Last Judgment, but in the modern sense it has application to any predicted moment of reckoning. Doomsaying is a latter day perversion of the Middle English word "dooming," which was the ancient art of forecasting the end of a single individual or of society as a whole.

In any case, it may be suspected that the practice is as old as man himself. Earliest man, given the twin gifts of memory and judgment, developed ceremonies of sacrifices and oblations in order to avoid catastrophe. The Old Testament records that the patriarch Noah was wise enough to heed to the wave of the future, while Homer relates that Priam, the king of Troy, was not. Cassandra, Priam's daughter, sharp-tongued and voluble, dulled her own gift of prophecy with over-statement and the words which might have saved Troy were unheeded. There is also in man's wonderful store of folklore the tale of the boy who cried "wolf" too often, a lesson which Cassandra herself should have known.

Dooming, or doomsaying, is always to be found in the human condition. There are times in which the stridency of its exaggerated rhetoric reaches higher levels than in normal periods, and such abnormal eras are usually coincidental with other factors. First of all, in specific moments of high dooming there is a related tendency toward higher general neurosis or anxiety. This last may quite obviously be rooted in very profound disturbances—war, for instance, or pestilence, famine, the general dislocation of society, and a higher mobility within that specific society. This last must never be downrated for it is within the breaking up of traditional stability and familial relationships that there are radical dispositions to change preexisting moral standards. This is not meant to imply that doomsaying is to be found only in unstabilized societies, but it does argue that the virulence of the disease is affected by that factor.

Outside of a few natural phenomena such as the appearance of Halley's Comet, there are really few other explanations of doomsaying than those given above. When a society is touched by any or all of the apocalyptic possibilities, it virtually always produces an excess of Cassandras. A society which tends to stability along with prosperity and peace rarely tolerates much dooming. It is as simple as that.

Who are the doomsayers? History illuminates them in differing ways. They are crushed idealists who have never found success in impressing society with their own personal goals. Occasionally they are hardened revolutionaries who seek to exploit social discontent through extensive use of dooming. They are liberals or conservatives out of power. They are relics of the ancient regime who see the old order perishing. They are fanatics who cannot achieve victory through any other means but compromise. Historically they would include Jonathan Edwards, who preached of "sinners in the hands of an angry God," and who warned his followers that failure to return to the old ways would bring doom upon them before the end of the year. They include Karl Marx, a thwarted revolutionary, who predicted the end of capitalism a century and a half ago. And there was Earl Grey, a British cabinet minister, who saw the lights going out all over Europe in 1914; it was the old order crumbling.

Over the last three hundred years doomsaying has flourished at a frenetic level, a strange development indeed in view of the increased literacy in the Western world. In a sense, however, this is easily traceable to a higher level of instability occurring over that length of time; this along with the more frequent demises of old orders. The American Revolution, for instance, marked a juncture of both of these conditions. The Appalachian barrier was being torn down, and the stability of almost 170 years of British domination was coming to an end. For Daniel Leonard, one of the more literate members of the old order in America and the ablest Tory pamphleteer, it was the beginning of the end. He wrote:

> May the God of our forefathers direct you in the way that leads to peace and happiness, before your feet stumble on the dark mountains, before the evil days come, wherein you shall say, we have no pleasure in them.[1]

The French Revolution was, by far and away, one of the most important events in the early days of the American Republic. It was a time of tremendous dislocation in Europe, of strange and alien ideas, and of the apparent end of an old order. The era produced the usual pattern of paranoia and exaggerated rhetoric. From the very opening of this political cataclysm there was a surfeit of both. What more perfect example of either can be found than in the hyperexaggeration of the significance of the Bastille. The royal prison was, in the words of street activists, filled from entrance to exit with political prisoners. Who knew what could be found inside? Men and women who had been imprisoned for years with the infamous practice of the lettres de cachet? When the smoke had cleared and when the mob had dismembered its quota of the Swiss guard, a mere handful of prisoners was set free. Two of those were criminally insane.[2]

France was not a poor country in 1789. By European standards of the time it reeked with affluence. But France was experiencing the flashpoint of contact between instability, mobility, and the decline of an old order. The Great Fear, an event of the early months of the Revolution, was another perfect example of paranoia and rhetoric. This development was a result of wild rumors which flew about the countryside. Chateaus were burned and looted, and there were peasant demonstrations in the hinterlands. The rumors which caused the unrest were groundless ones, and to this day there is little scholarship to indicate their exact origin.[3]

Republican America could not remain extant from the maelstrom which was the French Revolution. The impact of the resultant wars in Europe plus rational and irrational discourses on the virtues of the Revolution not only helped to create the two-party system but caused an appropriate proportion of paranoia in the United States.[4] Alexander Hamilton, born poor but a successful example of upward mobility, saw the French developments from the viewpoint of a possible old order. What was going on in Paris, according to Hamilton, was a prelude to "clouds and darkness." Thomas Jefferson, born rich but a member of the radical chic of 1791, saw the excesses of the French Revolution as minor ones. He was quick to imply that great goals were achieved through relatively small sacrifices. In reference to all those lives at the guillotine, he wrote: "The liberty of the whole earth was depending on the issue of the contest, and was ever such a prize won with so little innocent blood?" It was precisely this kind of talk which frightened the Federalists enough to cause them to seek a rather paranoic solution to dissension in America—the Alien and Sedition laws.

Throughout the early part of the nineteenth century, it was the success of American republicanism which formed a considerable part of the doomsaying in Europe. Prince Metternich, the brilliant exponent of European conservatism, typified the old order's fear of the new. "If this flood of evil doctrines and pernicious examples should extend over the whole of America," he wrote, "what would become of our religious and political institutions?"[5] Fears similar to those of Metternich found expression all over Europe. They were the foundations of a trenchant and virulent anti-Americanism which flourished in that period, and which even today is voiced by individuals in the French and British intellectual communities. Men such as de Tocqueville and Crèvecoeur in France, and Cobden in England, did portray the American with probity and wisdom, but in general their views did not gain acceptance in the upper levels of European society.

There were times when the vicious anti-Americanism of this latter class lapped upon the shores of paranoia. Thomas Moore, the Irish poet from Tralee, so disliked what he saw of American society that he wrote:

> Thee showy smile of young presumption plays,
> Her bloom is poison'd and her heart decays.

Moore's half-wishful prediction of America's death in a sea of corruption has been echoed by European intellectuals and European visitors to America for well over a century and a half. Any 1974 *London Times* in-depth piece on the decay of present-day American society is merely in the tradition. Harriet Martineau as well as de Tocqueville, time and again, noted the prevalence of talk and rumor to the effect that the "republic is at an end." One foreign visitor to America in the 1840s faithfully echoed a contemporary American maxim in his own literary efforts. "America is always going to the devil," he wrote, "but never gets there." An earlier visitor, Le Chevalier Felix de Beaujoir, forecast the doom of the United States because of the very nature of its society. The people of the United States, he said, had too much an "unbounded love of money"—Americans will become the "fatal victims of their own dissensions," and the country would dissolve before it could be formed into the "great body of a nation."[6]

The famous Captain Marryat, another visitor to the United States, was later to predict almost the same fate, that the "acrid jealousies" of the various states might prove too formidable an obstacle for continued union. A German visitor, F. J. Grund, carried the same prediction of doom and gloom into countless lecture halls on the other side of the Rhine. Sidney Smith, a Whig publicist, did not even have to tour the

43

states to express his positive opinion on the future of America. In the forty years of their independence, Smith asked, what had the Americans achieved? Where were their Foxes, their Burkes, their Sheridans, their Davys, Malthuses, Kembles, Byrons, Moores, and their Wilberforces? "In the four quarters of the globe," contended Smith, "who reads an American book or goes to an American play or looks at an American picture or statue?"[7]

Smith's blindness to an already substantial American achievement was typical of his class. In one single statement he had ignored the American-born Benjamin West, one of the more highly regarded "British" painters of the eighteenth century. He had ignored the already apotheosized Benjamin Franklin and Thomas Jefferson. But, as indicated above, Smith's attitude was par for the course among British intellectuals during his century. There was indeed a considerable amount of wishful dooming in Britain about America. One British newspaper correspondent in America once titled his dispatch to the homeland with the words "The Daily Bulletin from the sickbed of civilization." Another correspondent in the same period referred to the United States as the "Gehenna of the United States." Gehenna is a word from late Latin which had the nineteenth century meaning of "counterglow." Translated to twentieth century usage it might imply "the boondocks," or "hell hole."[8]

One of the more potent and yet pungent of European wits dedicated to dooming about America was Charles Dickens. Though in his own time and now, his literary talent seems almost without fault, he stands in his own country as a monumental reformer who dramatized the evils of the time. It was truly strange then that on the subject of the United States he suffered from an advanced case of myopia. There were financial reasons for this. His volumes had been pirated in the United States, and after investing and losing huge sums of money in land speculation in Illinois, he developed a broad anti-American streak to his nature. It may also have been that he discovered, long before the appearance of Oscar Wilde, that American society seemed to suffer from a touch of masochism.

Once Dickens had suffered his huge financial losses in the American West, he was never again quite the same. His *American Notes* written prior to the American Civil War particularly reflect his biases. Almost to his end he felt this way, writing in 1865:

I believe the heaviest blow ever dealt at Liberty's Head, will be dealt by this nation in its ultimate failure of its example to the Earth. . . . Look at . . . the desperate contests between the North and the South: the iron curb and brazen muzzle fastened upon every man who speaks his mind. . . . The stabbings and shootings. . . . The nation is a body without a head and the arms and legs are occupied in quarreling with the trunk and each other and exchanging bruises at random.[9]

The reportage produced for European readers by such writers as Dickens was so derogatory of American life that most later visitors to this country entered with already strongly affixed prejudices. What happened to some was a complete turnabout; a shock at having found an America they never knew to exist. Saint-Saens, the French composer who toured the United States in 1900, expected to have his "artistic sensibilities" stretched to the limit. On his return to Paris he delightedly told French newspapermen that his American visit had provided fresh daily delights. "Everywhere I found excellent orchestras," he announced, "everywhere excellent conductors."

It is true that many European visitors to this country after 1900 adopted a greater tolerance during their visits. Lord James Bryce, eventually the most able European interpretor of America to the world, tended to argue that much European doomsaying and exaggerated rhetoric about America was based upon the ordinary American's own proclivities along those lines. The American, contended Bryce, was too much inclined to view his own country's future in darkish terms. There was, in the United States, even at the turn of the century, too much talk about the "sickness" and death of American society, the standard American deprecations about immoderation, apathy, materialism, and the loss of old values.

What Bryce saw in 1900 or thereafter in America was a highly perceptive vision of the flaw in the structure of American society as a whole. Bryce noted, for instance, the existence of solid and resolute pockets of pessimism among the intellectual class of the country. Down below, in the great mass of the people—Middle America might be the appropriate term—there was a great "reservoir of force and patriotism." Another English visitor—not Bryce—saw an added characteristic. The country was full of "men who make a bluff at pessimism," but who always "surprise you finally by adding 'Still it's all coming out right in the end.'"[10]

One British visitor at the turn of the century who falls outside the characterization of doomsayer was the famous or infamous H. G. Wells, later to be regarded by American intellectuals as the beau ideal of British scholastic circles. His early book, *Future in America*, published in 1906, proved to be a beginning-of-the-century version of the more recent book, *Without Marx or Jesus*, by Jean-Francois Revel. Like Revel, Wells was a socialist, albeit a very mild one who kept an eagle eye on royalty figures. He saw America as a burgeoning, industrious, and promising land. It was not without problems and, in this regard, Wells laid heavy stress upon the aspect of racial confrontation. Yet his version of American life seems extraordinarily well balanced and intuitive.

This was not so with another socialist, the Russian Maxim Gorky, who came to the United States at almost the same moment as Wells. Gorky wrote of a dying civilization in which New York City looked less like the "fun city" of America than it does now. It was a monster, cried out Gorky, with a "huge jaw with black, uneven teeth." It belched "forth clouds of smoke into the sky" and seemed more like a "glutton suffering from overcorpulency." The people were nothing less than automatons, pushing, shoving, hurrying, without direction, "all hastily driven by the same force that enslaves them."[11]

As Bryce had intimated, if America lacked enough denigration from the outside, it was then perfectly happy to provide it from within. Frustrated reformers, the old order dying, change and instability—all worked a kind of occasional ferment in American life. It had been true of the Jacksonian period especially. Then, almost every phase of inner society was examined for the purpose of experimental change. Women's equality movements, crusades to change the penal system, and even the emancipation movement itself drew sustenance from the Jacksonian ferment. There was, along with all of this, the inevitable hand wringing and doomsaying. "O Americans! Americans!" passionately cried one speaker. "I call God—I call angels—I call men, to witness that your DESTRUCTION *is at hand,* and will be speedily consummated unless you *repent.*"[12]

The similarities between Jacksonian dislocation and the 1960s are obvious and pertinent. Both had communal experimentation. Both saw experimentation in religious exoticism and extremism. Both were witness to college disturbances. In the period before 1830, for instance, Harvard had been the scene of violent riots. Half the senior class of one specific year was expelled. The same held true for Princeton, and Nassau Hall at one time resounded to the thud of bricks against doors and the echoes of pistol shots on campus. Gentlemanly Yale likewise had its problems, though not in such a broad vein of violence.[13]

There was a plethora of sexual experimentation in the period prior to the American Civil War, dozens of little ecology movements here and there, and even a score of interesting food fads involving "natural" ingredients. Such was the frenzied activity of the reformers that the good Ralph Waldo Emerson in 1844 could take no more. "What a fertility of projects for the salvation of the world!" he proclaimed. Emerson was tired of being told that no man should buy and sell, that the "use of money was a cardinal evil," and that "we eat and drink damnation." He was tired of natural food faddists, tired of being told that vegetables grown in manure had higher food qualities. He was tired of hearing the insect world defended as a diminishing species; he was tired of new forms of social experimentation. And he was tired of "solitary nullifiers who throw themselves on their reserved rights . . . and who embarrass the courts of law by non-juring . . . and the commander-in-chief of the militia by nonresistance."[14]

Almost every decade has had a normal quota of doomsayers: some have had a glut. A writer for *Harper's Weekly* in 1857, for example, saw no way out for the world. "Never has the future seemed so incalculable as at this time," was his complaint. What was wrong with everything? Depression was abroad and everywhere, and "thousands of our poorest fellow-citizens" had been turned out to face a winter's cold. The political cauldron bubbled loudly in France and that bode little good. Russia, hanging "like a cloud," rested on the horizon of Europe. The British Empire, sorely tried, was faced with insurrections and with disturbed relations with China. "It is a solemn moment," concluded the writer, "and no man can feel an indifference . . . in the issue of events."[15]

So it went through the remainder of the century. James Russell Lowell concluded·in 1876 that the country was in such bad shape that the revolution one hundred years earlier had all been a mistake. In the 1890s William Jennings Bryan began crying doom in gold, redemption in silver. And then there was Edwin Lawrence Godwin.

Godwin was one of America's finest intellectuals in the last half of the nineteenth century. He was that period's equivalent of Walter Lippmann, and like the latter he tended toward an innate pessimism. In 1892 Godwin was half inclined to accept the notion that democracy was a complete failure, and that Alexander Hamilton was correct in his fear of an undisciplined "mobocracy." Four years later Godwin wrote that he was sick of American politics, and he now forecast "very evil times" for the Great Republic. Still two years later, in 1898, he confided to a friend that the United States was filled to the brim with a hundred million "puerile people," and that there was no hope for the country. As he phrased it, he was "glad to be so near the end of my career"; there was such "an awful prospect for the world." Godwin's brainchild, *The Nation,* was left to carry on the tradition, however, a duty which that magazine has seldom shirked.[16]

The United States at the turn of the century seemed especially beset by what writer Mark Sullivan was to call the "Jeremiads." "Exposure," proclaimed a writer in the *Atlantic Monthly* for August 1907, "forms the typical current literature of our daily life. . . ." And what was being exposed included the "depressing rottenness of our politics," the apathy of the good people, the "remorseless corruption" of the rich, the "gangrene of personal dishonesty," and so on. Walter Lippmann, entering the literary jungle as a veritable youth in 1913, bewailed the "misery of the country." A host of other writers whom Theodore Roosevelt called "muckrakers" detailed a multitude of sins and evils throughout the nation.

It required a writer such as Finley Peter Dunne, the irascible "Mr. Dooley," to put everything in perspective. On perennial reformers he wrote:

> The noise ye hear is not th' first gun iv a rivolution. It's on'y th' people iv th' United States batin' a carpet. Ye object to th' smell? That's nawthin'. We use sthrong disinfectants here. A Frinchman or an Englishman cleans house be sprinklin' th' walls with cologne; we chop a hole in th' flure an' pour in a kag iv chloride iv lime. Both are good ways. It dipinds on how long ye intind to live in th' house. What were those shots? That's the housekeeper killin' a couple iv cockroaches with a Hotchkiss gun. Who is that yellin'? That's our ol' frind High Finance bein' compelled to take his annual bath. Th' housecleanin' season is in full swing, an' there's a good deal iv dust in th' air; but I want to say to thim neighbors of ours, who're peekin' in an' makin' remarks about th' amount iv rubbish, that over in our part iv the wurruld we don't sweep things undher th' sofa.

Then, on another occasion, there was Mr. Dooley, sick in body and spirit from being forced to read such articles as "Graft in the Insurance Comp'nies," "Graft in Congress," and "Graft: Its Cause and Effect: Are They the Same?" The old Irishman opined:

> An' so it goes, Hinnissy, till I'm that blue, discouraged, an' broken-hearted I cud go to the edge iv th' wurruld an' jump off. It's a wicked, wicked, horrible place, an' this here counthry is about the toughest spot in it. Is there an honest man among us? If there is, throw him out. He's a spy. Is there an institution that isn't corrupt to its very foundation? Don't ye believe it. It on'y looks that way because our graft iditor hadn't got there on his rounds yet.

Then there was Mr. Dooley on doomsaying:

> I had no idee it was so bad. I wint to bed last night thinkin' th' counthry was safe, so I put out th' cat, locked th' dure, counted th' cash, said me prayers, wound up th' clock, an' pulled into th' siding f'r th' night. Whin I got up I had a feelin' that somethin' was burnin', th' same as I had th' mornin' iv th' big fire. But I cudden't find anything wrong till I opened up the pa-apers an' much to me relief, found that it was not me pants but the republic that was on fire. Yes sir; th' republic is doomed to desthruction again.[17]

The 1920s was certainly not a decade for reform, at least not in the United States. In France, Britain, and other countries of Western Europe there was a new hedonism, however, and it was spawned by dislocations, disillusionments, and in some cases affluence brought on by the war. Berlin and Paris were the centers of the cult, and this fact in rather unusual ways was to affect the United States. Paris was, during the twenties, the city of Picasso, Modigliani, Isadora Duncan, James Joyce, John Dos Passos, John Steinbeck, E. E. Cummings, W. B. Yeats, Kay Boyle, Ezra Pound, Ernest Hemingway, and F. Scott Fitzgerald. As William L. Shirer so vividly relates in *The Collapse of the Third Republic*, there were subtle fermentations and changes working their way into the subfoundation of French life. The political ambitions of the far right and the far left, the blind affluence of the French middle class, and a certain senility in French leadership served to prolong the disillusionments and agonies of French intellectualism.[18]

The pessimism brought about by the natural impossibility of achieving the high aims of the war eventually drifted across the Atlantic. Various antiwar dramas such as *What Price Glory* and *Journey's End* were supplemented by Fitzgerald's beautifully composed novels about the new hedonism. As Fitzgerald saw them, the new youth had been fertilized in the vapidity of President Wilson's war goals, and incubated in the new affluence. The motor car, with its attendant impact upon the familial influence of the American middle class, created a generation gap similar to that which existed in the 1960s.

It was one thing to recognize the gap as Fitzgerald had done, and it was another to exploit it as Sinclair Lewis was to do. Lewis's iconoclasm touched upon a series of flaws in American society, including small town provincialism, honor as opposed to baser motivations in the medical profession, chicanery in religion, and a supposed streak of fascism incipient in American character.

Another developing trend in the 1920s was to be found in a new and determined pacifism. Stimulated by the writings of Hemingway, Erich Remarque, Dos Passos, and a score of other writers, the new pacifism rippled into the depths of the American intellectual community. Scarcely a single American college was left untouched, and the same held true for universities in Britain. In the early 1930s, for instance, a goodly segment of the Oxford student body took an oath never to fight for God, country, or the king, no matter the cause. It goes almost without the necessity of saying that they did.

The similarities between the 1920s and the 1960s are obvious. A wide and strong tendency toward nihilism on American college campuses reached expression in both decades. There was a minor drug problem in the 1920s as well, though the level of usage seemed higher in both Britain and Germany than in the United States. There was a good deal of frenetic concern over so-called repression, especially in the instance of the famous Sacco-Vanzetti case. These two Italian immigrants, convicted of murder by the state of Massachusetts, were the "political prisoners" of the American left in the earlier decade. There were riots in many cities throughout the world protesting the conviction and the later execution, and almost every American campus was the scene of some form of organized protest concerning them. Recent historical research in the 1960s reveals that at least one of the two was truly guilty, and that the trial was marked with more justice than had previously been supposed.

Yet, all of these developments were to imbue much of the American intellectual community with a kind of hidden political activism. As Stuart Chase, a noted American economist of the time, put it: "Each of us, God help us, in those dreadful years, was trying to see how far he could go in wrecking the community about him, in tearing apart the bonds which yoked him to his fellows, in gnawing at the hands which held him up."[19] How contemporary to the 1960s that statement seems to be!

It was natural then that new levels in doomsaying and rhetoric were reached in the 1920s. Among socialist groups, and there were many of them, it was commonly held that capitalism was a dying institution—that it simply could not afford "another patch." The new generation, emerging in a somewhat disintegrating society, responded with the typical hedonistic approach of living for today while letting tomorrow ride. The old order was appropriately castigated for not getting out of the way of the new. One writer expressed the thought accordingly:

> The most hopeful thing of intellectual promise in America today is the contempt of the younger people for their elders; they are restless, uneasy, disaffected. It is not a disciplined contempt. . . . Yet it is a genuine and moving attempt to create a way of life free from the bondage of an authority that has lost all meaning. . . .

At the beginning of the decade twenty-three-year-old John Franklin Carter, later a well-known diplomat and public affairs specialist, described the parameters of the generation gap in an article for the *Atlantic Monthly*. The rhetoric is so similar to that of some forty years later that one needs to change only a few words for the piece to fit the tone of the radical left of the sixties.

> I would like to observe that the older generation had certainly pretty well ruined this world before passing it on to us. They give us this Thing, knocked to pieces, leaky, red-hot, threatening to blow up; and then they are surprised that we don't accept it with the same attitude of pretty, decorous enthusiasm with which they received it, 'way back in the eighteen-nineties, nicely painted, smoothly running, practically foolproof.

Obviously Carter had never read the works of Ida Tarbell or Lincoln Steffens before writing his polemic. The vacuity of the article finds sad similarity to the sixties. Elders in the 1920s had grown up in a world dominated by prudishness and poisoned by hypocrisy. The old had brutalized the young. The new generation had been forced to "mature" midst peculation, greed, malice, and an unforgiving society. What was needed was a new morality, and Carter told what it was to be.

> This is the quality in which we really differ from our predecessors. We are frank with each other, frank, or pretty nearly so, with our elders, frank in the way we feel toward life and this badly damaged world. . . . We actually haven't got much time for the noble procrastinations of modesty or for the elaborate rigmarole of chivalry. . . .

Not only did the new generation tell how it was, but it was anxious to take on the troubles of the world with vigor and determination. Carter described the wave of the future.

> We're men and women, long before our time, in the flower of our full-blooded youth. We have brought back into civil life some of the reckless-ness and ability that we were taught by war. We are also quite fatalistic in our outlook on the tepid perils of tame living. All may yet crash to the ground for aught that we can do about it. Terrible mistakes will be made, but *we* shall at least make them intelligently and insist, if we are to re-ceive the strictures of the future, on doing pretty much as we choose now."[20]

Carter's brave new world, as history proved, turned out with all of the flaws of the old and a few new ones hitherto unseen. It was neither a charitable world nor one free from deceit, and when Carter himself passed it on to the next generation it was just as "red-hot" as it had been in 1921. But Carter himself need not be faulted. His atti-tude was subscribed to by a good many individuals whom Fitzgerald once called "sad young men." Hemingway once wrote that it was a notion that the United States had "made a bloody mess of it." After all, Carter was not too far removed from T. S. Eliot who, in the same dec-ade, pronounced that faith alone could "renew and rebuild civiliza-tion and save the world from suicide."

Arthur Ponsonby, a British observer of America in the 1920s, wrote in his *Casual Observations* that life in the United States was too ma-terialistic, and that the new generation was dominated by machines, apathy, and contentment. He further contended that America had, by the 1920s, reached such a level of prosperity that both "effort and individual initiative" were being destroyed.

Ponsonby's claims, standard for British intellectualism then and now, were without foundation. The 1920s were neither repressive, as John Franklin Carter had proposed at the beginning of the decade, nor was the period unproductive. Rather, it was in an intellectual sense a kind of golden age for American arts and letters. The printing presses fairly sang the names of Eliot, Fitzgerald, Hemingway, Pound, Lewis, Sherwood Anderson, Willa Cather, and H. L. Mencken. Galleries were exploding with the colorful creations of John Marin, George Bellows, and Georgia O'Keefe. Eugene O'Neill and a host of brilliant dramatists lighted the stages of the country. There was Frank Lloyd Wright, George Gershwin, Aaron Copland, Lorado Taft, and all that jazz—Dixieland and Chicago style. Chicago, along with all if its unspeakable crime and grime, had a "left bank" of major significance, with names such as Carl Sandburg, Edgar Lee Masters, and Lloyd Lewis. In fact, all through Sinclair Lewis's supposedly dull and endless Midwest, there flourished an enormous renaissance in art and culture.

Of course, the trouble with Lewis and all of the other "doomed young people" of the 1920s is that they were never in their own minds able to match the roots of their own careers with the soil which produced them. Some few could, of course, but they were the more pristine intellectuals such as Van Wyck Brooks, who wrote in 1921:

It remains true that, if we resent this life, it is only a sign of our weakness, of the harm we have permitted this civilization to do us, or our imperfectly realized freedom; for to the creative spirit in its free state the external world is merely an impersonal point of departure. Thus it is certain that as long as the American writers share what James Bryce called the "mass fatalism" of the American people, our literature will remain the sterile, inferior phenomenon which, on the whole, it is.[21]

What Brooks seemed to be saying is that the nation is only as good as it thinks it is. The French for some several hundred years had thought of themselves as in the vanguard of Western civilization; it was perfectly natural, it was supposed in Paris, for others to wish to imitate them. The same could have been said for the British. Who was really to say that George Bellows and his Stag at Sharkey's was any less significant that Van Gogh and his Bridge at Arles. What outside judge could really determine the value of a Childe Hassam or a Prendergast? The real estimation of one's artistic value is seemingly determined by the egotism of one's society.

If it was an intellectual pessimism from which the United States suffered in 1925, then all was to be effected by titanic developments. The "self-indulgence" of the 1920s, as Jonathan Daniels called it in The Nation, was to be replaced by depression. The eventual identification of American intellectualism with the New Deal and with Franklin Roosevelt was to metamorphasize some important mutations into American arts and letters. The change was so dramatic in concept that its magnitude is even now difficult to comprehend. A current American history textbook, now used in a great many colleges and universities, tried hard to limn the details of the great revolution of the 1930s. Liberals, imply these historians, were "relatively optimistic"; conservatives were pessimistic. Moving one step further in the direction to which the authors point, one may very well conclude that since most intellectuals were liberal, then they had become by nature optimistic in the 1930s. If true, that certainly represented a switch from the previous era.

Of course it was not all that unassailable in terms of logic. There were numerous exceptions, as there always are. Charles Beard, who would certainly rank with Van Wyck Brooks as a pristine rather than a quasi-intellectual, did not always see virtue in the social dogmas or international policies of the New Deal. One is reminded here of Beard's laconic little observation that it was the Democratic Party which had brought on the War of 1812 and World War I, and that now the nation could expect World War II.[22]

But the 1930s were years of turbulence. Wilsonian liberalism, Progressive insurgency, and rural Bryanism were all swept away in the floodwaters of the New Deal: all drifted helplessly as flotsam and jetsam in the new revolution. The very nature of the New Deal, its twistings and turnings, its very experimentation, not only involved American intellectualism within the change but placed it in a position of responsibility from which it could not escape. Like a snake caught in a trap, American intellectualism was forced to bite its own tail—and that was not easy. American materialism and "boosterism," which had long been vilified by Sinclair Lewis, now became a "future" to be shaped by intellectuals. How strange it was to listen to the words of Rex Tugwell, the archetype of a New Deal intellectual technocrat.

> The program we must adopt for the immediate future is compounded of a natively American mixture, some of the elements of which are: mass production, machine processes, scientific management, constant invention, scope for initiative, democratic methods, decentralized administration, and judgment by results.[23]

It was almost like good old George Babbitt in his maiden speech before the Zenith Rotary Club. The truth was that Tugwell sounded almost exactly like Herbert Hoover of two years previously; even though Hoover had said that if the country abandoned Republicanism, then grass would grow on the streets of the nation. Yet Tugwell was an optimist of 1934; Hoover a pessimist of 1932. How could that be? The answer was all so simple—the liberals were now in, and the conservatives were out, and that is the way things tend to go with the ins and the outs. Of course the conservatives did not seem to help matters much, with Hoover claiming that repression would soon follow and that free speech and free press were on their way out. And then there was the *Chicago Tribune*, with its owner and publisher Robert R. McCormick playing a threnody of doom. The nation, implied the *Tribune*, was well on its way to a dictatorship.

It would seem that within these changes alone there is a mighty message. Almost two decades later the radicals of the 1960s were to decry the "Amerika" of rightist dictatorship, the end to free speech and press, and repression, repression, and repression. It is amusing indeed to conjure up the vision of Charles Beard and Robert R. McCormick sitting around a campfire with a dozen hipsters of the Sixties, all agreeing that the United States would not long survive.

The welter of voices which was to be heard during the New Deal period was just that, and it is difficult to sort out just who was who. A good *Tribune* editorial might observe, for instance, that the British "aren't going communistic—yet," but that the emergence of British radicalism was heralding the beginnings of radical revolution in America. Yet, on the other hand, right smack in the middle of the liberal optimism of the 1930s, Sinclair Lewis hacked out one of his lesser novels, *It Can't Happen Here*. Not a few liberals hailed this second-rate effort as proof that a fascist dictatorship for the United States lay just over the horizon.[24]

What confounded the entire issue of a supposedly optimistic liberalism as opposed to a theoretically pessimistic conservatism in the Thirties was the total picture of democracy, fascism, and communism. A rather significant chunk of the intellectual left in the United States and Western Europe had committed itself not only to the success of Russian communism, but to its very survival. The peregrinations of Russian ideology made this increasingly difficult, and not once but many times did the American intellectual left find itself going one way while temporary Russian revisions called for another. This was especially true during the Soviet purge of the 1930s, the Russo-Nazi Pact of 1940, and the subsequent Russian invasions of Poland and Finland. Once again, these changes called for the biting of one's tail, a requisite easily met by most American leftists.

The opening of the war in Europe in 1939 fixed a few intellectual positions, however. Many Americans in this category assumed that it was absolutely necessary for the United States to aid Britain, even if it meant playing a game of international brinksmanship which would have made John Foster Dulles green with envy. The proper technique was to equate failure to aid the British with the notion that civilization was in its death throes. Robert Sherwood, the playwright, set the tone by writing an ad for the Committee to Defend America by Aiding the Allies—a title which says a good deal in itself. "We Americans have

naturally wished to keep out of this war," Sherwood wrote. "But...,"
so ran the inevitable qualifier, "Hitler is striking with all the terrible
force at his command. . . . We can help by sending planes, guns, muni-
tions, food."[25]

So the full circle had almost been completed. The "sad young men"
of the 1920s, handed a "red-hot world" by their forebears; exposers
of devilish conspiracies which brought the nation into World War I;
writers of novels about decayed flesh on barbed wire: they had come
full about. War was now an absolute necessity. And still the circle
would not end—for far out in the American heartland, a young university president, J. W. Fulbright of the University of Arkansas, was
raging because he was censured for making a pro-war speech at
graduation ceremonies at the University of Missouri.

It was indeed quite strange that when Pearl Harbor finally came,
optimism was never higher in the intellectual community, nor was
doomsaying never more absent. The American right did some grum-
bling about why Pearl Harbor had happened, but after a few sketchy
"investigations" of the circumstances surrounding the attack, it went
right to work to win the war. The American left, entranced by its own
inborn and egoistic dream of remaking the world in its own image,
not only temporarily found capitalism acceptable but necessary to the
saving of Russia. Doomsaying was mothballed for the duration of the
war.

Once the delirium of peace was passed, however, both were once
again abroad in the land. Conservatives were soon to see conspiracies
in high places. Paranoia swept the right with charges that "they"—
Communists in high places—were manipulating events. President
Truman temporarily stayed the assault with the rebuttal that the only
Reds in Washington were "red herrings." When some actual cases of
subversion were recounted in the instances of Alger Hiss, Klaus Fuchs,
the Rosenbergs and lesser individuals, there was an almost instant
rebirth of conservative hope. American liberalism, on the other hand,
retreated into a blue funk.

Though the Democratic Harry Truman did win the presidency in
1948, and though since that time he has entered the pantheon of
liberal heroes, Truman was no leader of besieged intellectual battalions from 1948 to 1952. Arthur M. Schlesinger, Jr., had already
suggested that he get out of the way for the politically undeclared
Eisenhower of 1947. Resident Senate intellectual J. W. Fulbright had
suggested that Truman resign, which action brought forth from the
President the suggestion that Fulbright was only "half-bright." It is
interesting to note that the 1974 vision of Truman as an unstained and
honest President was not the vision seen in 1948 and the four years

thereafter. The "five-percent" scandals and the image of Truman as a gut-level campaigner seemed to connotate the notion of a "Dirty Harry" in the White House rather than a "Mr. Clean."

Of course it is generally accepted today that Harry Truman was a man of many parts—truly an honest and determined President who worked hard at his job. But the intellectual left of 1948-52 rarely regarded him in that light, and at the end of his tenure as President the mention of Truman's name in any intellectual gathering was to bring on an epidemic of embarrassed shuffling. Adlai Stevenson, a veritable Galahad among the same intellectual circles in 1952, found it quite difficult to accept political aid from Truman during the campaign year.

Since it appeared obvious that the urbane and talented Stevenson was to lose to Dwight David Eisenhower in November of election year, doomsaying got up, put on its clothes, and prepared to walk with liberalism into the night. While resurgent Republicans optimistically chanted "I like Ike," more liberal Democrats bespoke the black curtain which was about to fall upon humanity. There were to be no more social gains, Eisenhower was merely a pawn in the hands of subtle machinators, and, as Truman was to argue, not a single new dam would be built in the West. Even Stevenson joined in, calling the twentieth century the "bloodiest, most turbulent era of the Christian age. . . ." There would be no gains "without pains," he said, and no victory was to be won without a "long, patient, costly struggle." Only the last could save Mother Earth from "war, poverty, and tyranny. . . ."[26]

With Eisenhower in the White House the paranoid doomsaying of McCarthyism faded into the past. For on to six years there was a relatively placid period of peace and prosperity marked only with what could have been labeled by the most expert as second-class dooming. They were merely echoes of thunder in the distance, and yet they were sounds of leftish-inclined intellectuals practicing on the rifle range. The charges against Eisenhower during his early years were much the same as some used against Nixon during his presidency. Eisenhower was really a sick man, the rumors said, there was a nameless fear on the land, and there would soon be a depression which would "curl your hair."

On the whole, however, the political atmosphere of the nation during the mid-Fifties was diffused with the kindly light of a popular but sometimes indecipherable Eisenhower syntax. Yet, regardless of a poll of historians which placed Eisenhower somewhere between Chester Arthur and Andrew Johnson in effectiveness, this kindly President was something of a politician. His handling of Congress was superb. He did well with the press, even though its reporters had difficulty understanding the President's prose. And, of course, he was in essence a peacemaker.[27]

A number of events turned the last three years of the Eisenhower period sour, and in the turning the liberals recovered much in vigor. A mild recession was accompanied by the successful Russian launching of a satellite. The latter event was accompanied by an outbreak of attacks against the education system. One single book alone—*Educational Wastelands*, by Arthur Bestor—caused a furor almost on the level of that achieved by the Flexner Report on the medical profession written almost fifty years before.[28]

Though the Bestor attack was mainly one based in educational conservatism, holding that quality rather than quantity should be stressed, its effect was exactly the opposite. Tremendous forces were unloosed on the land, all translating the meaning of "quality" in terms of sheer quantity. State after state, either through bond issues or other revenue plans, poured money into higher education. The federal government plied colleges and universities with grants from both the Department of Health, Education and Welfare, and the Department of Defense. Small, inadequate, and poor state colleges soon became big, inadequate, and poor state universities. Faculties, hastily recruited and poorly matured, were set to the task to teaching hastily recruited and poorly matured students.

Such was the rapid growth of some university graduate programs that, in some cases, curricula exceeded demand. Departments were created to meet demands which didn't exist. And, in the end, those same departments were forced to hypo their attendance by simply buying students off the rack, so to speak. Later, when the Vietnam War required increasing draft levies, it was many of these same programs which offered safe havens for increasing numbers of deferred students.

The issue of "sputnik" and its concomitant results breathed new life into the American left, and it is almost possible to mark chronologically the growth of campus radicalism with the uncontrolled expansion of the university system. Looking back, it does seem quite strange that much of the impetus given to the new radicalism came from elements of the American Jewish community. Perhaps it is true, as Joseph Epstein wrote for the *Chicago Tribune* in 1972, that the 1950s marked the "last hurrah" of white and Episcopalian leadership, though it must be added that much of that claim seemed to be pure rhetoric itself. It may have been true, as Epstein seemed to claim, that Jews and Catholics attained a greater niche in American society, but to throw American Episcopalians into the picture seems a little rank.[29]

The truth seems to have been that the American Jewish community in particular made tremendous strides during the 1950s. That seems to be true in almost every category. The per capita income of American Jews outstripped all others by far, while the American WASP fell to an unenviable level in this statistic. And Catholics followed suit; Poles, for example, ranking high in per capita income by 1965. While American Jews were on their way to becoming the largest single ethnic element on the Harvard faculty, for instance, American Catholics tightened their tenacious position in the political establishment. Catholics became the largest part of the Senate, the majority leader of the Senate was Catholic by 1961, and in the same year so was the President of the United States.

But it was the new Jewish consciousness which had a most significant effect on the 1960s. The ethos of the Jew, his seemingly inherent motivation for the public good, and his drive to excel, all combined to add a new leavening to the American scene. As Norman Mailer was to put it, most Jewish youngsters of the Sixties came from the middle class. They were well educated, opposed to the conformity of their parents, and "radical pacifist" in the sense that they had taken "the vow of nonviolence." Noting the tendency of Jews to the new radicalism, Mailer wrote:

> His act of violence is to commit suicide, even as the hipster's is to commit murder, but in his absent-minded way, the beatnik is a torch-bearer of those nearly lost values of freedom, self-expression, and equality which first turned him against the hypocrisies and barren culturelessness of the middle class.[30]

The reinvigorated left of the late 1950s was stimulated by a number of strangely paradoxical issues, among them an exaggerated fear of atomic conflict, the supposed failure of the educational system, a proclaimed overconformity in American life, the declared evils of a consumer economy, the civil rights movement, and the "missile gap." They were paradoxical in many ways, but the most obvious one of course was the direct contradiction existent in the left's fear of atomic conflict, while at the same time it was perfectly happy to exploit the fraudulent claim that Russia was moving far ahead of the United States in missile development.

Neither the left nor the right have been totally concerned with truth in the political arena. But what is amazing in looking back is that so many well-intentioned and able people lent themselves to what proved to be patently false arguments. The eminent theologian Reinhold Niebuhr, for example, pronounced severe judgment on President Eisenhower in 1960 for "letting the Russians get ahead of us . . ." A respected historian, Allan Nevins, publicly deplored the nation's "passive, complacent, and even apathetic mood," and implied that the nation might go down the drain if it did not elect a strong President.

Both Niebuhr and Nevins were on shaky factual grounds and the best explanation of their complaints is that they were caught up in the developing Kennedy campaign for the presidency.

Still, doomsayers as they are, they were no further wrong than the *New York Times* in 1960 which happily pronounced: "In this winter's sunshine, peace and prosperity are widespread: the clouds are no bigger than the hand of man, and no stronger than his will."[31] Clouds were on the horizon, and they were building up in the manner of a Kansas tornado. The successful Cuban revolution of Fidel Castro had unleashed demons from the box, and already the Fair Play for Cuba Committee had been formed. Shortly Lee Harvey Oswald, a future presidential assassin, was to begin working for it. The Student Peace Union, organized in Chicago in 1959, quickly gathered force and in that same year was able to put 5,000 demonstrators before the White House. The National Committee for a Sane Nuclear Policy was operating from bases throughout the nation in 1960. Everywhere and anywhere, a vigorous left was grasping at any straw which might bring it to power. A lone student had conducted an antimilitary protest in the early months of 1960, but in February of the same year sizeable demonstrations were whipped up to save from death the condemned rapist, Carol Chessman. And in May 1960, some 8,000 students plus faculty members held a rowdy confrontation with police in San Francisco.[32]

It was, of course, to be a decade of unprecedented dooming. Already the thunder from the left set an ominous tone. The San Francisco riot had been against "repression," a popular item for doomsaying in the ten years that followed. There was an increased stridency to the call for "priorities" in order to save the nation. Walter Lippmann's equivocal response probably typified the thoughts of the nation. "In the absence of clear ideas and defensible standards," he wrote, "the victory is likely to go to the loudest battalions."

The loudest battalions were on the left in 1960. The American right, huddled in massed confusion, seemed unable to defend the simple and effective argument of eight years of relative peace. Among the few Americans with minds free enough to shuck aside political considerations and to make some daring predictions were five contributors to *U.S. News and World Report*. The resultant article was impressive, and it still is. Precluding their specific arguments, the five men concluded that there appeared to be a rapidly changing moral standard. Specific examples were to be best illustrated by the increase in juvenile delinquency, the widespread cheating in American colleges, and by the increase in police irregularities.

The five men—Robert Fitch, Detlev Bronk, Mortimer Adler, Herbert Muller, and the Reverend John LaFarge—saw most distressing signs

59

of a turbulent decade. Fitch, pointing up that most young people in the coming decade would be affected by middle-class affluence, argued that parental permissiveness had given the new generation everything but "moral standards and moral imperatives."

Muller emphasized corruption, slackness, and softness. Adler saw the indications of a "silly sentimentality" and the need for more work for children. LaFarge contended that the growing rootlessness of American society bode ill for the future. The latter pushed the concept of self-discipline as the basis for true democracy. He added:

> A good many parents who really don't believe in coddling are still rather helpless. They don't know exactly what to do. They would like to be sterner with their children, but they're up against the environment, the social atmosphere, around them.[33]

At almost the same time, relatively speaking, the Commercial Associated Network in Great Britain produced a transatlantic television interview and commentary on American society. Twenty-five American critics, described by one source as assorted "beatniks" and eminent university professors, were allowed to range freely on the existing flaws in American culture. Among those involved were Alger Hiss, Dalton Trumbo, Mort Sahl, Norman Cousins, John Kenneth Galbraith, Robert M. Hutchins, Norman Mailer, Jules Feiffer, and Harold Call. Call was a representative of the Mattachine Society of the United States, Feiffer a cartoonist, Sahl a humorist who made a living from satirizing the Eisenhower administration, and Trumbo a Hollywood script writer with markedly leftist leanings.

What happened in the way of doomsaying was almost incredible. Sixteen hours of complaint were recorded in the sessions, and these were eventually boiled down to a ninety-minute program. What was left amounted to an almost unalloyed colloquy on the vacuity of American life. It was dooming in the most extraordinary sense of the word. It might be pointed out, perhaps needlessly, that the event took place long before the large American participation in the Vietnam War. Yet what is surprising is that their tone was to a great extent that which marked the entire left during the 1960s. Alger Hiss, for instance, was allowed to express a "fear, a sort of nameless fear, of the unknown and of unexpected things . . ." It was typical 1960s rhetoric. Perhaps good old Norman Thomas, the dean of American socialism, made more sense than any of the other participants—which gives one a notion of what transpired—when he claimed that to get ahead in the United States, one had to wear a grey flannel suit.[34]

A fair number of these individuals were to be ardent supporters of the Kennedy campaign in the coming months, and that probably says a good deal about the sense of what they seemed to be saying. They were "outs" and people in that category tend to construct a vision of the world in more apocalyptic terms. But even Kennedy himself, at almost the same moment, was orchestrating along the same line. So were the members of his political team. In January 1960 Kennedy called for a stronger man in the presidency and vowed that, if elected, he would exercise the "fullest powers" of the office. Seven days later Governor Robert B. Meyner of New Jersey accused President Eisenhower of too much "smilesmanship," and said the President was dancing to a Russian tune. The nation was becoming a second class power, Meyner added: "We are so far behind in the missile race and in the development of new weapons that it is a serious question whether we can ever catch up."[35]

The United States was not really behind the Russians in 1960 in an overall sense, and the Cuban missile crisis of the Kennedy period was to show the falsity of liberal charges. What was going on was a beautifully developing campaign of deception; dirty tricks might be the term used in later years. The U.S. Army was a fit arm of national defense, and in infinitely better shape than it was to be in 1970. The American Navy could claim absolute superiority on the high seas; something it could not do ten years later. There was no missile gap.

But the pro-Kennedy press was substantial, and leading Democrats presented a picture of precipitous American decline in military strength. Kennedy himself stated on January 23:

We are not enjoying a period of peace—only a period of stagnation and retreat, while America becomes second in missiles, second in education and, if we don't act fast and effectively, second in production and industrial might.

The statement was not only a clever bit of dooming, it was sheer demagoguery.

Senator Hubert Humphrey, trying to match the pace of the Kennedy campaign, followed suit by laying the responsibility for the possible end of a "period of peace" at Eisenhower's feet. Humphrey said:

He cannot avoid responsibility for the erosion of our national power and prestige which has taken place in the last seven years. He cannot dodge or duck responsibility for the slowdown in our national growth which has taken place in the last seven years. He cannot beg out of the stagnation in our national morality and character which has taken place in the last seven years.

Herblock, the Washington cartoonist and a confirmed "dove" in later years, whipped out an appropriate offering in mid-January. There stood a beleaguered President, carrying a sign shot full of holes. The caption: "I know more about defense than almost anyone in the country."[36]

Besides that of the "missile gap," Democrats in 1960 raised other issues which implied doom and ruin for the country unless their party was successful at the polls. Candidate Kennedy, speaking in Indiana, referred to seven "years of economic failure" in connection with the Eisenhower-Nixon team and interjected, parenthetically, that Ireland had been subject to "foreign oppression" for some 700 years. This was a strange admixture of arguments, indeed, especially for the Hoosier state. Later the young senator was to develop a more cogent message—or at least one which had a broader appeal. He began to argue that the country was required to have a higher priority than that of the creation of a consumer society. As Kennedy put it, America had to make a choice between "public interest and public comfort." America had begun to slip in terms of power, he claimed. "I don't want historians writing in 1970 to say that the balance of power in the 1950s and 1960s began to turn against the United States and the cause of freedom," he said.[37]

The Democratic claim that President Eisenhower had taken the country to the brink of disaster was skillful politics, even though without factual support, and neither Eisenhower nor Nixon could really devise effective answers to it. It is almost axiomatic in politics, American politics at least, that a successful candidate is one who attaches as many evils of existing or future society to his opposition, and then promises that only he can lead his people down the long hard road to the promised land of security and peace.

Given the present methods of transmitting the news, such a candidate needs to keep the media friendly so that by repetition he hammers his message home. The "ins," those having to defend policy, are hard put to answer all charges. It is far less appealing, politically speaking, to argue that everything is proceeding in good order than it is to proclaim supposed dangers ahead. In 1960 both the President and candidate Nixon had great difficulty in counteracting Kennedy's charges. Eisenhower stated that Democratic charges of American military weakness were "spurious." "Our defense is not only strong," Eisenhower argued, "it is awesome and it is respected elsewhere."

History has proven that Eisenhower and Nixon were both right in their claims about the strength of the United States, and it was President Kennedy himself who provided the ultimate proof during the Cuban missile crisis. But the victories go sometimes to the loudest battalions, as Walter Lippmann had indicated, and here was the classic case. The President could inveigh against the "political morticians" who were so engaged in "breast-beating pessimism," but the words were unheeded by many. Richard M. Nixon was to argue that what the country needed for the next four years was a man "who won't go off half-cocked and give appearance of leadership when, actually, his speaking out might be disastrous to the whole world." That kind of argumentation was not what the country wanted, either.[38]

Kennedy did win, of course, and his victory was traceable to his charm, his seeming youth, and his success in creating a vision of doom. Yet, it is fascinating to relate retrospectively both Kennedy and Eisenhower to the American left in the later 1960s. By 1969, for instance, Kennedy was seldom quoted in terms of the 1960 campaign for the presidency, and the movement preferred to picture him as part of a golden Camelot which, in reality, never existed. Eisenhower, however, assumed a dual role in the movement's dialectic. He was a "do-nothing" President who, at one point in his life, was granted one extraordinary moment of perception. This revelation came during the Eisenhower "farewell address," when the outgoing President warned against the "acquisition of unwarranted influence, whether sought or unsought, by the military-industrial complex."

The selective citation from President Eisenhower's speeches and writings is typical of the manipulation of reality by the movement. Nothing is ever said, for instance, about words in that same farewell address which explicitly warn that the national arms must always be at the ready and that there can no longer be any "emergency improvisation" of our national defense. Nor is it ever remembered that in 1969 Senator William Proxmire of Wisconsin was to conclude:

> I do not claim nor even suggest that any conspiracy exists between the military and the 100 largest defense contractors. I do not believe in the conspiracy theory of history. I charge no general wrongdoing on the part of either group.[39]

Such is the course of history and of doomsaying over the years, and one can well wonder how, through it all, humanity has managed to survive. It has, and the obvious proof is that, through a thousand real or imagined disasters, man is still here. Progress is painfully slow, as the real humanist has come to understand, and it is sometimes only as evident as the crumbling of the bank on some slowly shifting riverbank. Perhaps Lord Kenneth Clark has best summed it in his personal credo on the state of mankind:

> I believe that order is better than chaos, creation better than destruction. I prefer gentleness to violence, forgiveness to vendetta. On the whole I think that knowledge is preferable to ignorance, and I am sure that human sympathy is more valuable than ideology. I believe that in spite of the recent triumphs of science, men haven't changed much in the last two thousand years, and in consequence we must try to learn from history. History is ourselves.[40]

3
Rhetoric on the Campus

The levels of distance between Old Siwash of 1939 and the University of California in 1973 are almost too great to comprehend. The older notions of the academic community as opposed to those of the new, the enormous change in all standards of campus morality as well as the sheer size of the American university campus, represents a generation gap of considerable proportions.

The college student of 1939 most generally walked from his privately owned and rented quarters to his classrooms. Today much of the university campus space is taken up with parking lots for student automobiles. Students of 1939 may have read a little of John Steinbeck, Hemingway, Santayana, or Joyce. Today, among those who do read, one finds the names of Marcuse, Heller, and Herman Hesse ranking high in popularity.

The greatest change of all came in the manner in which universities and colleges acquired their students. In 1939 those who attended institutions of higher education did so either because they had acceptable grades and sufficient money, or because they were adequately prepared and had enough drive to work their way through the system. Most of the young people of the pre-World War II era were necessarily driven by a compulsion to be educated regardless of hardships caused by empty stomachs and empty pockets. In the Sixties, when times were "a-changing," so was the type of young American entering the university as a freshman. It is true that for some there was the old compelling drive to further their educations. For others, however, universities meant either a haven from the draft or a fulfillment of a parental rather than an individual dream.

As one contributor to the *New York Times* was to write in the 1960s, "no one has successfully or fully explained the changing moods and styles of campus life." At the beginning of this chaotic and colorful period, American institutions of higher learning were in a remarkable and enviable position. Public sentiment had moved behind the cause of the university community, partly because of favorable publicity relating to facilities and salary scales and partly because of the Russian successes in space. The order of the day in the early Sixties was that faculty salaries had to be raised, and great amounts of money had to be poured into the educational pipeline in order to improve the product.[1]

Truly nothing was too good for American universities and colleges during these years. Salary levels went up. State legislatures rarely quibbled about budgets, and private colleges were almost immediately successful in raising money for expansion. Harvard University, for instance, was able to announce in 1959 that its three-year drive to raise $82.5 million had gone over the top and that, along with accrued interest, the fund had leveled off at $88 million.[2] Increasingly available loans, both from federal and private sources, made it increasingly possible for students to "borrow" their way through four years of college.

All over the nation the entire university community kept contractors in the black with huge building programs. High-rise dormitories which did nothing to balance the state budgets or the emotional well-being of students went up everywhere. Change was in the air. *In loco parentis* went out as a university principle and the drug traffic came in; the last not as a university principle of course, but as a result of having no principles at all. The old order was disappearing and a new one was coming in.

The time was to come later in the Sixties when a score of differing notions were developed concerning the causes of the so-called student revolution. One noted educator, for instance, was inclined to believe that the preoccupation of school administrators with neatness and order had tended to trigger among students a sense of repression.[3] The contention does not hold up under scrutiny, particularly when one views it in a historical context. The Presidential Commission on Campus Unrest heard dozens of ideas of the causes of the revolt, including the usual ones relating to the Vietnam War and the supposed need of university responsiveness to change. In his testimony before that committee Senator Ted Kennedy argued the Vietnam theme. So did President Robben Fleming of the University of Michigan. President S. I. Hayakawa of San Francisco State offered a differing argument, stating:

> Campus disorders come not from those who are in school because they want to be, but from those who are trapped there, whether by Selective Service or by social pressures.[4]

Stephen Kelman, a former Harvard student, added a newer slant to the discussion when he testified that "campus violence will continue as long as students continue to regard the American people not as potential allies in resolving problems, but as an enemy to be confronted."[5] Bruno Bettelheim argued that the Vietnam War and the so-called atomic bomb issue were only screens for what really ailed the students. "Youth feels its future is bleak not with the prospect of nuclear war . . . ," he claimed, "but because of their feeling that nobody needs them, that society can do nicely without them." To Bettelheim, America had made the mistake of prolonging adolescence. Pointing out that there were few campus militants in engineering, medicine, and chemistry, he further contended that "our institutions of higher learning have expanded too fast." Public pressure had created a forced growth. "With no more open frontiers left," he concluded, "our society has no special place for adolescents today, with the single exception of our colleges and universities."[6]

Much of what Bettelheim said seemed to have been true. Dozens of normal schools had exploded into "universities"—places like Kent State and Southern Illinois University—their high-rise dorms overfilled and poorly policed. A great many of these schools had lowered their academic standards in response to the call for growth, though in all honesty it must be admitted that unrealistic grading practices existed throughout the whole educational community from Harvard on down. Everywhere, colleges and universities had become corrective institutions. They corrected the inadequacies of students with poor high school records by means of so-called precollege courses. They offered "relevant" courses which were designed to correct society's inadequacies. In some colleges it became almost next to impossible to flunk out. Semivocational schools operated by some of these schools kept on campus the student who simply could not crack the liberal arts or science courses. Furthermore, the new and emerging universities failed to maintain rigorous transfer policies, making it possible for any poor student to drift from institution to institution.

Thus did many students float from campus to campus, seeking in many cases the "in" spot, and rarely bothering to correct their own basic inadequacies. So loose did university policies become in many instances that the large high-rise dormitories became wayfarers' inns for itinerant young people. Drifters, some of these not even of college age, had little difficulty in staying overnight in these structures, or in cadging meals or in attending school functions. And if a demonstration had been planned, their numbers helped to swell the crowd.

It was in the traditional difficult liberal arts areas in which standards seemed to suffer the most. The impulse toward relevance helped speed the decay. Political science departments seemed to become overloaded with instructors whose political inclinations assumed a higher degree of importance than their intellectual attainments. With the hindrance of very little scholarship indeed, it became incredibly possible for such departments to offer courses in revolution, while at the same time ignoring the possibilities of more practical courses in the meaning of capitalism.

Much the same perversion swept over history departments in both major and minor universities. Oscar Handlin, a most respectable scholar, speaking at the American Historical Association convention in 1970, expressed something of the sense of change in his area of study. American historians, he said, had "allowed their subject to slip into the hands of propagandists, politicians, dramatists, novelists, journalists, and social engineers."[7]

A case in point during the 1960s was to be found in the creation of so-called black history courses. The mania to develop such ethnic studies departments not only called upon the need for invention in a broad sense, but it exceeded the real need for experts in these reputed fields. Peter Chew, writing an excellent commentary on the subject for *American Heritage*, decried the "rummaging about" within black history for "any kind of accomplishment" on the part of the Negro race. In particular he pointed to a "relevant" lesson plan distributed by the Washington, D.C., Teachers' Union, a plan which likened the burning and destruction of the 1960s' Washington riots to the Boston Tea Party. He further noted that a "black heritage" series by CBS was so erroneous that Roy Wilkins, the executive secretary of the NAACP, called it "hopelessly flawed."

As Chew argued, the publishing press got in its licks as well in the search for immediate profit. Arno Press, he said, had published a series of advertisements showing or indicating that Crispus Attucks, an American killed in the Boston Massacre, was a black who had died while "leading the patriots." There is considerable evidence, said Chew, that Attucks may have been Indian instead of black, and that he was less patriotic in his behavior than he was irrational.[8]

History is particularly vulnerable to mistruth, of course, for a clever writer may choose his facts to fortify a partisan case or he may be accidentally misled by circumstances. With time and effort most histori-

67

cal errors are eliminated, although it must be added that some persist with incredible durability. As an example, the Sacco-Vanzetti case of the 1920s has remained in many American history books falsely representing a miscarriage of American justice.

Nicola Sacco and Bartolomeo Vanzetti were Italian immigrants who were found guilty of having committed a holdup murder in 1920 and were sentenced to death. Liberals in America and Europe immediately sprang to the barricades with the charge that the two had been framed because they were ardent socialists. There were riots before American embassies overseas and great protests in the garment district of New York City. Radical chic entered to the rescue. Edna St. Vincent Millay stopped burning her candle at both ends long enough to write an indignant book about the case. Maxwell Anderson wrote a brilliant play called *Winterset* which was based upon the theme. James Thurber produced a kind of comedy, *The Male Animal*, which was based in part upon the last letter written by Vanzetti. Years after the end of World War II, CBS and Edward R. Murrow, the noted news telecaster, produced a series of recordings called "I Can Hear It Now," in which the two men are apotheosized.

It wasn't until the 1960s, however, that the historian Francis Russell really examined the case in retrospect. He found that ballistics evidence was unquestionably on the side of the government in the case and that some of the individuals who had supported the two men during the course of the trial were convinced of the guilt of one or both of the accused. What is really tragic about Russell's astounding piece of detective work is that so many intellectuals in the decades following the case, and so many college students along with them, became convinced by the cant that the Sacco and Vanzetti case was the perfect illustration of the existence of a corrupt and rotten legal system.[9]

Even more tragic was the further indoctrination of a generation of American college students with the writings of such radical historians as William A. Williams, D. F. Fleming, Gabriel Kolko, Diane Shaver Clemens, and David Horowitz. Some if not all of these writers invariably saw the United States not only as a flawed society, but as the villain of international diplomacy during the last thirty years. This country rather than Russia was the cause of the Cold War. This country, because of the rapacity of its peculiar brand of capitalism, had pressed for American economic expansion abroad. Only the Soviet Union, its motives pure and unsullied, stood between the United States and a kind of world oppression.

In 1972 Robert Maddox of Pennsylvania State University examined the work of the radical historians in a book entitled *The New Left and the Origins of the Cold War*. His conclusion was that their writings are not only based upon the "pervasive misusages of the source material," but they involve a revision of much of the so-called evidence or documentation. Williams, said Maddox, was guilty of constructing "speeches and dialogues by splicing together phrases uttered at different times and on diverse subjects." Maddox discovered among the revisionist historians a tendency towards the misused quotation and the alteration of what actually was said upon certain occasions. Maddox's most serious charge was that there were "misstatements of fact, quotations, wrenched out of context, and unsupported allegations. . . ."[10]

If Maddox was right, then the impact of the writings of such historians might have been serious. After all, the forced growth of so many universities had compelled the employment of many new and barely qualified instructors. Misleading materials plus the other factors of immature teachers and bored students all added up to trouble. The signs of all these can easily be seen in the Sixties. Too many grammar instructors, bored with freshman composition courses, moved their students to the activist and emotional discussion of current events. Similar instances existed on almost every campus in the areas of history, political science, sociology, and psychology. Errors of fact were not only compounded by the ignorance of both instructor and students, but they were unfortunately passed to incoming generations of students as what was or ought to be.[11]

If those same errors had been committed in similar magnitude in university chemistry buildings, then entire communities might have been blown sky high. But in the general area of liberal arts they were allowed to ferment into a kind of thinking which was revolutionary in its framework. Carl Oglesby, a radical leader of the 1960s, provides the perfect illustration. His comments on the Watergate issue of the early 1970s contained the following items of logic. The primary issue in American society, he claimed, was the conflict between the "Yankees" and a frontier-oriented "cowboy" element. Lyndon B. Johnson and Richard M. Nixon, seemingly disparate types, were both products of the latter.

Oglesby then lays a most heavy gravamen upon his readers. The logic is so granular that it can only be given by direct quotation. "Whether or not the Cowboys killed Kennedy in Dallas in 1963 in order to make the Vietnam War," Oglesby writes, "the ascendancy of LBJ still amounted to a transfer of the base of federal power. . . ." Upon the assassination of Robert Kennedy, writes Oglesby, "it must have become clear to leading Yankee activists (Clifford, Vance, Ball, Harriman?) that the Cowboys would not permit the restoration of Yankee power. . . ."

How does Watergate enter the picture? Oglesby explains: "Watergate opens onto this Yankee-Cowboy split most revealingly, stunningly, if we entertain the notion that McCord may be a double agent acting in behalf of Yankee interests." Oglesby's mental gymnastics may leave one aghast, but it is imperative to remember that he is only the product of the historical training he has received.[12]

During the 1960s Oglesby had been a leading figure in Students for a Democratic Society, an organization which heralded the campus revolution with the "manifesto" of 1962. That document, so often marked as the beginning of the radical assault upon the university system, contained the usual number of platitudes—among them the charge that the Fifties had been a decade of apathy and that college students had been too undemonstrative. But there was a significance in the document as well. It did not plead for an end to radical inactivity, but it unequivocally indicated that the time had come for "breaking the crust of apathy and overcoming the inner alienation. . . ." It is indeed strange to note that last word—alienation—used in the context of 1962, at least three years before the large American troops commitment to Vietnam.[13]

Slowly but surely did the old order begin to crumble, and it was to be helped on its way by some unusual assistance. In 1964 Grayson Kirk, himself a victim of activism in later years as the president of Columbia University, portrayed the beginning of the end of Utopia. In words he would doubtlessly regret in years to come, he stated that the "search for common social values must begin in our own back-yard." Some years later his office at Columbia was occupied and despoiled, but in 1964 he contended that the ideal society could not be reached if the "men in the vanguard are restrained for the fear that they are too far ahead of those struggling in the rear ranks. . . ."

By the time that Kirk made these remarks the grand march toward campus disorder was well underway. The University of California at Berkeley, its campus honeycombed with such organizations as the Young Peoples Socialist League, the Young Socialist Alliance, the Student Society for Travel to Cuba, and the Independent Socialist Club, had fallen victim to the first successful large-scale student strike. What were to become familiar campus scenes were all acted out in Berkeley—the initial calling for a strike over some ultimately innocuous issue, the sudden appearance on campus of prominent supporters of the strike (in this case Joan Baez), the provocation of police, and a resulting campus confrontation. It is interesting to note, parenthetically, that at least one of the strike leaders was in his fifties and that a disproportionate number of the remainder of the leadership was Jewish.[14]

By the spring of 1965 campus activism had spread beyond the borders of California—much of it imitative of the Berkeley example and much through the encouragement of the SDS. In March 1965 the first "teach-in" was held at the University of Michigan. In the following May another was held back at Berkeley and it was attended by such prominent liberals or leftists as Senator Ernest Gruening of Alaska, Norman Mailer, Benjamin Spock, Staughton Lynd, Isaac Deutscher, I. F. Stone, and representatives of the Progressive Labor Party.

Student revolts then began to pop up across America with increasing frequency. In a great many instances the various university administrations involved capitulated ignominiously to the strikers almost before the activities had gotten underway. The president of Cornell University sat at the feet of revolt leaders while they lectured him from the stage of an auditorium. Teachers at San Francisco State were harassed and threatened, and fire bombs were placed near their offices. In almost every instance of the campus explosions occurring during the middle 1960s, the university or college newspapers had previously fallen into the hands of student editors with leftist points of view.

This last may have occurred without plan, but it was well within the aspirations of the growing radical left. Carl Davidson, a movement leader of some dimension during the decade, had already laid out the steps by which campus domination could be attained. First, he wrote, "try to gain control·of as much of the establishment campus cultural apparatus as possible." Secondly, if control of such outlets is not possible, then activist organizations should attempt to "influence" them. Thirdly, if influence is not possible, then activists should "organize and develop a new counter-apparatus" of their own. Action, said Davidson, should include gaining control of campus newspapers, radio stations, local magazines, and other media. Student and faculty meetings were to be harassed, if necessary, and deans burned in effigy. "Reactionary" professors were to be tormented in larger sections, where disruptions would be difficult to control.[15]

Thus came into being what was euphemistically called the movement, or the campus revolution. What ought to be added here is that, generally speaking, the entire campus flux as it existed in the Sixties was based upon a premise written in 1945 by Dave Dellinger, one of the movement's leading philosophers. "This is a diseased world in which it is impossible for any one to be fully human," Dellinger wrote in that year. "One way or another, everyone who lives in the modern world is sick or maladjusted."[16]

The movement, as it developed, tended to care less about the issue of the moment than it did about long-range goals. A park was fought over in 1964 in Berkeley and, as Fred Hechinger of the *New York Times* pointed out, it was eventually turned over to its "former users, predominantly muggers. . . ." The important thing was that the university had been bested in a struggle for power.[17]

The movement was also to be trendy, sliding quickly whenever necessary from one issue to another. One week might see the lionization of the Black Panthers; another the emphasis upon ecology. Buckshot salvoes were to be fired at almost everything so that, in the final analysis, the movement might claim to have unrooted a potential evil.

Nonviolent in theory, it was to sanction and support more violence than the country had seen in decades. The national capital was bombed and so were individual post offices. Banks were burned. Even mistruth was to be supported in the attainment of specified goals. Emotion was to be exploited. As Professor Alisdair MacIntyre of the University of Essex explained it, "It is the taste for pretentious nostrums describing in inflated language which induces excitement rather than thought."[18]

While most American students stayed outside the perimeters of thought control as exercised by campus activists, there was a definable romantic appeal exercised by the movement. It was as Saul Bellow wrote in *Mr. Sammler's Planet:* "They sought originality. They were obviously derivative. And of what—of Paiutes, of Fidel Castro? No, of Hollywood extras. Acting mythic. Casting themselves into chaos. . . ." The romantic appeal had a further historical connotation. John Aldridge described it in 1970 in terms of "U.S. army tunics of World War I . . . the broad-brimmed hats and plunging sideburns of the Western plainsmen . . . the headbands of Comanche braves . . . Edwardian suits, the smocks of French Bohemian painters, or the gaudy saris of guruland. . . ."[19]

It was an acting out of the past—Goethe's Werther and England's Robin Hood. Yet with all of it—the sexual overtones, the drug craze, and the growth of cultism—the movement leaders did have an early effectiveness. They did manage to establish radio grids throughout the country—a radio grid so well constructed that a student strike call on Cambodia was passed throughout the nation in hours.

The adherents of the cause seemed possessed of demonic drive and devoted far more energy to the movement than was ever shown in academic work. They could man the phones for hours, as they did at Amherst in 1970, shouting out periodically that "Connecticut is out" or "New Mexico is out." They had enough force to persuade prominent faculty members to join them. At Amherst, Henry Steele Commager, whose *Pocket History of the Second World War* had sold widely, became a Vietnam dove with flourish. At a 1970 Amherst rally he managed to quote Pericles to hundreds of students spread out in aisles with their dogs—"do not idly stand aside at the onset of the enemy," he proclaimed. All of them—activist students, faculty supporters, drifters— were all part of a vast colorful struggle to be portrayed perhaps by some future David. *The Trumpet*, a California underground paper, best expressed it when it stated: "It happened in France, in Russia and, yes, it happened here two hundred years ago. The Bourbons, the Romanoffs, and George III of England did not understand neither the causes nor the power of the forces which they tried to subdue."[20]

If there was a kind of ineffable vagueness to the windmills against which they tilted their lances, it was understandable. The goals and objectives of revolution were too often colored by emotional and herd instinct factors. Early on in the movement there were some campus activists who saw themselves in the vision of a Castroite revolution. Hence the appearance of beards and coarse clothing in the late 1950s and early 1960s. By 1965 the Cuban experience offered rationale as well. "The Fidelista understands all the ailments of Cuba, and of Guatamala, Haiti, the Dominican Republic, and all the hungry nations," wrote one theoretician, "and he intends to translate this knowledge into action." But how does one adapt the Castroite revolution to the American university campus? It is simply done. The Fidelist "knows the meaning of misery and exploitation, of disease and illiteracy . . . , the campus rebel, lacking the Cuban experience, nonetheless *feels* it."[21]

Among the more fanatical campus activists it was difficult to make the constant readjustment necessary to the flux of the movement. The emotional toll among some university revolutionaries was heavy. A Berkeley official wrote of constant visits from *sturm* and *drang* leaders who, once behind the closed doors of his office would cry out: "I am at the end of my rope."[22]

When one considers the shiftings and turnings within the total movement during the 1960s, it is little wonder that psyches were damaged. There was a montage of charges against one branch of the establishment after another. Consider too, the barrage of overstatement and rhetoric which began early in the decade and reached its peak in 1970. The Canadian publication *Sanity*, which had a considerable U.S. circulation, provided the opening scene. In 1964, for instance, this underground sheet began a furious campaign against nuclear armament by publishing the partial content of a speech by a Manhattan College professor that because of atomic fallout, insects would eventually control the earth.

A year later, but still prior to the massive American commitment to Vietnam, *Sanity* reported upon large-scale anti-American demonstrations throughout the North American continent. Students were urged to distribute leaflets for the cause—leaflets which stated in part that "ours must not be a mere alliance of words. We must use our intellectual wills to draw up a blueprint for world peace. . . . Our generation will solve it, or be the last generation."

As President Johnson increased aid to South Vietnam, so did *Sanity*

73

spur a general anti-U.S. crusade. In April 1965 the paper argued that American imperialism was the bane of world peace, and that students everywhere should indicate their opposition to that evil. Plans were published concerning a proposed Washington demonstration designed to protest wars of aggression "conducted by the U.S. . . . ." Toronto students were urged to join in with a twelve-hour peace vigil —using a technique which was to become familiar later—by parading with lighted candles. British students were to march at the same time upon High Wycombe, the headquarters of the British Bomber Command, and New Zealand students were planning to hold a four day "activity" camp in Wellington. Swiss students planned a march as well, as did those of Germany.[23]

The hyperactivity which was to mark later phases of the movement was seen in the 1965 Washington demonstrations. Banners indicating the origination point were handed out to each state delegation, thus providing the appearance of emotional solidarity. In demonstrations elsewhere there were other signs of things to come. In Boston, for instance, long before the Tet offensive, long before the My Lai massacre. students taking part in the peace demonstration were entertained by a program of Vietnamese folk music.

Later in the same year the tempo was speeded up, and so was the rhetoric. At the "peace" demonstration held in Washington, D.C., in October, Carl Oglesby pronounced a litany of U.S. sins. United States Marines were in the Dominican Republic, he said, because of American capitalistic interests in the sugar production there. Some tortuous logic provided the proof. Ellsworth Bunker, who was ambassador to the Organization of American States, was a board member and stock owner in the National Sugar Refining Company. Abe Fortas, a close associate of President Johnson, was on the board of the Sucrest Company, which, according to Oglesby, imported molasses from the Dominican Republic. But there was still more! Adolf Berle, an oldtime New Dealer, and Roland Harriman, the brother of a leading Democrat, were officials of the National Sugar Refining Company. All would come out right in the end, however—so said Oglesby: "Nuns will be raped and bureaucrats will be disembowelled. Indeed revolution is a fury."[24]

By 1966 the movement was reaching frenetic levels of activity. *New Left Notes* out of Chicago advised that fasting was an excellent way of getting attention from the nationally established media. It served to "arouse people's sympathy. . . ." Charges and claims began to verge upon the ridiculous. Dick Gregory, the activist comedian, as cited in *The Fifth Estate* of Detroit, had inside information that President Johnson would not run for reelection in 1968. The President was suffering from cancer, it was claimed. Mark Lane's book, *Rush to Judg-*

ment, likewise received much attention. Using Lane's peculiar logic as a base, *The Fifth Estate* opined that President Kennedy had been assassinated by insiders—the FBI perhaps. The paper precluded any further "truth" about the assassination by claiming that future witnesses would be silenced by "trumped up charges of drug addiction."[25]

Berkeley Barb, a leading West Coast underground paper and a significant influence on the movement, presented its own interpretations of President Kennedy's assassination. The paper printed a set of murky and virtually incomprehensible photographs purporting to show the presence of Jack Ruby, Lee Harvey Oswald's killer, near the site of the President's assassination. Slowly but obviously the *Barb* moved in the direction which implicated President Johnson in the killing. There had been a radio show in London, and on it Gore Vidal, the novelist, had supposedly stated that Mrs. Kennedy had caught Johnson "chuckling over her husband's corpse."

A month later another *Barb* contributor claimed that President Johnson had "ordered Earl Warren to prove that Lee Harvey Oswald . . . killed President Kennedy. . . ." The logic in this theme would soon be proved by an irresistible public pressure to exhume the dead President's body.[26]

Following the advice of Carl Davidson, a movement leader, more and more university newspapers and lecture committees fell into the hands of activist elements. More conservative speakers were virtually driven from the college lecture circuits and the long arid desert of leftist cant was broken only by an occasional appearance of moderates such as Harry Reasoner or Howard K. Smith. So solid was activist control established at such places as Brandeis, Tufts, Amherst, Brown, Howard, and Trinity that one radical speaker announced that he had been on a "triumphal tour" of speaking engagements at these institutions. Felix Greene, a North Vietnamese sympathizer, was in great demand in the late 1960s and appeared at colleges large and small in exchange for large and small fees. Greene had the knack of leaving his audiences with the assumption that the North Vietnamese and the Viet Cong were noble both in aspiration and deed. At Berkeley he ran his slides showing alleged American-inflicted bomb damage in North Vietnam through the machine so quickly that few questions could be raised. Nevertheless, *Berkeley Barb* accepted with alacrity Greene's excuse that he had speeded up his lecture because he wished to avoid "possible damage to them [the slides] caused by the intense light of the projector's arc lamp. . . ." To the few who realized that valued negatives are usually duplicated, this seemed a lame excuse.[27]

By 1970 the conservative point of view had virtually vanished from the American university scene. Those who were moderates in 1965 now held the right. At the so-called "counter-commencements" held in the spring, campus radicals exercised complete control. Joan Baez and Phil Ochs sang their songs of dissent to students at Tufts and the graduation ceremonies there consisted partly of contrapuntal arrangements of readings from the university catalog and the names of six graduates killed in Vietnam.

At the University of Massachusetts it was decided that a "joyous commencement" would be inappropriate. At American University the more activist students attended graduation ceremonies in black robes and white masks with Oriental features. On hand was Nicholas von Hoffman, a columnist, who launched a bitter attack upon the national administration. Other commencement speakers that spring were George Wald, the Harvard antiwar biologist, former Attorney General Ramsey Clark, Julian Bond, the columnist I. F. Stone, and Senators Muskie and Kennedy. Both of the latter legislators had voted for the Tonkin Gulf Resolution by which springboard President Johnson had launched the Vietnam intervention.[28]

Through the late Sixties the impact of leftist rhetoric upon student thought was both effective and ponderous, especially in view of the fact that there were few college newspapers which sought to question that rhetoric. A black militant speak-in at Wayne University in 1966 had pronounced the following dicta: President Johnson was censoring the press; America could be saved only by defeat in Vietnam; the "only solution to the condition of the Negro in the U.S. was Black Power"; and there was torture in Vietnam by Americans because the war there was against "black people." The last bit of slapdash was explained away quite simply: all people are "black if they're not white."[29]

Needless to say, much of what was written and said and believed by campus activists during the 1960s enters into the vein of the ridiculous. Gregory Calvert, the SDS president in 1967, presented one of his more moving lectures at Princeton, of all places. There he lauded his listeners as the "trainees" of the "next working class." And *East Village Other*, quoting radical leader Frank Zappa, spun the following crazy quilt of information. The power structure in the U.S., said Zappa, was similar to that of Latin American countries. Then, in a historic lie of incredible proportions, Zappa argued that the "original Americans," the Plymouth settlers, came out of debtor's prisons. They "probably lived [survived he meant] because they ate the bodies of the ones that died." The same settlers soon set up an "industrial society." As for George Washington, Zappa said in a parting shot, "pretty soon we're gonna find out that he was a sodomist."[30]

It seems incredible that such words could have been uttered with sincerity or conviction. Yet Zappa seemed to be expressing the will of the New Left—especially when he wrote: "I think the kids are in a very ambivalent situation right now. They actually control the country." Everybody else in all other age categories was essentially greedy. All—including "their own mothers and fathers, man." How should the young strike back? asked Zappa. One must look at his father and "see that he's a coward . . . he's an alcoholic, and if he's not an alcoholic, he's taking pills of some sort, and he's a liar, and so's your mother, and they're all just *rotten*, man. . . ." Zappa's final commentary—all young people should say: *"Because my folks were so rotten, I'm really gonna be pure."*[31]

Resist, another underground newspaper with a campus following, presented similar material to its readers in the 1960s. Frank Mungo, writing for the paper in April 1968, warned Americans that "this country is on the verge of civil war, and I am glad of it." Who constitutes the classes in the U.S.? The gospel according to Mungo was that the "bourgeoisie and the ruling classes" owned the country. They represented the "new fascists of America," the people who rise to cheer "their fuehrer when he makes a war speech, when he talks of assembling the greatest concentration of firepower in the history of the world over the tiny nation of Vietnam. . . ." The other "class" were the young who had "nothing to lose by the hypocrasy [sic] and the despair they have know [sic] in the world of the fathers." "I belong to this group," said Mungo. "I want to make love when I am in it, to smoke pot when my mind is not at ease, to meditate when I feel I need it, to rebuild in man's image what has been built and destroyed too many times over in the witness and image of a foolish and irrelevant God." Who were the specific Nazis of American society? President Johnson "may be," said Mungo, ". . . so is Romney, so is Kennedy, so is Nixon, so is Rockefeller, so is Dirkeson [sic]. . . ."[32]

Kenneth Keniston, writing for the paper *Motive* in March 1970, described in particular terms the characteristics and symptoms of the movement as it existed in the college community. He was merely echoing Hofstadter's comments on paranoia when he stated:

> The quest for ethical integrity may become a self-righteous and compulsive search for total moral purity at the expense of all else. The world becomes simplified and divided into two moral camps, the pure and the impure; on the one side stands good (the free world, the people's democracies or the Third Reich), and on the other hand stands evil (the Communist Threat, the capitalist-imperialist menace or the liberal-Jewish conspiracy). People also are divided into two groups, the pure and the impure; and the impure are experienced as not fully human, but as hyenas, Jewish scum, white racists and so on. Only if they join in the struggle of the pure are they entitled to their full human right, in the meantime, they deserve no empathy, compassion, insight or understanding; they possess no inner complexity; they become purely and simply, The Enemy.[33]

It is obvious that, as the Sixties rolled by, the New Left was possessed of a fanaticism which matched that of any other fringe movements in American history. Yet student radicals never saw themselves in the Nazi tradition, for instance, or as the forward patrols of the Red Guard. When they stormed through classrooms in order to disrupt, when they carried rifles and wore uniforms or when they broached no opposing opinions, the actions were all seen as in the order of moral justice. Might on their side meant right; might on the opposing side meant repression.

Daniel Moynihan, at one and the same time one of the wisest and most misquoted intellectuals of the decade, tried to capsulize the crisis in American education in 1970. There was altogether too much "crisis mongering," said Moynihan; an almost classic "nihilism" was flourishing among the children of upper and middle class American society. Out of this, declared Moynihan, had come a frustrated outrage of the kind Lenin might have described as an "infantile disorder," but which increasingly Americans are told "is a virtuous rage to off the pigs and generally to punish working class groups."

It was almost as George Orwell had written, stated Moynihan— "nearly every modern intellectual has gone over to some form of total-itarianism." Or it had come to truth in Norman Podhoretz's remark —"the barbaric hostility to freedom of thought which by the late 1960s had become one of the hallmarks of [the radical] ethos." But who was to blame for it all? From whence did it all come? Moynihan wrote:

What is at issue is an adversary culture firmly entrenched in higher edu-cation. The patrician tradition and leadership of the most prestigious universities seems to me to have been painfully vulnerable in its initial encounters with this new reality. It would seem to me that the individ-uals involved by and large could not understand or could not believe what suddenly was before their eyes and in varying degrees panicked, collabo-rated, or simply collapsed.[34]

As Moynihan and others pointed out, it was customary for the stu-dent left in the 1960s to employ the Nazi theme in much of its litera-ture. Blind to its own latent totalitarianism and to its paranoia, it played havoc with the facts of history. "Amerika" was racist, greedy, imperialistic, corrupt, and evil. The young leftists, on the other hand, were pristine and moral. Yet there was, in all of this, a sense of the inanely dramatic: a ridiculous playing at games. A writer, visting counter-culture in action at Woodstock in New York, found among those present a conscious portrayal of hardship roles. Boys and girls were clad in military paraphernalia—webbed army belts, dog tags, shoulder patches, army boots, etc. "Those who have guitars," he stated, "never seem to put them down or to become accustomed to their burden. The instrument, like a soldier's rifle, is held, petted, caressed, even pointed, and kept always at hand like a 'best friend' it is said to be."[35]

The year 1970, with the invasion of Cambodia and the unfortunate occurrences at Kent State University, marked the high tide of both leftist alienation and romantic fatalism. During the months from May to December of that year the apogee of the movement was reached. Rhetoric on the campus exceeded all previous limits. Consider the single issue of "racism" as it was posed by the student left during these months. Underground and campus newspapers whistled up stories about students in Tennessee, presumably black, who were forced to go through the contents of garbage cans in order to find enough to eat. There were other wild charges as well, among them the implication that 37 percent of American soldiers stationed in Vietnam were black. Other campus papers heralded the onset of a white policy of genocide in regard to blacks.[36]

In New Haven, Connecticut, movement leader Tom Hayden announced that the United States should be forced to end its "systematic oppression" of such "political dissenters" as the Black Panthers—and masses of Yale students cheered. *The Roosevelt Torch*, published for Roosevelt University students in Chicago, contended in May 1970 that the university could not be a neutral institution. "How much racism is permissible?" asked the paper. "Can we vote on it? One dead Black Panther? 10 dead Black Panthers? 28 Black Panthers?" The writer concluded:

> To sit in the classroom, to sit in the tomb of the mind and human spirit, that is 430 S. Michigan is something that I cannot put up with any longer. My five years here at this university has been a daily atrocity—a continual process of this school using it's [sic] to grind all it's [sic] racism, all it's [sic] male chauvinism, all it's [sic] elitism into my soul. It has corrupted, and humiliated, and destroyed me more than I ever thought was possible. It has been a literal hell.[37]

Vortex, a racially militant publication catering to students in Lawrence, Kansas, offered excellent illustrations of the new nihilism in its May 1970 issues. One of its writers gleefully reported: "Another Savings bombed, Gambles burned, Judge Rankin's house bombed, and the attempted burning of the White House." How could one attend classes in the excitement of the moment? Were these not romantic times? Whites had joined blacks in Lawrence in the struggle against the "pigs," for after all, "their area was occupied, their life style threatened. . . ." The total mood of white radicalism was "in line with the struggles of the black people"—whites "felt it necessary to emphasize their solidarity, as comrades in the struggle against a common enemy. . . ."[38]

Space City of Houston offered up a call for a new "people's party."

Only Marxism and Leninism could relieve blacks from 400 years of "inhuman treatment" for, after all, there were "people in power" who were "trying everything they can think of to keep black people under their control. . . ." Calling for freedom for all blacks in all jails, and no military service for blacks, *Space City* passed the word on "genocide":

> The terror is growing closer by the day. The power structure will never change its nature, the nature that killed off the American indians [sic] and took their land, that enslaved blacks and dehumanized them, that dropped bombs on Japanese women and children, that wages a war against the poor Vietnamese people, that killed brother Fred Hampton as he slept and that will continue to kill until it is cut out. . . .[39]

The truth was all on one side, it was obvious. But what is amazing about that middle part of 1970 is that the words, whatever their source, seemed to be cut from the same cloth. Martin Hirschman, editor-in-chief of *The Michigan Daily*, appeared to swallow wholesale the story that a host of "black political leaders" had been "shot down on the streets of our cities. . . ." At Western Illinois University, the leftist activist John Froines argued: "We are an emerging nation in a dying empire . . . , all power to the people must become a reality in Amerika in order for us to survive."[40] Far off in London, *Red Mole*, a leftist student paper, pointed out that fascism had a chance in England. "We are living in a fool's paradise if we believe for one instant it could not happen here," the paper claimed. As for the blacks in America, *Red Mole* followed the line of campus activism in America.

> In America, the Panthers, the only effective voice of the Black people, are suffering a vicious and deadly campaign of Police persecution. Computerized systems are enabling them to track down and harass Panther Party members, whether or not they are legally justified in doing so.[41]

As Arnold Beichman has pointed out in his *Nine Lies About America*, it has been customary ideological cant to tie racism to some unidentified "repression" peculiar to the Nixon administration. How strange it was, however, to find the theme echoed and re-echoed in establishment journals! *Time, Newsweek,* and the *New York Times* paraded the same line as many underground radical papers. *Time* asked: "Specifically, are the raids against Panther offices part of a national design to destroy the Panther leadership?" The question itself implied conspiracy. Edward J. Epstein, in his cleverly researched piece for the *New Yorker* (February 13, 1971), not only destroyed the whole leftist thesis of police murders of Black Panther leaders, but ended forever the notion of a guilty Nixon or "national design."[42]

For those who were determined to accept the student-left view of race in America, however, there was no alternative position—even when faced with the real facts of the Epstein inquiry. Far out in the boondocks of higher education, at universities such as that of Western Illinois, where black students represented approximately 3 percent of the total student body, a student "radical manifesto" set forth the creed. The university, so said the statement, was a "rascist [sic] institution," and "intellectual whorehouse," a "cosmic cop-out," a school whose administration was guilty of allowing "continuous racial discrimination to occur. . . ." Furthermore, and much to the surprise of most of the faculty, Western Illinois University was also guilty of cooperating with the military-industrial complex to "further the Indochinese war and other counter-revolutionary activities of the U.S. . . ."[43]

These were the reactions of a white world, however, and when federally enforced guidelines on minority hiring began to impinge upon what had been the white world of opportunity, the slow amelioration of white attitudes began to take place. By 1973, for instance, the Supreme Court of the United States was being called upon to consider the case of a white student who had possibly been denied admission to law school because of his race. Even Dick Gregory seemed to be less in demand, though some predominantly white schools such as Knox College of Illinois called upon him for programs. There in Galesburg—where Lincoln and Douglas had once debated—the student body listened in rapture to Gregory's one-liners. A student editor of the school was constrained to advise the alumni that the comedian had opened the eyes of students "to the real America." Most appealing, apparently, was Gregory's call for a white and black unity which would "turn the whole system over."[44]

The high noon of campus violence was reached in May and June of 1970, and the crescendo of exploding bombs was accompanied by a strange and eerie carnival atmosphere. Frightened administrations, occupying headquarters far removed from the trenches, prayed for immunity to "incidents." Much of the violence or intended violence —fire bombs which were discovered before exploding—never found its way into the newspapers. Beneath the show of contempt for the law there were, on each campus, finely knit organizations which kept the pot boiling. This last was a helter-skelter of apparati which included underground newspapers, various campus publications, radio stations operated within dormitories, and "free universities." The so-called free university reached a level of expression on almost every campus, and the courses taught therein ranged from political indoctrination to "rap" courses. At San Jose, for instance, one could sit in on gay liberation studies, "Massage #5," "Being a Free U Together [where one could appreciate 'love']," "Massage-E-14 [where beginning and advanced techniques were taught]," chanting, "Tripping," Yoga, Zen, Basic Buddhism, and Tarot.[45]

Following the confrontations at Kent State and Jackson State, the accepted pose of the campus leftist was one of complete hopelessness and depression. The country might not be safe; in fact, it was possible that it would not last the night. Douglas Kneeland, writing for the *New York Times*, saw the campus as a place where "people are unhappy, but they don't know where to go." "Is there a tomorrow?" seemed to be a common theme for the campus press. Kneeland catalogued the predictions of radical and liberal students. There would be "another widening of the Vietnam war, such as the invasion of Cambodia . . . another Kent State or Jackson." Others opted for predictions for an indefinable future wreathed in chaos.[46]

Truly many students were echoing teachers or writers who should have known better. Frederic Morton, a novelist and essayist, sadly admitted in June 1970 to having broken into tears when some little girls threw a frisbee at him. "I wanted to cry about the world's loss of America . . . ," he lamented. "Here is a Goshen going down the drain. The country that had snatched us away from the gas ovens now burns another people elsewhere." Morton's conclusion: "It is an awful thing to know what only our ghettos (and our Thoreaus) have known all along—that the United States can be as monstrous as any giant."[47]

There were others who were as equally guilty as Morton. I. F. Stone, the leftist publisher in the national capital, wrote: "The race is on between protest and disaster. . . . The only hope is that the students can create such a plague for peace, swarming like locusts into the halls of Congress. . . . The slogan of the striking students ought to be: suspend classes and educate the country." James Reston, in a column titled "Amherst, Mass.: Memorial Day 1970," proclaimed the "decline in the belief in the sanctity of human life." Gloomily Reston added that "it is easier to regard the universe as merely a great machine, pointlessly grinding its way toward ultimate stagnation and death." Both I. F. Stone and Reston were widely read by American students in 1970.[48]

What was amazing about many student publications, or underground and establishment papers, is that there was an astounding similarity in language from medium to medium. The words sounded so much the same—the echoing of thoughts from one writer to another. A candidate who was running for a $7,000-a-year student position at Roosevelt College told why he wanted the job. He wanted to "challenge the authority of the academic pimps, hookers, and voyeurs that constitute this sado-machistic whorehouse plagued by the venereal disease of self-interested perversity." He did finally add that he was in the race "primarily for the money." Downstate, at Western Illinois University, the verbiage was the same—the institution being portrayed as an "intellectual whorehouse."[49]

Hofstadter's paranoid style was truly running wild and free in those spring months of 1970. A reporter for the *Harvard Crimson* was quoted as saying: "What used to be frustration is now just total desolation. The great majority just don't see anything they can do that can have any effect. They'd rather do nothing." At Stanford University another student was reported to have said: "I haven't seen anything in twenty years that the military has been used for that was not pernicious. I would leave the country but I want to stay here and do political work. Remember what Guevara said: 'You Americans are lucky, you live in the heart of the beast.'"[50]

Almost invariably during the months of May and June, the American university campus was the scene of well organized activities designed to promote the sense of doom and gloom. Displays of the cross, the ritualistic burning of candles (seen ten years earlier in Toronto demonstrations), chanting, street theater, and prolonged and silent demonstrations were all among the techniques used. At Stony Brook in New York, the graduation ceremonies included a musical work entitled *Requiem for a City*. No threat to Beethoven's Ninth, it did offer variety—a taped offering of the sounds of city life, a gloomy poetic offering called "Doubting," and the inevitable moment of silence. At Rutgers the graduation ceremonies included both a moment of silence and a jazz interlude. At NYU the commencement was entitled "A Convocation for Peace," and it was a conglomeration of emotional student speeches, spirituals, and readings from the Gettysburg Address. The *New York Times* account of the NYU ceremonies failed to include an explanation of how one could extract "readings" from Lincoln's noble statement of rededication.[51]

The sickly panorama of self-pity was played out on every campus. And sometimes off campus as well. A number of seminary students knelt in prayer at Grand Central Station in New York City. While these young people were praying for peace, at almost the same instant NYU officials discovered a $3.5 million computer to be wired with explosives. Small student groups from various colleges in New York City attempted to snarl traffic and one young man, emulative of paintings of the French Revolution, was heard to cry "Let's take the Brooklyn Bridge." One girl, interviewed at the height of the May demonstrations in New York City, admitted to having a great time. She had demonstrated at City Hall, Wall Street, Union Square, NYU, and was now on her way to a "candlelight procession." Later she was planning to attend the movie *Woodstock*. In between all of these incidents she had managed to burn a black flag at St. Patrick's Cathedral, and she had doubtlessly listened to a set of revolutionary speeches at the junction of Broad and Wall streets. There an orator had told the crowd: "You brought down one President and you'll bring down another."[52]

Everywhere, on campus and off, the message was essentially the same: it was doom, gloom, and self-pity. Martin Flumenbaum, editor-in-chief of the *Columbia Spectator*, regarded his society as "disintegrating before our eyes." To work in the slums was no answer to the world's problems. Such meaningful activity "would bring us no closer to ending the war in Vietnam, to ending political repression in our own country, to guaranteeing adequate medical services for all our citizens, to providing food for twenty million starving Americans, to ending corruption. . . ." A writer for the *Western Illinois Courier* intoned: "For many here at Western and all over the country, the dream is dying, poisoned by self-interest, indifference, maimed by violence and silenced by a psychological scare." *Red Eye* of San Jose, California, saw the country in terms of Nazi Germany. "Every young man that cooperates with the draft system," it argued, "that cooperates in any way with research programs which are tied in with the military . . . is no better or worse than a German burger [sic] who sits outside of Dachau, and pretends not to see what is happening inside."[53]

From the fall of 1969 to December 1970 the incidence of violence reached an incredible level. Not all of it had to do with the Kent State or Jackson State affairs, or even with the Cambodian invasion. In the latter part of 1969 the National Guard Armory in Madison, Wisconsin, was bombed. Other attempts were made at Baraboo, where an ammunition plant was located, and at the Dane County Selective Service office. In April 1970 windows were trashed in the vicinity of the University of Illinois campus in Champaign-Urbana, and within a five-day period a Kroger supermarket was gutted and two dozen other fire bombings carried out. At Southern Illinois University an ROTC building was damaged and a mob of 5,000 students broke into the home and office of the president. Of the 760 protests recorded on various campuses after the Cambodia invasion, some 5 percent ended in violence. The ultimate event occurred in Madison, where a U.S. Army Mathematics Research Center was blown up and a research assistant was killed.[54]

An insight into the type of people who now composed the "bomber left" was given in Amitai Etzioni's "Lunch With Three Prospective Bombers," printed in the *Wall Street Journal*. Etzioni makes some interesting observations. All three of the radicals he interviewed were not really young; they were approaching thirty years of age in each case. Two were from affluent families—one the son of a top executive in a New York firm; the other the son of a retired commodity broker. The third was the girl friend of one of the men. The parents of the two men were responsive and sympathetic, with one of the fathers indicating that "the system is rotten to the core."

Etzioni found one to be living off his parents. He slept late each day and tended to flit from one sexual liaison to another. The other man had flunked out of two law schools before finally obtaining his degree from a lesser-known institution. He too was a late sleeper. Etzioni's conclusions were that these people had been brought up in an ultra-permissive level of society and that their philosophy was a "selfish, indulgent one."[55]

Eventually the pace and intensity of radical action in 1970 was bound to diminish. The aim of the movement had been to bring down the government and, despite the violence which had occurred, the goals were not reached. It was precisely during this stage of the assault against life and property that student radicals made their final break with the bulk of the liberal community and, in fact, with the majority of Americans. Senator Margaret Chase Smith, as she had done in the McCarthy era, clearly defined the limits between acceptable and unacceptable trespasses upon civil rights. "Trespass is trespass—whether on the campus or off," she stated. "Violence is violence—whether on the campus or off. Arson is arson—whether on the campus or off. Killing is killing—whether on the campus or off." It was as simple as that.[56]

The liberal-radical parting of the ways was made heavy with vindictive rhetoric. A Roosevelt University student, admitting that she was still in school and still taking "daddy's money," tried her hand at chastising liberal thought. "Liberals don't understand the concept of alienation . . . ," she argued. "They can not really imagine the system becoming so meaningless that they would openly admit to defying the law." Some student liberals began openly to air their opinions of more recent expressions of radical sentiment. "Products of postwar prosperity's suburban culture," wrote a Yale student about the radicals on his campus. They are "raised on instant breakfasts and TV-dinners, educated in 'progressive schools'. . . ." A Harvard professor, apparently having reached his limit on radical student behavior, defined leftist dissent as "the malaise of the spoiled." "The great majority [of Harvard dissenters] just don't see anything they can do that can have any effect . . . ," was the kiss-off by one college liberal of his former radical friends.[57]

At no time did the student radical movement represent the will of the majority of the national university community. Even at places like Kent State and Southern Illinois University, refuges for white suburban students from heavily populated areas, the activities of May and June 1970 were basically the results of indiscipline and overindulgence. There were even some universities in which the student bodies reacted very adversely to the campaign of violence. The graduating class of Virginia Polytechnic Institute took out an ad in the *Richmond Times-Dispatch* which made the point of thanking the taxpayers of Virginia for "preserving the principles of a country that makes it possible to obtain an education."[58]

As 1970 passed rapidly into the past the aging student radicals moved into other activities. The lesser ones opted for the good life by taking jobs within the hitherto hated corporate structure. One radical leader went into a form of Buddhism; another was arrested and charged with being an agent in a drug ring. Some found their way into obscure byways in search of the illusive perfect society. A young Canadian girl, for example, greeted the end of a Buddhist ritual in New Delhi with the same enthusiasm with which she had taken part in the movement. "It's all so beautiful," she gushed. "These people are beautiful. India beautiful. Wow!"

The ultimate and crushing blow to many fringe dissenters, especially to those in the liberal arts, was the declining availability of jobs. No longer could graduate students write their own tickets during job interviews, and the resultant change was a fantastic one. Martin Lipset, the Harvard sociologist, expressed it most appropriately when he stated: "I've rarely seen such deference from Ph.D. candidates. They're becoming obsequious again."[59]

4

The Education of the University Establishment

Despite the inadequacies in American life as seen by liberals in 1960, the United States still appeared to the world as a shining example of the accomplishments of the democratic system. The truth was evident in immigration figures for the twenty years from 1950 to 1970. In that period the number of people coming into the country, legally that is, jumped from 249,187 in 1950 to 373,326 in 1970. The rise in annual immigration was steady, even through the troubled Sixties when many of the young people in America gave evidence of having lost faith in the country.

More importantly, a so-called brain drain into the United States continued through those two decades. Until the mid-Sixties the major part of these trained and skilled individuals came from such countries as the United Kingdom, Germany, and Sweden. During the late 1960s and until 1973 the greater number tended to emigrate from Africa, Asia, Central and South America. What is most interesting about the flow of these latter types into the United States is that, despite the constant complaints about American racism from the radical left, there was not one single year after 1950 that the immigration of Orientals and Africans to the United States diminished in annual numbers.

One reason for the steady rise in immigration figures lay in the enormous expansion of educational facilities from 1958 forward. Slowly but surely, during ensuing years, American education became one of the major industries of the nation; that is, in terms of people employed and in what public and private monies were spent in the maintenance and expansion of the system. By 1970 more than sixty million Americans were connected in some way with the educational establishment. Of these, some 58.6 million were in the educational pipeline as students, 2.7 million were employed as teachers, and 200,000 served as administrators or the equivalent thereof. There were also some 100,000 Americans who were on school boards or in related activities. Altogether, a little less than one-third of the population of the country was tied into the operation of the national educational structure.

The economic impact of the educational growth was fantastic. Beyond the new purchasing power which rested in the hands of 2.7 million teachers and administrators, there was an incredible building program which began in 1958. Huge bond issues were floated, additional tax levies were approved by voters, and federal money appeared in ever-increasing amounts. Some of the last seemed to be pushed off on colleges and universities which, in turn, spent the allocated sums as if the money might spoil if kept. Colleges and universities recruited as vigorously for students as did big business for the graduates of the system. Not only were students cajoled and flattered by one college after another, but high schools arranged "college nights" for graduating seniors so that colleges and universities might contest for pledges to enroll.

A study of the student population during a part of this period reveals some startling facts. By 1970 some 29.5 percent of all American citizens were in the national school system, with 3.7 percent of the population enrolled in college. Actually a larger percentage of the black population was in the educational pipeline, some 33.8 percent, though a lesser 2.2 percent of American blacks were enrolled in college. These represented important signs of progress, however, for the percentage of blacks in the American college establishment exceeded similar figures for nine other major countries. In other words the percentage of blacks enrolled in colleges in the United States exceeded the percentages for college students in the USSR, Japan, France, Argentina, West Germany, Italy, Sweden, the United Kingdom, and Switzerland. Only Canada's college enrollment percentage equalled the percentage of American blacks enrolled in colleges and universities. But it must also be pointed out that all in all, there were more American blacks in higher education than the total number of Canadians listed as college students.[1]

Looking backward to 1960, it is possible to see now that several variants were present within the educational system which pointed toward trouble. Schoolteacher income went up 26 percent from 1950 to 1960, a fact which at the time seemed to be necessary to attract better types into the profession. At the same time, however, there was a forced growth of the entire system. Teachers came temporarily into short supply and this fact, coupled with the draft evasion possibilities offered by the teaching profession, pushed into the educational establishment a different kind of teaching recruit.

There was another foundation upon which dissension would build, however. A new type of college president appeared. While the older version had been strictly political in nature and in tune with the various boards which governed him, the new tended to be either quasi-intellectual or quasi-corporate in character. As it turned out, the new model seemed less able to handle controversy than did the old.

But most of all, the major change in the American college and university seemed to be the overidentification of liberalism with truth. An intellectually dominant view at first, but a mania by 1968, academic liberalism reached the position that no applicant for a faculty job could be considered unless he or she possessed the standard precepts of liberal ideology. First and foremost among these seemed to be a commitment to activism. As early as 1960 David Lawrence had seen something of this when he wrote:

> We find in intellectual circles today a growing sympathy with statism. Our universities abound with professors in all fields who feel that the abstract interests of the state must supersede individual freedom. Indeed, we are told that the state exists for the sole purpose of promoting the "general welfare," even at the expense of individual freedom.[2]

The new breed in the university community seemed to be responding to John Kenneth Galbraith's call to activism. In his book, *The New Industrial State*, Galbraith urged the college teaching profession to shun passivity. "Writing, lecturing and even determined conversation" were to be considered as much to be weapons as bombers possessed by a general. What the Canadian-born Harvard professor seemed to be saying was that activism was the wave of the future.[3]

If that was the case, then Galbraith was right. By 1965 there was a steaming kind of activism—mostly then in California, but later to spread across the country. Its origins in that state were partially rooted in the state's natural affluence. In the late 1940s the high salaries offered by various institutions within California acted as a magnet to growing numbers of liberal intellectuals from the East. Nonmaterialistic though these teachers may have been, that characteristic was never applied to their constant search for increased salaries. In the

1950s a new "master plan" brought under a Board of Regents more of the smaller institutions supported by the state. As was to be the case in every master plan adopted by other states later in the Sixties, there was a concomitant increase in administrative personnel and students.

In the last category there was a new breed as well. It included "floaters," young men and women who moved casually from campus to campus in search of a richer social climate. There were student radicals who sought more fertile soils in which to work. There were increased numbers of black and Chicano students who brought activist sentiments with them when they registered in the California system.[4] And there were hundreds of easterners; young people who had been raised in either activist or affluent families and who sought the kind of liberal surroundings which the Sunshine State seemed to offer.

The president of this vast multiplicity—which he called a "multiversity"—was Clark Kerr. Smoothly dressed, able and genteel, Kerr was truly the image of the quasi-intellectual and corporate style university president. He had led the fight in earlier days to forestall a "loyalty oath" for California state employees, and that had earned him good marks among liberals in the state. In 1960 when he refused to take action against faculty members and students who had taken part in a riot against the appearance of the House Un-American Activities Committee in San Francisco, he was made into a liberal folk hero. Shortly thereafter he became the recipient of the Alexander Meiklejohn award for his contributions to academic freedom.

Between 1960 and 1964 other metamorphoses were occurring within higher education. The high-rise dormitory and the campus computer became symbols of a brave new world—in California and elsewhere. On the other hand many of the older and closer relationships between faculties and students were disappearing or changing. The ticky-tacky university "hotels," each housing several hundred students, faculty members who were now prerecording their lectures, mass lectures of ungovernable size—these were all working into the kind of ferment which was to mark the decade. In the end, all of these signs of bigness, though not of progress, were to come to fruition at Berkeley.

As Clark Kerr was to find out, the multiversity complex was not a guarantor of better students, a better faculty, better governance, or more stability. Older students in the system, intuitive to the issues, whipped the students to a frenzy over a relatively minor issue. Numbers of other groups moved into the scene in order to expand upon their own provincial aims. Frustrated faculty members saw the issue as a means for self-aggrandizement. The media filled in the excitement and emotion needed for its own audiences. Everything but everything was predictive of things to come elsewhere in the United States during the 1960s.[5]

The Berkeley outbreak had numerous causes, but in this instance as with others to follow, the leaders or instigators were not fuzzy-cheeked youngsters fresh from high school. These last were merely the foot soldiers of the crusade. Nor was the issue one of academic freedom. What the Berkeley episode was to show more than anything else was the relative weakness of the educational system to handle such problems. Gone were the old-style administrators who drew the line and dared any to cross. Given the Vietnam War plus the civil rights issues, those who had become college administrators in the 1960s seemed the least fitted to deal with crises. The change in leadership had been gradual, and was perhaps best illustrated in the attitudes of Dr. Buell Gallagher, the president of the City College of New York. On the question of student expulsion Gallagher stated: "If you expel the top man, there's another one who'll step immediately into his place. . . ." On the question of professors who were so activist that they threatened academic freedom itself, Gallagher argued: "I think about all we can do —when we cannot win over him—is to try to win him over, and keep the dialogue going."[6]

The conservative Jeffrey St. John was to say in 1970 that America's major universities were "no longer strongholds of scholarship, learning, and reason."[7] That was a minor bit of doomsaying but, sadly, St. John was partly right. Scholars and rationalists had by 1970 given way to activists and cause-seekers.[8] Everywhere, and especially in the "better" institutions, this appeared to be the case. An administrator at Harvard, for example, castigated the university faculty for its "loss of nerve, its clarity about and confidence in espousing a few central values of a university." At a campus in Buffalo some forty-five faculty members occupied the president's office and were arrested. At Emory University a leading professor advocated the end of ROTC academic credit by stating that the disavowal would eliminate the university's guilt for the Vietnam War. Twenty-one teaching assistants at the University of Wisconsin were convicted of civil contempt for taking part in a riot in 1970. At San Francisco State a faculty group backed a movement to end a program to upgrade the training of Micronesians as merchant seamen. At the University of Texas a professor of philosophy was fired after whipping up a mob by shouting: "The bloody mess has got to go. You can't get a revolution by marching in peace parades."[9]

Obviously, as Robert Nisbet wrote in the British magazine *Encounter*, most faculty members kept their respective feet on the ground. But there was a minority, a powerful one "containing within it Nobel Prize winners and others of equal stature" who helped the student revolt get off the ground:

> Most of them have long since fled to other campuses or retreated behind locked institute doors, but in the beginning they served the student

revolutionists well. Granted that they only rarely ventured forth into the open, and that under the iron security of academic tenure they had nothing to fear from administration and regents, their role in the revolution was a vital one.[10]

Among the lower professional ranks were the ambitious instructors who sought to use campus unrest for self-aggrandizement. M. Brewster Smith, the chairman of the University of Chicago psychology department in 1970, stated: "The position of a junior faculty member is a very difficult one, because he is . . . under a great deal of pressure to prove himself in a relatively short time." But S. I. Hayakawa, the president of beleaguered San Francisco State, laid it right on the line:

> The worst enemies of American higher education are professors, or a minority of professors within it. They've got an awful lot of routine undergraduate teaching to do, and they are bored stiff. The only way they can get a little excitement . . . is to appeal to their students for admiration, and they appeal therefore to the most radical and most immature of their students.[11]

The sense of boredom about which Hayakawa wrote seemed to be endemic in the university establishment during the 1960s. It was fed by a sense of doom and frustration exuding from the intellectual world in general during the decade. Richard Todd, the editor of *The Atlantic*, in writing about a costume ball he attended, portrayed the gloom-and-doom postures of faculty members and students present at the event. It was all Berlin in 1929 or Vienna in 1930: an "end-of-the-world" costume ball, including individuals in peasant blouses and dirndl, and Marine Corps lance corporal's dress blues. Quotes and snatches of conversation recorded by Todd include: "I don't know if there is anything worth saving here"; "If you have nothing to die for, you have nothing to live for"; and "I've looked into working. It's a drag."

Other quotes from the Todd article include the following:

> The environment's going up in smoke. We can't deal with 200 million people. How can we deal with 300 million? We live on the back of the beast. It will take a complete revolution to get the earth back to livable proportions. The world is a world, it is not the U.S. We are all in the same movement, we're all together. The Vietnamese may all die before we get out. There's going to be a war in Korea. The U.S. is napalming South America. This country is on a death trip.[12]

What happened to the teaching profession by the middle Sixties seems, at least in retrospect, to stretch the limits of credibility. A young teacher from New Haven appeared at a rock festival wearing only a bead and shell necklace. "It's too peaceful here," she was heard to say. "It's like really relaxing. It's like getting your sanity back. It's easy to be really open and honest with everyone in a setting like this."

A teaching assistant at the Chicago Circle Campus of the University of Illinois—a chemist—was asked to appear as a witness before the Illinois Joint House-Senate Committee on Campus Unrest. His uniform was of brown and green camouflage material with a Mao Tse-tung medal pinned to it. It was later testified that the same teacher had taken groups of individuals to firing ranges in Wisconsin where they were taught to use M-1 rifles on targets marked with signs reading "pig." Other instructors attempted to blow up university computers in New York City, while still others went the route of living in communes with their students. A Queens College lecturer in biology was arrested in 1970 as a "major supplier of marijuana on that campus."[13]

Even on the most prestigious campuses one could find opinions swayed by emotion rather than reason. One major college president was widely quoted as having said that Black Panthers, in particular Bobby Seale, could not receive fair trials in the United States. President Mason Gross of Rutgers, in May 1970, was reported to have urged that "faculties should indicate their support of the strike, too," a reference to the student strikes following the invasion of Cambodia. There were some in various faculties who, after having made a hasty start to the left, quickly reversed their fields. Professor Nathan Glazer, when at Harvard, demonstrated against civil defense, applauded Fidel Castro's speech in Central Park ("who knew what he was saying?"), and supported other liberal or leftist causes. Later, as he wrote in the *New York Times* in November 1970, he "realized how complex the world was and how important it was to preserve free inquiry and rational discourse."[14] It was too bad that he hadn't looked before he leaped in that earlier period.

On almost every campus there were faculty members who leaped into the sea of paranoia existent in the Sixties, or who used it to press university administrators for personal gain. A good deal of what was written and said by such people may seem, some twenty years or so from now, to have been concocted out of whole cloth. But it was true: faculty members and so-called scholars did utter those remarks! An assistant professor of a New York university informed his classes during the May 1970 troubles: "It's silly for us to be arguing about niceties like grades when there is work for peace to be done." Kenneth Mills, a professor of philosophy at Yale, reputedly told an audience of students: "The universities have got to shut down. We have got to mobilize. We will win." The same audience proceeded to dash out to the streets, tear the front entrance off a hockey rink—and spent the remainder of the evening roaming about the streets of New Haven shouting, "The streets belong to the people."[15] It was the speck of reason upon the sea of emotion.

Out in Long Island in the late Sixties, the noted writer and philosopher Paul Goodman, who incidentally recanted his revolutionary ardor in later years, spoke at Long Island University. Goodman heated up his audience by stating that America was headed for "nuclear destruction and death within ten years unless ten to twenty thousand American students . . . stood up publicly." Goodman then urged his listeners to fight the military draft. It was the same spirit of dooming that appeared in an article by a member of the faculty of the New School in New York City in 1970. He wrote about America: "The human suffering is immeasurable, the magnitude of the problems enormous."[16]

It must be admitted that some of the wilder notions and rumors of the hectic decade had their origins within the university or college classroom. The most interesting of these made the rounds of seminar sessions in the early part of 1970 and it became so commonly repeated that it eventually drew the attention of Daniel Patrick Moynihan. Moynihan, whose appearance at Fordham University in June was the signal for some fifty students to throw their mortar boards at the stage, spoke of the "increasingly nonrational, even irrational" fear and "growing distrust" of all social institutions by young people. He cited in particular a rumor then making the university circuit—that President Nixon was about to "cancel" the 1972 presidential elections.

It should be added that almost every underground newspaper pushed this rumor, though nobody seemed to know its real origins. Moynihan traced the story to a Newhouse National News Service item, printed first in the Staten Island Advance, and which stated that the White House had ordered a study on "what would happen if there is no presidential election in 1972." A Rand Corporation researcher was named as the individual to carry out the study—though he quickly denied any substance to the item. The Village Voice then picked up the story and it was quickly spread to the "political radical press" and to "one respectable West Coast newspaper." From there, in the classrooms and elsewhere, the story was elaborated upon and puffed to an incredible size.[17] A similar assertion occurred in the same circles in 1973, aided and abetted by the respectable media, that President Nixon had made a deal with the Mafia for the presidency. Actually hinted at in some classrooms was the notion that Nixon had persuaded the Mafia to do away with his chief roadblocks to the presidency—the two Kennedys —and in return he was to grant the organization certain favors.

Though most history and social studies departments were either directly or indirectly involved in this sort of thing in the 1960s, it must be added that the majority of teachers themselves kept to their assigned tasks. Still, the appearance of total activism was a major reality on the college scene. Some faculty members were even willing to spend *their* money for *Times* advertisements, in May 1970, carrying such slogans as "The killing must end," or "The war must be stopped."[18] A study by the Urban Research Corporation in 1970, as reported by the *New York Times*, noted a "sharp increase in active protest by faculty members." ROTC programs all over the country had been brought to an end by the votes of university faculties, though three years later at Boston University the same instrument of procedure was used to return the program to that school.

Representative Edith Green from Oregon, whose special House committee had studied the issue of campus unrest, brought herself to some solid conclusions. "I am convinced there would be no campus riots if it weren't for some faculty members," she emphasized. Douglas Hallett, a senior at Yale and the editorial chairman of the *Yale Daily News*, castigated faculties in general in 1970, claiming that they were breeding "in their students the kind of rigidity that comes only with one sided historical analysis." And the *New York Times* in June 1970 denounced university faculties by stating:

> The faculty cannot escape all blame for the campus disarray. Faculty members' confusion and frequent failure to stand up to coercive demands undermine students' respect for their teachers' integrity.

What was frightening in the 1970 aspect of the movement was the real academic weakness bared by campus violence. It should not be forgotten, however, that the participation of faculties in the strikes of the time was often motivated by impulses other than that of a moonstruck radicalism. Hayakawa of San Francisco State seems to have been partly right at least when he pointed his finger at faculty boredom. Hans Fink, a noted psychiatrist, added something of the same line in the following 1970 comments:

> There is no doubt in my mind that it must be extremely confusing to the student when some faculty are using drugs. It is also disconcerting to the student when the teacher announces his dislike for a particular course or subject matter he is teaching.

In any case, one could not possibly generalize about faculty activism in 1970 and in previous years. It was true that many faculty members, some impelled by a desire for power, aided and abetted the movement in its activities. A great many others, on the other hand, sought to keep the university system in good order. While it was always heralded that certain Nobel prize winners were in the camp of the activists, the media tended to gloss over those other distinguished Americans who heroically tried to do their duties. One had to search long and hard for the news item concerning Dr. Isador Rabi and his attempts to teach his class on May 7, 1970. A Nobel prize winner as well, he struggled to reach his classroom by walking through the picket line—only to be physically pushed away. Academic freedom was, at least in his case, not one of the goals of the movement.

A number of developments tended to turn the impact of the movement about, however. A Czechoslovakian student, disgusted at what he saw, put his thoughts on paper and, surprisingly enough, they even saw the light of day in some college papers. As reported in the *Roosevelt Torch*, he wrote:

> I don't wish you to try really what it is to be a political prisoner—for example, in a socialistic country. For me . . . this sentence seems funny. I'll tell you something about a political prison; we cannot travel—we must stay in our country (Czechoslavakia is smaller than Illinois); we cannot express our own ideas, own opinions; we cannot get objective information from the rest of the world; we cannot have meetings; we cannot gather; we cannot change our occupation.[19]

Other students began to react as well. Five Harvard classmen, writing in the *New York Times*, mocked the "carnival atmosphere" on that campus—the cantish phrases surrounding "these times of crisis." To these young people, the virtual abandonment of "academic standards by a university faculty previously considered among the world's greatest," indicated the extent to which baser elements had gained control over the educational establishment.[20]

For those among the faculties gifted with common sense, it really took little effort to see the deterioration which was taking place in the area of standards. Bad and substandard undergraduate programs had been introduced at most large schools across the country. Entrance and transfer standards were in decline. "Floaters" moved from campus to campus, dabbling briefly at each stop in whatever courses caught their fancy. The University of Wisconsin, for instance, was troubled with some 5,000 such young people. They panhandled on the campus and off, and many used drugs openly within sight of the administration building.[21]

One of the factors that turned the tide of the campus movement was the growing sense of elitism associated with faculty members and students involved in campus activism. Richard Hofstadter noted this in 1970, writing at length about students whose "elitism is based on moral indignation against most of the rest of us." To Hofstadter, those individuals had very little sense "that anything preceded this, or that there are parallel failures in the history of other nations." The noted historian's conclusions were fascinating. He saw nothing positive emerging from this period, and he was determined to call his own chapter of written history of the Sixties "The Age of Rubbish."[22]

Nevertheless, that sense of elitism was there—in prolonged sneering at "rednecks" who couldn't see the light on the great issues of the day, or in passing and snide references to blue-collar America. There were not a few among these elitist elements who would have done well to have read Robert Burns's "*To a Louse.*" If they had only been given the gift to see themselves—shouting down an appearance by Hubert Humphrey on one occasion or pelting Senator Strom Thurmond with marshmallows on another. Or even a chance view of a television program in the 1960s—a panel of "superior" students who, while arguing about the uselessness of democracy, uttered forecasts that "we will take over" in the establishment of rule by class.[23]

While there were some historians such as Andrew Hacker who continued to write about the "end of the American era," there were numerous others who saw much in the vitality and drive of the American system. Daniel Boorstin, for one, skillfully defended the nation during those hard days of 1970. Though he deplored the media's reverence for youth and for the "culturally deprived," he looked upon America's troubles as a temporary hypochondria. Boorstin urged a new sense of history—the academic field most perverted by the movement. "To be really persuaded that things can be otherwise," he wrote in connection with the possibilities of man, "we must see how and when and why they have actually been otherwise."[24]

The most substantial force in curbing the faculty activists in 1970 was the extension of the movement from a romantic and idyllic radicalism to violent and almost uncurbable excess. When the movement reached the latter stage in 1970 it was the faculties of the various universities who bailed out first. Some of the same individuals who previously had counseled activism now realized that the movement could neither support nor allow the freedom which they had themselves exercised. Slowly but irrevocably the movement began to turn in upon faculty liberalism—as one paper put it, those "bad . . . and boring" teachers who couldn't keep students awake with emotional inspiration. When the last break finally came in the spring of 1970, the movement let fly with an especial venom against those "liberal" professors who had failed the cause. *The Roosevelt Torch*, for instance, noting the lukewarm response of the faculty of Roosevelt University to a strike call, described them as instruments "in the hands of the rich for active suppression and murder of the people."[25]

Then, too, a few college presidents began to draw a bead on faculty and student protests. Dr. Miller Upton of Beloit College (a conscientious objector in World War II) vented his frustrations in a widely quoted statement. There was oppression in the land, he conceded, but it came mostly from the left which had disrupted college campuses and curtailed university freedom of speech. "We in the colleges and universities," he argued, "have tolerated unspeakable intimidation and thought control on the part of radical students, faculty, and others."

Out east, President Nathan M. Pusey of Harvard also entered the lists. Reflecting the sentiments of a majority of his faculty, Pusey blamed campus disruptions on students and faculty members who wished to see "our colleges and universities denigrated, maligned, and even shut down." He noted a new McCarthyism abroad in the land—the Hitlerian tactic of the big lie—especially in the radical claim that the university "is a hopelessly bigoted, reactionary force in our society which serves the interest of the hideous military-industrial complex."[26]

Columnists Rowland Evans and Robert Novak, after visiting some California universities in 1970, noted a distinct waning of the movement's activities—particularly in the activism of the faculties. They reported that the University of California regents were now asking some serious and pertinent questions about the abrupt decline in standards; in particular about one psychology class which had ballooned from 150 students to 600 enrollees at one institution. The regents got their answer. The instructor of the class had passed the word that "late registering radical students" could receive a full semester's credit for the course.

Furthermore, Evans and Novak found a new resistance on the part of more moderate professors, particularly in respect to the "eroded academic standards in the black studies program" of the San Diego campus of the University of California. To Evans and Novak as well as to other acute observers of the California scene, the corner of Berkeley-style radicalism seemed to have been passed. Coveys of teachers who had been drawn into the California system by the promise of high salaries were now fleeing eastward to the Midwest, partly because of their fear of radical violence and partly because the California taxpayer had reached the limit of his tolerance. In fact, it could be added that by midsummer of 1970, Americans in general were simply fed up.[27]

In the earlier years of the movement, when the moderate instructors in the trenches were absorbing the onslaught of the untutored, there was little concern exhibited by most university administrations. The demands of the movement were quickly ameliorated or satisfied with concessions—usually at the expense of moderates or conservatives on the campuses. But inevitably, of course, the outer patrols of the revolution had to reach a line of conflict with both university administrations and the boards which governed them. Demanding the right to fire and hire faculty members, to evaluate them for pay raises, and to determine the manner in which taxpayers' monies were to be spent—all became pivotal issues in the movement's advance.

As more and more university administrations felt constrained to oppose these aims, more and more university presidents felt the lash of the movement's will. Obscene telephone calls, threats against the

families of university officials, and real violence—all of which had been
the lot of some moderate teaching professors for years—now became a
part of the life of university presidents. One of the more interesting
cases was that of Kenneth Pitzer of prestigious Stanford University.

As William Buckley noted in 1970, "ideologically, Pitzer was perfectly respectable." He publicly deplored the Vietnam War. He was
active in condemning Brigham Young University because the Mormon
faith, which supported the school, denied priesthood to Negroes. He
had gone far out of his way to include students in various university
committees. He publicly deplored the draft. He persuaded his trustees
to agree to student demands to close the university research institute.
When one of Stanford's buildings was burned during a demonstration,
he took a most tolerant attitude toward those who may have perpetrated
the crime. In the end, his reward for not acceding to further student
leftist demands was elegant. Rocks were thrown through his office
windows, and a can of paint poured over his person. Pitzer promptly
quit.[28]

By August of 1970 some 10 percent of the universities and colleges
in the nation were lacking presidents. Those who stuck to their posts
began to take tougher lines with dissenters—many because of a fear of
retaliation on the part of that vast and hidden Middle America. The
New York Times editorialized:

> A shortage of money to pay the bills is less dramatic than a student boy-
> cott of classes, but bankruptcy can close a school down more completely
> and more permanently than any strike. The possibility that some institu-
> tions may soon go under and others—even some of the most prestigious—
> may have to close down entire divisions of departments is an ominous
> development that is now being openly discussed by the presidents of
> American universities.[29]

To many Americans, the guilt for college violence rested solely upon
university permissiveness. The mayor of beleaguered Madison, Wisconsin, where trashing and murder had become part of the campus
scene, laid the blame squarely upon higher education administration.
Acts of violence, said the mayor, had been the fault of universities that
had discarded rules, that had allowed faculty members not only to
encourage such demonstrations but had allowed movement faculty
members to "intimidate" students into taking part in acts of violence.[30]

By 1970 the tide of public sentiment, so in favor some ten years
previously of broad support for higher education, had reversed itself
completely. Father Theodore Hesburgh, the president of the University
of Notre Dame, stated the case as he saw it in October of that year:

> Feeling is running high against many visible universities and the witch
> hunters are out and at work. Both federal and state programs of support

for higher education have been reduced or tied to impossible conditions.
. . . The fact is that almost every state has considered some punitive
legislation against faculty and students.[31]

Hesburgh's statement was far too harsh and was typical of the type
of university president of the 1960s who tended to run alongside the
movement. No witch hunt ever really developed, and in the sense of
democracy it was within the right of the American taxpayer to wish to
express his opinions through his ballot. And his opinions in 1970 were
clearly along the lines of curbing expenditures for higher education.
Anybody, including Father Hesburgh, could have foreseen such a
development. Polls taken shortly after the May 1970 uprisings reflected
a range of disapproval of college disruptions from three to one to five
to one. Though it was true that a small percentage of students had
actually engaged in trashings and other violence, the public had assumed that such acts had won the tacit approval of the majority of
students—and perhaps they had. In any case, it was probably true that
most of the American people in May 1970 would have said "amen" to
a statement by Roger A. Freeman, a senior fellow of the Hoover Institution on War, Revolution, and Peace:

But even if all 7 million students on U.S. campuses disagreed with official U.S. policy—which, of course, they do not—what makes anybody
think that they would have the right to force the hand of the lawful government and the duly-elected representatives of 205 million Americans?[32]

The institutions which were to suffer the most from the general
public rejection of higher education were the private ones. At these
colleges and universities, so dependent upon bequests and gifts, there
developed a kind of economic panic. The reasons for the increasing
failure to raise adequate support went far beyond those most obvious
to the public eye. First, so many of the smaller colleges had ceased
instilling a sense of institutional loyalty among their students so that
those who were graduated had no sensitivity to the needs of the schools
which had sent them into the world. Secondly, many of the smaller
colleges had been so overcome with the concept of egalitarianism that
they had packed their dormitories with nonachievers. As it happened,
most of these students, upon graduation, continued to run true to
form—not earning enough to give to their alma maters even if they
had wished to do so. Private schools especially soon learned that grati-
tude could not be passed on to faculties in the form of pay raises.
Furthermore, some of the smaller colleges had lost heavily in declining stock market values brought on by a feeling of national malaise.
Still others found that it was far too expensive to replace burned out
buildings with structures of equal size. Insurance premiums went up
at an amazing rate. Northwestern University of Evanston, Illinois,

saw its insurance costs swell from $21,000 to $85,000 in a very short time. While Northwestern could afford such inflation, smaller schools could not. Parenthetically it should be pointed out that little Blackburn College in Illinois did not have any damage to its buildings from student violence in the Sixties—there the students paid part of their tuition costs by helping to erect such structures that the school needed.

Thus did a college financial crunch develop. William J. McGill, the president of Columbia University, reported his institution to be "overextended" and $11 million in the red. The Massachusetts Institute of Technology, at which there had been much tacit support of the movement, was reported to be $2 million in the red. Big and small private colleges and universities found the going increasingly tougher. Knox College in Illinois anticipated having to dig into its reserves. Ripon in Wisconsin was having trouble. The very small schools—like Lakeland in Wisconsin, Midwestern in Iowa, and John J. Pershing in Nebraska faced a dim future.[33]

Almost too late, boards of regents and private school administrations began to react to the situation. After all, when it came to the influence of money, both college faculties and their administrations were every bit as vulnerable as other aspects of American life. The University of Missouri, which was not private and which had a minimum of disturbance during the hot years, showed the way by adopting a policy in which the "destruction of property and interference with the rights of other members of the community will not be permitted." At Yale the regulations were more quietly changed in order to dispel student misconceptions about implicit immunities to civil prosecution.

Johns Hopkins followed suit by setting up a new code for its arts and science division. It outlined penalties for the abridgment of the rights of others and for any disruption of the functioning of the university. The University of California in Los Angeles relegated the infamous bullhorn to specific portions of the campus, and professors were directly informed that they should not use classes for antiwar protests. Nor were they allowed to change the course content of the subjects they were responsible for teaching.[34]

The University of Illinois, which had considerable trashing in May and June of 1970, laid out rules for the expulsion of students engaged in any prohibited conduct and the university threatened the revocation of financial aid for students involved in disruptions. Students at the University of Washington were given a six point code of conduct; a set of rules applied to the faculty as well.

The question to be asked at the end of the decade was why such rules had not existed before. The truth was that, in a sense, they had. Somehow, along the line of time, too many college administrators had given in to too many factions. Too many university presidents had failed to honor the traditional stance of the university structure in regard to American life; a stance which allowed for a variance of opinion within the confines of scholarship rather than emotion. Dr. Samuel B. Gould, the chancellor of the State University of New York, noted the extent of the dereliction when he stated in 1970: "I think there is a great tendency toward moving the intellectual life away from its central place in the university. . . ."[35] That was one of the great understatements of the decade.

5

The Intellectual-Media Establishment

One of the most interesting developments of the Sixties was to be seen in the emergence of a new internal balance of powers. The presidency as part of the executive branch of government had probably stabilized or at least peaked in its influence. Congress, on the other hand, having reached the nadir of its powers during the Johnson period, was attempting to reassert itself toward the end of the decade. Within the absolutely internal operation of the government the Department of Health, Education and Welfare had not only established itself as the chief feeder at the trough of the government budget, but had also become one of the most effective self-generating lobbies in the national capital.

But there was now an extragovernmental influence which had grown enormously in strength since 1950. A loose conglomeration of elements and areas, it included the mass of the liberal intellectual community, the purveyors of both written and spoken news, and the commentators. No one phrase or collection of words could be easily created which might describe the new power, excepting the rather inclusive phrase, the intellectual-media establishment.

Still, by 1970, it was possible to suppose that along with the executive, legislative, and judicial divisions of government, there was such

103

an outside force which, in some cases, almost seemed to overbalance the force of the legal divisions of government. The might of the intellectual-media establishment appeared to be so strong by the end of the decade that one eminent writer referred to its members as the "unofficial rulers of America." Samuel Beers of Harvard, describing part or all of the elements of the new force, wrote: "The media revolution is as powerful as the industrial revolution was. The word manipulators are on top. . . . My students leave here and go into journalism and wield enormous power."[1]

There were further evidences of the strength of the new force. It was possible during the first Nixon administration to publish the innermost decisions of government, and suffer no penalties for it. It was possible for elements of the media to copy grand jury tapes of private presidential conversations. International agreements were jeopardized by energetic operatives of the media. Secret Defense Department documents were printed and no action could be taken against those who stole the documents, or those who printed them. At least two Presidents were beaten into powerless executives before the end of their tenure of office—partly because of their own failures, but partly because of the power of the new establishment.

Not all of this passed unnoticed, and some who saw dangers in the new conglomerate tended to refer to it as the "Eastern establishment." The phrase had only a partial validity on a number of counts. First, the intellectual-media establishment operated with strength all over the nation. Secondly, not all of the intellectuals in the East or elsewhere conformed to the rules of the new power. Irving Kristol, Daniel P. Moynihan, James Q. Wilson, Sidney Hook, and Edward Banfield, plus others, tended to keep themselves free of the singlemindedness which characterized the mass of the establishment. Many of them paid the price—the needed exposure of a new book on television, or a favorable review in certain literary publications. The favorable publicity during the 1960s tended to go in the direction of the adherents to the cause. So did the profits.

But there were more explicit and torturous punishments for defectors. Banfield and Moynihan were repeatedly quoted out of context. Walt W. Rostow, an adviser to President Johnson, could not return to the Massachusetts Institute of Technology at the end of his government duties. But John Kenneth Galbraith, who had served in the Kennedy administration, was a mandarin who was welcomed by Harvard with open arms.

The unity of the liberal intellectual community and the liberal media called for an abnormal conformity within all aspects of their disparate worlds. Those who strayed were dealt summary punishments. Distinguished and conservative professors were forced to suffer indignities in silence. Sometimes "unperson" to their colleagues, they failed to match the promotions and salary increases of liberal and conforming colleagues. Those commentators in the media who left the common front suffered at least part of the same fate. Needless to say, the impact of punishment could be great, whether coming from the salary and personnel committee of Podunk University or the *New York Review of Books*.

Some who suffered in silence during the decade could hardly be called conservative. Elements of the intellectual community or of the media who preferred Hubert Humphrey in 1968 to Eugene McCarthy were suspect. Those who tried to moderate the tone of dissent by attempting to look at all sides of issues were placed outside the pale. By the mid years of the decade the pressure for conformity was so direct that Andrew M. Greeley, a Roman Catholic priest, thought he could define the rules. They were as follows:

1. Schools are the best places in which to accomplish social reform.
2. Marxism was the most effective way of creating social progress outside the United States.
3. Youth is the hope of the future, and the intelligentsia should be profoundly involved in what is happening to them.
4. Somewhere there are the "people"—to be distinguished in any respect from the "silent majority"—and that somehow this element would provide the necessary "power" to effect change.[2]

Part of the explanation for the growth of power of the intellectual-media establishment was in the slow accretion of access to the American mind. Television news broadcasts, for example, increased not only in terms of the length of presentation but in their potential public audience. The 1970 census reports indicated that, despite the fact that 25.6 million Americans were supposedly living below what had been arbitrarily established as a poverty level, some 95.5 percent of all American homes had television. That combination of facts alone represented a possible source of power for only one element of American culture—the producers of television news broadcasts.

There were other changes as well, part of them in the structure of the media itself. Rising at first as a thin trickle, the stream of advocacy news, both in the written and spoken word, became a freshet during the Johnson administration. Spurred by emotionalism surrounding the various assassinations of the decade, the Vietnam War and the civil rights struggle, the media may well have surprised themselves by the power they appeared to generate. The older straight journalists tended to fall into discard. Emotion brought larger viewing and reading audiences than did reason. Then, too, it must be added that the university community added a segment of the new activism. Liberal arts graduates as well as journalism school products tended to enter the media field as advocates. At least one journalism professor noted the tendency early in the 1960s. In another one of those classic bits of understatement, he explained the weaknesses of the younger journalists by stating: "I think basically it is a lack in our education."[3]

As indicated previously, there had been a deep throbbing of discontent in the intellectual-media community as early as 1958—the closing years of the Eisenhower administration. Much of it was standard flak from the left, but indeed a large part of it was generated by the seemingly natural Democratic inclinations within the media and the liberal arts. In 1960, for instance, Sidney Hyman, a political scientist, expressed the typical liberal view of President Eisenhower. The outgoing Chief Executive had been a failure. He had cut off debate about military matters. He had called his critics "noisy extremists." Hyman argued that Eisenhower had given the country eight years of dull leadership; there had been a loss of "elan and dash" within the country.[4] Norman Mailer followed up Hyman's assertions, and seemed to agree tacitly with the Hyman argument that the country was on the verge of falling apart.

President Eisenhower had indeed referred to his various critics as "political morticians exhibiting a breastbeating pessimism." It was the outgoing President's way of crying doomsaying. But what kind of doomsaying was it? Some of it reflected a revived passion for national adventure—a return to the "high seas of adventure" was the way Mailer put it. In other ways it was a kind of new nationalism which, as Richard Hofstadter pointed out, was often found at the root of the paranoid style. Hofstadter's words need little clarification. He wrote: "It [paranoia] is a common ingredient of fascism, and of frustrated nationalism, though it appeals to many who are hardly fascists and it can frequently be seen in the left-wing press."[5]

This is not to say that all of those who decried the Eisenhower period were paranoic. But there was a kind of nationalism entrenched within segments of American liberalism, and it was the force of this sentiment which was to lead the way into the calamity of Vietnam. It may well have been true that some of the nationalistic or jingoistic imperative in the doomsaying of the late Eisenhower years was present simply because it provided a convenient drum upon which to pound. Sidney Hyman, a liberal contributor to the *Progressive*, was depressed in 1960, for instance, because the country had lost its "elan and dash." Yet, in December 1973, on an ABC telecast, Hyman was still depressed and for almost the same reasons.

So it was that Norman Mailer longed for those high seas of adventure in 1960. Some ten years later he wanted to beach the boat, however, and he was emotionally anti-Nixon because he thought that the Nixon withdrawal from Vietnam was not proceeding fast enough. Walter Lippmann is cut from a different cloth than Mailer, but he too trumpeted forth during the doomsaying hysteria of 1958 to 1962. In fact Lippmann could be cited for real consistency in Cassandra-like soliloquies. In 1913 he mourned the conditions of misery in the country. In 1932 he seemed to be positive in his impression that Franklin Roosevelt was a poor choice for the presidency. In 1955 he had convinced himself that the U.S. was at a critical point in its history, and that the nadir of public morality had been reached. In 1962 Lippmann wrote that if President Kennedy was to "raise the American economy from the creeping stagnation which has come upon it in the second half of the Fifties, if he is to recover the industrial preeminence which we once had . . . the administration will have to do a mighty job. . . ." Still the nation survived all of these alleged crises, which may have proved that Lippmann may have suffered more from human flaw than from real insight upon each of the above occasions.

To have read Lippmann and Mailer consistently during the 1950s might have brought one to the same conclusion reached by Finley Peter Dunne some fifty years earlier—that the best thing to do was to go out and buy a gun. Yet, amazingly, Lippmann was back at the same old stand in 1965, complaining about the size of American cities, the inadequacies of American education, and a general situation so bad that the nation "can't wait another generation."[6]

There were a number of conservative members of the media who fretted at the prevalence of doomsaying in the early part of the 1960s. David Lawrence, with a good deal of prescience, warned that the country should not "look on history as the faded pages of some other generation's failures." Nicola Chiaromonte, in an earlier piece, had declared that it was the duty of the intellectual to expose "fictions and to refuse to call 'useful lies' truths."[7]

But the will of the nation's liberal intelligentsia was such that slowly but surely there occurred a dismantling of the national psyche. A phantasmagory of frightening visions was unloosed upon the public, partly out of an increased activism on the part of television producers and partly from within the intellectual community. Some of that activism was well meant and natural. Part of it rested upon either personal or group ambition.

Though no President had cozened the press as did John F. Kennedy, not all of the 1,034 days of the Kennedy administration were full of wine and roses. The President constantly complained about the manner and behavior of newsmen, and claimed that in some cases they were not really reporting the facts. He further contended that the media should not fill their pages "with analyses that cannot be proven, with statements that cannot be documented." Even that lead huskie of the old liberal tradition, Hubert Humphrey, backed Kennedy's arguments by saying: "I would suggest, in all humility, that fanning the flames of racial or religious prejudice—however unwittingly—is highly dangerous in a society based upon the dignity of man."[8]

The reactions of both Kennedy and Humphrey do indicate the extraordinary growth in the intellectual-media establishment after the advent of nationwide television. But the biggest step in that growth was yet to come. In September 1963 CBS made the fateful decision to expand its nightly news program from fifteen to thirty minutes. Other networks quickly followed suit. As Theodore White was to state some years later: "That was equivalent to driving the golden spike at the completion of the Union Pacific railroad."[9]

The change brought about by the expansion of national news coverage was phenomenal in nature. Much more time had to be filled. The ever-increasing amounts of taped news arriving in New York and Washington had to be culled for more interesting items. And what was more interesting, as it turned out, were segments of tape colored by advocacy. Newspapers were forced in time to "op ed" pages in order to meet the challenge of such presentations. And radio, which for a decade had floated upon a stagnant sea of pop music, began to adopt either instant and constant news broadcasts or advocacy conversational programs.

Though the major television networks admitted to little in the way of bias in the presentation of the news, evidence indicates the contrary. After Vice President Agnew's Des Moines attack against the media in 1970, there was a good deal of soul-searching by the networks and by elements of the print media. Surprisingly enough, there appeared to be a good deal of concurrence with Agnew's charges. *Newsweek* magazine allowed that there had been a liberal tendency in news circles. *Time*, in June 1970, gave considerable space to the argument and admitted the existence of an "Eastern establishment." To further buttress its piece, *Time* quoted Theodore White's description of the media "establishment" as an "opinionated mafia."[10]

What seemed to frighten many Americans in the hinterlands was the possible neglect on the part of networks in the presentations of both sides of any issue. A sizable segment of the American people seemed to resent the deliberate attempt on the part of some in the media to cram their personal opinions down the national throat.[11] Almost anybody of this persuasion could cite examples. There had been a radio news broadcaster who, thinking his microphone had become dead, had called a leading presidential candidate a "bastard." In September 1970, NBC had allowed its First Tuesday commentator Sander Vanocur to state that Liberia's brutal police force seemed to have been trained in the "Chicago style." Yet Vanocur was never forced to provide any proof that Chicago's police were any more brutal or inefficient than those of New York City or Los Angeles.

The search for advocacy news seemed to become an obsession with some network producers during the 1960s. A Fort Worth television station asked its network central news office if it wished tape footage on the peaceful integration of the local school system. Was there any violence on the tape? was the reply. If not, then the network office did not want it.[12]

In 1973, the networks and much of the print media were to use the Watergate issue in a serious attempt to expiate the possible errors of the previous decade. In fact, some commentators seemed to be using Watergate as evidence that the media in general had established a lily-white reputation. But the still unanswered questions concerning the potential influence of the media were many. How was government to regulate television and radio without infringing upon the freedom of the press? Did all of television constitute a lobby so powerful that even the American government could not touch it? While it was within the power of the television news producers to investigate all aspects of American life, who could be powerful enough to investigate the investigators? Who would check the growing influence of television upon national elections and upon Congress? Are the television networks above reproof?

These are serious questions and some thoughtful individuals, even in the media, have sought answers to them. A *Saturday Review* of March 1970 carried a biting piece on the problem which was entitled "Have the News Media Become too Big to Fight?" *Time,* the *National Observer,* and the *Wall Street Journal* have likewise carried similar pieces from time to time.[13]

What many liberal reporters were reflecting in the way of specific biases was to a great extent what was being thought by the general liberal intellectual community. Tom Wolfe's magnificent essay on "radical chic" refers to the latter as "serious-minded, morose, morbid to the point of gangrene . . . and quite out to lunch." Wolfe's analysis of rules for acceptance by the radical chic is clever and pointed. Intellectualism, he argues, is as much a way of life in America as it is anything else. It is a life style, so to speak. Those not conforming to the characteristics of that life style are either not acceptable, they are non-persons, or they are read out of any previous membership. William Faulkner was quite acceptable to the radical chic of the 1920s, but in 1960 he was dismissed from the fraternity because of his personal behavior. Buzz Aldrin, the astronaut, was not considered an intellectual during his NASA days, even though he held a doctorate from MIT.

Three years later Aldrin published a book which revealed his personal and psychological difficulties, and the book was given substantial television play.[14]

Wolfe's intellectual of 1970 rode a Volkswagen, kept brown bread in the bread box, wore muttonchops, played Beatle records, kept a stack of unread copies of the *New York Review of Books* about, and was capable of spewing out some highly emotional sentiments on the Vietnam War.

The rules of membership thus seemed quite firmly established. Sometimes in an almost indefinable way they touched upon the ridiculous and the sublime at one and the same time. The death of John Dos Passos, the great American writer, presented a good example of this in 1970. In his earlier years Dos Passos was a flaming liberal; in his late days he was conservative. The *New York Times* obituary described the turnabout in the sentence—"But in his middle and old age, he turned against his former idealism." It was a subtle rebuke of Dos Passos's rejection of "good values." Would it have been better to have said that in his late years Dos Passos had become a realist?[15]

The extent to which advocacy and doomsaying entered into the establishment media during the late 1960s rivaled the appearance of the same characteristics in the underground press. It was, as Senator Margaret Chase Smith had said, a "national sickness."[16] It was, in truth, a reflection of the general paranoia to be found throughout liberal circles in the intellectual and media communities. The *National Observer* in July 1970 made note of the illness by claiming that the intellectual-media elements of American society had "manufactured and propagandized an illusory concept of America, and more than any other group made a fashion of despair."

This paranoid style, as Hofstadter had defined it some years before, had been building through the decade. Joan Baez, who owed much of her popularity to radical chic, had declared in 1964: "People are starving to death in some places in the world. They look to this country, with all its wealth and all its power. They look at our national budget. They are supposed to respect us. They do not respect us. They despise us." It was a sentiment which made little sense both then and later, and it smacked of hypocrisy and deceit. People will always be starving to death somewhere in this world, unfortunately. Do they always look at our national budget in their last agony? Do they always go to their death cursing America?

Yet in that same year Dr. Benjamin Spock equalled Miss Baez in her emotionalism. It was a year before the large American troop commitment to Vietnam. Spock declared that young people in America "dread the loss of their parents and their own mutilation" from atomic fallout. American children, he argued, used to be "noted for their optimism"— but now, in 1964, "most of them want to join marches."[17]

The kinds of sentiments expressed by Baez and Spock preceded by many years the nadir of depression reached by the intellectual-media community in 1970. In that year, the psychosis had reached an almost parallel state in both the establishment and underground presses. In the *New York Times* of October 1970, Martin Hirschman, editor-in-chief of *The Michigan Daily,* was allowed a forum for his opinions. "Have not dozens of blacks, especially black political leaders, been shot down on the streets of our cities . . . ?" he asked. The question was a polemical one, and Hirschman added the conclusion. "Students have petitioned the government dozens of times . . . but there has yet to be a serious response."

Some months earlier, the underground paper *Red Eye,* of San Jose argued: "We are tied up in Cambodia and Vietnam because of poverty that strikes down thirty to forty million people in one way or another. That sends babies out in the streets of Appalachia with swollen bellys [sic] because one child must forego eating . . . so six can eat on that particular day." The writer further intoned that President Nixon was a "gross and insensitive man," that some 37 percent of American soldiers in Vietnam were blacks, and that the future for all Americans was bleak. His final shot was: "You've watched your parents go on into a system which corrupts them as much as anybody else."[18]

Thus it was that both in the *Times* and in the underground papers there appeared sheer exaggerations of fact. Black leaders were not being shot down on the "streets of our cities," poverty was not striking down thirty to forty million people in the United States, and far fewer than 37 percent of American fighting men in Vietnam were blacks. But, as the illustrations show, the hysteria and the rhetoric was to be found overground as well as underground.[19]

The manner in which elements of Hofstadter's paranoid style had filtered into the intellectual community, especially in terms of doom-saying, is further shown by example. Norman Cousins, one of the paladins among American intellectuals, wrote at the end of 1969: "Indeed, considering the human situation in the world today, the wonder is not that campuses are in a state of unrest but that they should be able to function at all." Indeed, continued Cousins, the generation of the late Sixties was the "first in history to witness a situation in which the survival of the human species itself . . . is deeply and perva-sively threatened." What else do people see today, Cousins asked, but a diversion of energies and resources into "ways of expunging and cheapening human life." Moreover, Cousins implied, the world was about to be overcome by pollution and by a possible depletion of oxygen in the air.[20]

The statements by Cousins typified the exaggeration which was endemic through the decade. Oxygen levels have remained constant since man was first able to measure them. To have argued that people,

American people, were engaged in a pursuit of "meaningless satisfactions" was to deny the great dollops of American aid given by those same people to the starving peoples of the world. As for that one moment when humanity was first faced with doom, Cousins should have restudied history—when, for instance, two-thirds of the people of Europe had been wiped out by plague in the early Middle Ages. Or when, in 1919, much of Europe was on the brink of starvation.

There seems little doubt that the pessimism which had emerged in the Sixties was, as Senator Smith had noted, the symptom of some evil disease. And progressively it was to be found on both the overside and the underside of American society. *Space City* of Houston illustrates that point in one of its April 1970 issues. A writer for the publication urged the establishment of a new political party in order to fight the 400 years of "inhuman treatment" given to blacks. The contributor *demanded* "freedom for all black men held in federal, state, county, and city prisons and jails," and no military service for blacks under any circumstance. As for the future and the present the writer concluded:

> The terror is growing closer by the day. The power structure will never change its nature, the nature that killed off the American indians [sic] and took their land, that enslaved blacks and dehumanized them, that dropped bombs on Japanese women and children, that wages war against the poor Vietnamese people, that killed Brother Hampton as he slept and that will continue to kill until it is cut out.[21]

The *New York Times,* which had started out the decade with a nice little editorial about the cloudless future, was some ten years later almost overcome with the notion that the country was on the verge of self-immolation. Its Op Ed page alone was loaded with so many predictions of gloom for the future that one must almost feel, as Keats put it, "half in love with easeful death." The doomsaying which had engulfed much of the media and the intellectual community reached its apex in the *Times* in midsummer of 1970. A chronological examination of the paper's descent into the abyss of despair offers interesting insights.

On May 2 Anthony Lewis, who personally seems like a cheery soul, saw fit to denounce President Nixon—which was almost a daily chore for Lewis during that period. Nixon, said Lewis, had reached a new low in ordering an invasion of Cambodia. As far as the American university community was concerned, the columnist asserted, one had to excuse the violence of rhetoric and the lack of maturity which appeared from time to time. After all, hadn't the nation been led by a President who chose to divide rather than to heal? About the future? "Nothing for years has cast so dark a shadow on America's future," he wrote.[22]

On the following day, Tom Wicker, another *Times* columnist, got into the act. In a column entitled "In the Nation: Further Into the Quagmire," Wicker charged that the Cambodian invasion had indicated that Nixon had no plan to end the war. The President, said Wicker, was "pursuing the bloody chimera of striking one final overpowering blow that will drive the North Vietnamese to their knees. . . ." As a parting shot Wicker accused Nixon of deception, demagoguery, and chauvinism.[23]

Two days later the *Times* editorial page implied that the nation was headed for a terrible self-destruction. In the same issue an article was headlined with the words, "60 Years of Quiet at Kent State Are Shattered in Era of Protest." Of course the editorial, as Mark Twain might have said, was a little premature in its assumptions.[24] In the case of the Kent State piece, Wicker's exaggerations might just as well have been applied here. The situation at Kent State was not a sudden explosion. In no context could it have been the result solely of Nixon's ordering of the invasion of Cambodia.

Reason, in that early summer of 1970, seemed hard pressed for survival. In the May 7 edition of the *Times* there appeared a letter from Walter Hickel, the former secretary of the interior. It contained the complaint that President Nixon was ignoring the lessons of the past. The American Revolution, Hickel asserted, had been led by such "youths" as Patrick Henry and Thomas Jefferson. Hickel and the *Times* should have checked the facts. Henry was born in 1736 and was forty years old at the time of the Declaration of Independence. Jefferson, born in 1743, was thirty-three when he wrote the Declaration. Both men were hardly teenaged demonstrators.[25]

What seemed to be happening to the *Times,* which was and is the reflection of intellectual tastes in America, was that it was separating itself from the general mood of the mass of the people. On May 8 the paper editorialized that the nation faced the "task of rescuing the nation's young from their growing dissatisfaction," and it cast a warning about the "great numbers" of students involved in the hue and cry of the moment. Unfortunately the *Times* missed taking any strong editorial stand concerning a speech recently given by Mayor John V. Lindsay on the nature of the Vietnam War. Lindsay rhetorized on America's draft dodgers, saying: "The ones I have unending admiration for are the guys who say, 'I simply will not serve in the Army of the United States in Vietnam and I am willing to take the consequence for it.' These are the guys who are heroic."

Was the mayor advocating resistance to the draft? Was he saying to the American people that young men could choose and pick the war in which they wished to fight? A later release from the mayor's office added a codicil which read: "I personally do not advocate draft resistance, but those who resist and accept the lawful consequence of their beliefs rather than turning to violence deserve our respect even if we disagree with them." The rhetoric had now moved beyond understanding.[26]

Through the remainder of May, the Eastern branch of the intellectual establishment, with occasional assistance from scattered areas elsewhere, kept up a drumfire of recrimination and doomsaying. Mayor Lindsay, who had done well on issues of doom and gloom in the past, again entered the fray by advising: "Our hold on the future is very frail. That future—all that we are and all that we can be—dies a little bit each day the war goes on. . . ." Three days later the *New York Times* chipped in with an apocalyptic vision of its own. America had become a nation of "doubts" and "fears," full of a "sinister mood," overwhelmed by a "deeper crisis," a meeting of "unmet demands by confusion and contradictions," and a spontaneous outpouring of "concern from the nation's campuses."

The nation had lost its sense of direction, moaned the *Times*. Protests were coming from masses of old and young who, though they appeared to be crying out in anger, were really "calling for help." The editorial closed with a quote from John W. Gardner, a former cabinet officer and the organizer of Common Cause. "The danger is the creeping disaster that overtakes a society which little by little loses a commanding grip on its problems and its future"—so Gardner had said. That phrase "little by little" seemed almost an echo of Mayor Lindsay's comment about the nation and the future dying a "little bit" each day.

James Reston, a senior member of the *Times* staff and one of the more reasonable contributors to the paper in 1970, appeared to be swept along by the general frustration and disillusionment found in the media. By mid-May it was possible that he had accepted a notion held generally in the East, that every one of the nation's university students had embraced the principle of revolt. Scattering visions of gloom, Reston described the nation's capital as being "more divided and pessimistic" than in previous times. A speculation by a Washington lawyer, John Lord O'Brian, was run into the Reston column—whether or how long "congressional government could survive under existing political and economic pressures." John W. Gardner was also resorted to in a quote which proclaimed: "While each of us pursues his selfish interests and comforts himself by blaming others, the nation disintegrates. I use the phrase soberly. The nation disintegrates. . . ."[27]

Even if the nation wasn't really disintegrating, as Gardner implied, the intellectual-media establishment was. Joined by opportunistic politicians and television personalities, its members turned the lights of the national future down low. Henry Steele Commager, the historian, burst forth in *Look* magazine in July 1970 with an article entitled "Is Freedom Dying in America?" Freedom may not have been dying but

Look was. Shortly thereafter, it heaved over on its corporate side and sank in financial ruin.[28]

Whole segments of the Eastern seaboard intellectual-media establishment seemed possessed with the desire to contribute to the confusion of the moment. When Senators George McGovern and Mark Hatfield wanted to make television spot tapes expressing the dovish point of view on Vietnam, Madison Avenue advertising firms provided free assistance. "We had to make opposition to the war respectable," was the rationalization.

Hugh Downs, who had gained a considerable amount of fame as a side man on a nighttime conversational program, threw his own contribution into the pot on the NBC "Today" show of July 30, 1970. It was in the form of a convoluted question on the "corroded values" of the older generation. And out in South Bend, Indiana, where stood the golden dome of Notre Dame University, Reverend Theodore Hesburgh, the university president, stated: "I think we're at some kind of watershed in American history. Until we can get this generation convinced that the system can work, we cannot get back to education as we have known it." It might be added here that Notre Dame eventually did return to something in the nature of the past. Its football teams not only played in the Sugar Bowl and the Cotton Bowl in following years, but won the mythical national championship in 1973.[29]

By mid-1970 the pessimism of the nation was bubbling to the surface in a dozen different quarters. Ernest F. Hollings, a Southern senator, told University of Georgia students that "like 100 years ago, the politics of hope have given way to the politics of despair." Despite Hollings's arguments, the South, more than any other part of the nation, kept its equilibrium on national issues. Atlanta or New Orleans were far removed from the spirit of Cambridge and Greenwich Village, and in many ways a great deal more vital and spirited.

On the other hand, the pessimism of the East seemed centered in New York City, Washington, and Boston. Saul Bellow, a solid and accomplished Midwestern writer, visited New York City in 1970 and found Greenwich Village "gray-bearded and hugely goggled" and as densely covered with protest buttons as a fish is with scales." As for the whole of New York City, Bellow wrote:

> New York seems to thrive also on a sense of national deficience, on the feelings of many who think themselves sunk hopelessly in unsatisfactory places, in the American void where there is no color, no theater, no vivid contemporaneousness, where people are unable to speak authoritatively, globally, about life.[30]

The last third of 1970 brought varied viewpoints from the intellectual-media community about the possibility of American survival.

Tom Wicker of the *New York Times* discovered a wisp of hope after flying across the country. "The Great Plain is even reassuring," he wrote. "It makes it possible to believe for a moment that, on such a continent, men with such a heritage may yet be saved by the land and the past, from the worst nightmare of the future." The statement seemed a faint acknowledgment that the East—or at least the intellectual-media segment of it—was in dissonance with the remainder of the nation.[31]

Shortly thereafter, however, the *New York Times Magazine* produced an article by one Philip Green, a professor. Green saw the world as in a terrible shape, brought on mostly by "repressive American politics at home and abroad. . . ." Furthermore, Green added, police were harassing the Black Panthers and he claimed that in Oakland the police had "harassed and shot Black Panthers before any black had ever pulled a trigger. . . ." Though most of Green's claims were refuted by Edward J. Epstein's 1971 *New Yorker* article on the police and the Black Panthers, the lack of research was no hindrance to Green. "To predict that repression will come is redundant, since it's already here," he claimed.[32]

James Reston's most interesting contribution to the temper of the times in the last third of 1970 was published in an October issue of the *Times*. He expressed a mild concern that perhaps President Nixon's actions in Vietnam might have the support of a majority of the American people, and that was bad. The majority was not always right, Reston opined, and he offered up as proof the instance of the use of atomic bombs in World War II. The two themes involved in the Reston argumentation—that is, that there was a misdirected Middle America, and that the dropping of atomic bombs in Japan was bad—were standard fare in most underground newspapers of the time. *Space City* of Houston had argued exactly these two points earlier in the year. Now they were in the establishment press.

The half circle traversed by the *New York Times* from 1960 to 1970 was completed with an editorial message in December. There was, said the paper, the possibility of the emergence of a "plutocracy" in the country. This was another theme present in the underground press. The *Times* argued that it was difficult to be merry on the Christmas of 1970, for the situation in the country was most difficult. Young men were dying in Asia, refugees were rotting in camps in the very birthplace of Christ, tidal wave victims were suffering in Pakistan, and small children in many places knew nothing but hunger and deprivation The last applied "even in the United States," though the paper gave no examples.

Some days earlier Tom Wicker had paved the way for this final bit of doomsaying with a sad complaint about the hungry people in

America. At least in this instance the columnist did not engage in other wild estimates of the moment, estimates so fantastic that foreign visitors could have expected to see people dying on the streets. But Wicker did have hard words about a bill in Congress which would have required at least one member of a family on relief to work in exchange for food stamps. One of the reasons for the introduction of the bill in the first place had been the large numbers of collegians who were applying for and getting the stamps, a fact which Wicker seemed to overlook.[33]

What seemed to bother a great many Americans during the entire year of 1970 was the application of standards by doomsayers to the United States which were seldom met anywhere else. Robert Conquest, a British writer, noted this in a *New York Times Magazine* article in October. Entitled "The American Psychodrama Called Everyone Hates Us," the piece indicated that the phrase "America has gone mad," long used by doomsayers in the United States, had even penetrated European intellectual circles. Professor Sacher V. Scapegoat is Conquest's imaginary American anti-American intellectual whose "jaw muscles crack with politely repressed yawns at his tales of how corrupt, how imperialist, how rich, how unutterably vile his country is." America's sins are not really all that bad, Conquest concluded, and the United States seemed to be "no more than one of those outpatients with chronic hypochondria, bothering a hospital by constantly trying to get one of the beds urgently needed by the truly ill."

Conquest's most interesting point was made against those in America and elsewhere who attempt to remake history. Almost as if to anticipate the rash of books and articles on the theme, Conquest denotes the beginning of the attempt in 1970 to imply that convicted spies Julius and Ethel Rosenberg were actually innocent. It was the beginning of another attempt to find martyrs on the left in the mode of Sacco and Vanzetti, despite the firm evidence that Kim Philby, the master spy for the Russian government, had implied the guilt of the two.

Conquest further claimed that many intellectuals were quick to arrive at conclusions which were invalid and immoral. He saw it as a kind of "antithought" which forced many within the intellectual-media element to ignore the "accidents, cross-currents, and sudden switches" which compose real history. "The failure to carry out the will of a minority is therefore labelled 'totalitarian' democracy or 'repressive tolerance,'" Conquest added. As to whether the United States had witnessed irrationalism within its intellectual community, Conquest fell back upon a quote from George Orwell. "The direct, conscious attack on intellectual decency comes from the intellectuals themselves," Orwell had once written.[34]

Intellectual decency was not a byword in 1970, however. Over-statement and rhetoric were the vogue. David McReynolds, the field secretary of the War Resisters League, described his America in these terms:

Is the revolution here? Something is happening, Mr. Jones, but I'm not sure what it is. The bombings. The campus unrest. Hundreds jailed for resisting the draft, thousands jailed on drug charges, tens of thousands fleeing to Canada, black leaders shot to death in their beds by Chicago cops. Listen to the rock music. Observe the culture heroes of the youth.

McReynold's fanciful vision of the day of reckoning was almost equalled or excelled by those writers of the liberal overground and the radical underground. Richard Rovere, a contributor to the *New Yorker,* sensed that American society was "deteriorating" but that the shape of that possibility had not "reached the masses." What Rovere did not seem to understand is that it had reached the masses; the results were to be shown in the 1972 presidential election. A member of the Peace Corps argued that there were people in leadership positions in the U.S. who were "fascists" and who wished to murder the young and the blacks. This government-subsidized young American had reached darkening conclusions. There should be nationwide strikes, the dis-ruption of the Justice Department by "liberal" lawyers, and huge street demonstrations. These actions would serve to free such "political prisoners" as Huey Newton and Bobby Seale, and would force the country to negotiate "reparations with blacks, Indians, Puerto Ricans, Mexican-Americans."

All of these sacrifices and oblations would and could not atone for America, so said the Peace Corps representative. He urged the "even-tual dissolution of the United States"—"dissolution before decay" was the way he phrased it. "I often think that the name of the thing we are headed for is not fascism, not revolution, but national suicide," he concluded.[35]

A few years later, Fred Hechinger of the *New York Times* looked back on the 1960s and sought to recall some aspects of the puerile rhetoric of the decade. What came to Hechinger's mind were such men as Charles Reich, author of *The Greening of America,* and Pro-fessor Frederick Rudolph of Williams College. The first had once said for posterity: "This is a Revolution; the rebirth of people in a sterile land." The latter had compared the Woodstock rock festival to a trip to the moon—as he put it, "for now the most significant of all. . . ."

As Hechinger noted, the movement was finished by 1973. The so-called youth movement had been a myth in terms of enjoying mass support from America. The most incredible phenomenon, according to Hechinger, had been the self-delusion of the intellectual-media class during the entire decade of the Sixties. As Hechinger pointed out, Samuel Lubell, the pollster, had discovered that at the height of the movement, only about 10 percent of the nation's college students were "in serious disagreement with the aims, values, and politics of their parents." A Michigan Research Center study made in 1968 could have added significance to the Lubell findings. Its research found that possibly 30 percent of those in conservative George Wallace's camp in 1968 were under the age of thirty. A third clincher was a Yankelovich study which found that 48 percent of college students and 70 percent of noncollege students were conservative in their own estimation.

But hypocrisy and self-delusion, both symptoms of paranoia, were rampant among the liberals of the Sixties. As Hechinger argued, the fatal error of many of those on the left was the assumption that the youth culture was immune to the "same viruses that made the older generation vulnerable and corrupt." The young were just as subject to "mindless fascination with slogans"—they were even more vulnerable to cant. Where the radical leaders had succeeded was in convincing most liberal and media people in the United States that they represented a major force in political change. They didn't, of course, and that was because their sheer banality and quasi-intellectualism caught up with them. America's liberals, unfortunately, were too slow in picking up the contradictions in radical logic. The great American middle class was not.[36]

The enormity of the liberal self-rapture was astounding. America's work ethic, especially the WASP work ethic, was reprehensible and corrosive; but the thousands of Chinese seen sweeping snow from the streets of Peking seemed so admirable in the eyes of many liberal newsmen. Racial integration was absolutely necessary on one hand, but black nationalism was to be promoted. There was much that was good in the Black Panthers, but military trappings and murderous tactics in other groups were bad. America or "Amerika" was dying— but somehow the American ethos was admirable as seen in other peoples.

As Hechinger pointed out, the movement suddenly found itself drifting rudderless on an open sea after 1970. Meaning and support seemed to have disappeared. Only the older and more cautious liberals were available to reactivate the cause of the American left, but many of these individuals had been decimated in the radical drive to power in the 1960s. Though George McGovern took the Democratic nomination in 1972, squeezing out the old stalwarts from American labor and the local Democratic machines, it would not happen again in 1976. Few intellectuals could even agree with George Fraser, who pronounced on a CBS *Spectrum* program in 1973 that the movement had been right in so many areas of concern. As Fred Hechinger put it, there had been some "mildly beneficial reforms," but the intellectuals had "seen the future and it does not work, not without something more concrete than emotions and consciousness."[37]

Even so, doomsaying in the intellectual-media complex offers an interesting study in development. It is mind-boggling to read Richard Goodwin's January 1969 article on American political life in the *New Yorker*. A long-time supporter of liberal political campaigners, Goodwin preluded Watergate by writing:

> In addition, the expanding machinery of secret police, investigation, bugging, and wiretapping must be halted and dismantled. Fear and suspicion are the more paralyzing agents of all, and the most likely to provoke unrest.[38]

Since the article was published in the same month in which Richard Nixon was inaugurated as President of the United States, one must suppose that Goodwin was referring to presidents who had preceded him.

But Goodwin also writes of a divided America in 1969—a situation for which Nixon was to receive considerable blame in 1970. He complains of power blocs which used the government for their own ends, and of "unreasonable" government. In view of Goodwin's insights into American political practices, it is amazing that the media-intellectual circles were so shocked at what happened three years later at Watergate.

It may be true that a dual morality exists in the think tank centers of Washington and New York. Fred Hechinger of the *Times* seems to think so. And so did Aleksandr I. Solzhenitsyn who, in 1973, saw many flaws in the post-Watergate onslaught carried out by American liberalism. The Nobel prizewinner pointed up the silence of American and European intellectuals after the Hue massacre of 1968, an incident which at least one liberal had indicated was understandable because it had been perpetrated by a retreating army. Solzhenitsyn was astounded by the "hypocritical, clamorous rage displayed by the Democrats," and he asked the question:

> Wasn't that democracy full of mutual deception and cases of misconduct during the previous election campaigns, except, perhaps, that they were not on such a high level of electronic technology and remained happily undiscovered?[39]

It is impossible to detail all the examples of doomsaying and rhetoric from the intellectual-media complex in the Sixties. There is ample evidence that the paranoia on the left was of gigantic proportions, however. Irving Howe, writing for the liberal *Saturday Review* in 1970, indicated some understanding of the phenomenon when he warned: "For what the New Left, in its thoughtless fascination with apocalypse, fails to consider is the probable line-up of forces in this country if there is to be a polarization during the next few years—to say nothing of the probable victor in the showdown."[40]

What is frightening about it all is the obvious power resting in the hands of media and intellectual circles within the United States. David Halberstam, in his *The Best and the Brightest,* took note of this aspect when he wrote in description of McGeorge Bundy, one of President Kennedy's chief advisers: "He was the favorite of that predominantly liberal part of Washington which sets the tone of the city, deciding who is good and who is bad, who is in and who is out, what is legitimate and what is not, who has power and who does not."

That sentence alone merits a Pulitzer Prize, because it recognizes the very existence of an Eastern Establishment. Halberstam does not say it, but it could be added that it was this same establishment which responded so quickly to the sense of depression and paranoia which swept the country in the 1960s. A shotgun-blast montage of some of the more memorable items during the period would include the following:

1. Senator J. W. Fulbright, though raised in Arkansas, has spent a goodly portion of his life in Washington. He was also a Rhodes scholar. In the *New York Times,* May 18, 1970, he is quoted as saying that the invasion of Cambodia was a "serious international disaster" which had clearly "weakened our power to influence the situation in the Middle East or nearly anywhere else."

2. Anthony Lewis, in a column entitled "But Britain Did Not Die at Yorktown," writes in the *New York Times,* May 11, 1970: "Judging by the reaction of the educated Briton, the United States faces a crisis of confidence among her friends in Europe."

3. An advertisement in the *New York Times,* May 1970, states reasons why "defeat" in Vietnam would be a good thing for the United States.

4. John Gardner is quoted by James Reston in a column entitled "Reflections on Election Day in New York":

   In the downward spiral—diminishing a confidence on the part of the individual that he can possibly affect the system. . . . At the bottom of that downward spiral will lie the wreckage and the memory of a free society.

5. Russell Baker, the *New York Times,* May 7, 1970:

   . . . indeed, it may prove to be the war Orwell foresaw in 1984—that endless war politicians invoked from time to time to justify a ruling tyranny.

6. Charles Reich, *The Manchester Guardian,* international edition, June 23, 1973:

The striking fact about Watergate is that it is happening despite the indifference that greets it, despite the wish that it would go away. Though reformers or activists or rebels brought it about, Watergate came from within. The system has begun to self-destruct.

7. *The Manchester Guardian*, international edition, August 18, 1973:

Not only have they had to contend with Watergate, Agnew, Vesco, and the Ellsberg trial sensations; last week truckloads of beef were being hijacked in Massachusetts, cattle rustling was reported to be increasing enormously in Wyoming, petrol was running desperately low across the country, the cost of borrowing was shooting up to over 9 percent, the stock market was soaring, and Skylab, above it all, was in dead trouble.

8. John Gardner, in the *New York Times*, May 16, 1973 [Before reading this, one should recall more doleful remarks made by Gardner in 1970. This came after Watergate]:

All those proud regimes (the Holy Roman Empire, the Venetian Republic, the Chinese Empire, the Japanese Shogunate, Tsarist Russia)—and scores of others—have passed into history; and among the world powers the only government that stands essentially unchanged is the Federal Union put together on the East Coast of North America. It will survive.

Excepting Gardner's remarks, how many of the above statements turned out to be essentially true? Fulbright's comments, which appear to be directed to the American Jewish community, evaporate before the truth. Despite the Cambodian operation, which turned out to be successful, the United States was by far and away the most influential power in bringing the 1973 Yom Kippur War to an end. Lewis's observations that the U.S. was losing prestige in Europe falls flat in view of what has happened to Europe, and especially to Britain, since May 1970. Gardner's initial comment is cancelled out by his last. Baker's Vietnam War was not an "endless war," and Reich's commentary is ridiculous. *The Guardian*, whose American correspondent echoes the feelings of the Eastern liberal set in the United States, was wrong on all counts. Even Skylab was able to carry out most of its missions.

It might be well here to point out that the American far right was mildly active in the 1960s and early 1970s, but in a greatly diminished sense.[41] The general tendency of conservatives and moderates was to cleave to the flag, particularly in the crisis year of 1970. They wore it, they plastered it to their autos, and they flaunted it from hastily erected flagpoles. Some right-wing intellectuals like Ayn Rand, author of *The Fountainhead*, identified with the masses. Miss Rand wrote:

Physically, America is not in a desperate state, but intellectually and culturally she is. The New Left is the product of cultural disintegration; it is bred not in the slums, but in the universities; it is not the vanguard of the future, but the terminal stage of the past.[42]

In the middle of the whole of the American intellectual community there remained a harried but consistent covey of moderates, best exemplified by such men as Daniel J. Boorstin and Sidney Hook. Boorstin was one of those scholars whose record was so impeccable that liberals were forced to give him audience. He saw the nation not as a sick society, but as having lost its sense of history. Colleges and universities had fallen victims to relevancy and a "voguish reverence for youth." Too many people, said Boorstin, had been persuaded that the immediacy in education should be the yardstick for what the young should know. "To be persuaded that things *can be* otherwise," he stated, "we must look into the whole Historical Catalogue and see how and when and why they have actually *been* otherwise."[43]

Hook paralleled Boorstin to a great degree, and so, strangely enough, did the writer James Michener, who had lived abroad for a number of years where it had not been difficult to encounter criticisms of America. Foreign intellectuals, said Michener, seemed to derive perverse satisfactions in pointing up the flaws in American life. Yet, said the novelist, were the United States to lower the immigration barriers, it would see "from those countries which criticize us most severely an exodus of people hungry for a new life in the United States."[44]

Though Michener was essentially right in castigating the views of foreign intellectuals, it would be well to point out that some of America's strongest defenders came from abroad during the 1960s and later. Jean Revel, the French socialist, saw the United States as the beacon of the future. Henry Fairlie, a British conservative writer, was likewise quick in the defense of this country.[45]

A third European who deserves mention was Romain Gary, the French writer. In 1970, when so many American intellectuals appeared to have lost all balance over the Vietnam issue, it was Gary who pointed out that the USSR as well had lost ground because of the war. In fact, said Gary, Russian credibility had become far more suspect than that of the United States. China had been confined to "immobility" by the war, and the common Communist front in Europe and Asia had been shattered.[46]

Among the sillier moments of the decade were those which occurred in 1970, when the radical left and radical chic attempted to establish a common ground. Mr. and Mrs. Leonard Bernstein entertained selected members of the Black Panther Party in their Park Avenue apartment. Mrs. Randolph Guggenheim gave a spaghetti dinner for the Puerto Rican Young Lords, and Andrew Stein invited a number of Cesar Chavez's Mexican-American grape pickers to his palatial mansion in Southampton. Stein later gave a huge cocktail party on Manhattan's Upper East Side in honor of "the American Indian." Guests at the latter soiree included Senator Fred Harris and his wife, Comanche, Mrs. Eleanor Searle Whitney, a Kiowa Indian named Perry Horse, and

Senator Jacob Javits ("he's always been a great friend of the Indian," said Comanche Harris).[47]

Apparently none of the above had read any of Finley Peter Dunne's hilarious account of a similar gathering at the end of the last century. Dunne's radical chic consisted of "Mrs. Vanderhankerbilk" and her friends, and the entertainment provided was a "musical sorre f'r th' ladies iv th' Female Billyonaires Arbeiter Verein. . . ." The theme told the story—the "futmen were dhressed in th' costume iv the Fr-rinch Rivolution, an' tea was served in imitation bombs."

The most serious reaction to this and other excesses of the intellectual-media community came in June 1970, when construction workers in New York City attacked a group of college demonstrators. The average worker who took part in this confrontation had some gripes of his own. He was, in essence, an optimist who did not share the "gloomy conclusion" of John W. Gardner "that the country is disintegrating. . . ." A *New York Times Magazine* contributor analyzed the blue collar explosion:

> They know but do not suffer the dark fear that a complex and subtle civil war is wasting the land with hate and with overt and invisible violence; white against black, conservatives against liberals, workers against students, old against young.[48]

How strange it was that then—in 1970—few in the intellectual-media community could read the message of the blue-collar revolt. While they, the intellectuals, continued to rush the Democratic Party to the edge of radicalism, the blue-collar worker had reached another conclusion. To save his party—the Democratic Party—he would have to risk its destruction.

In the end the oldest political party in the world was not saved by liberalism, or by the blue-collar workers. It was saved by Watergate and by some incredibly fumbled chances to redeem the errors of it. By 1973, due to the latter, the Democratic Party was healthy enough again—but it was not the party of 1972, and it was doubtful that it ever would be again. A new folk hero was Senator Sam Ervin, a Southern Democrat. George Meany, the president of the AFL-CIO, seemed to be back in the fold. The ineffable Mayor Daley of Chicago was back in favor again. And Governor George Wallace of Alabama was being courted by Senator Ted Kennedy of Massachusetts. The old coalition was triumphant once again.

6

The Underground Press and Days of Doom

A few years ago a large Midwestern university library enlarged its special collections section with the addition of back issues and microfilms of the so-called underground papers of the 1960s. In order to explain the nature of the acquisition, the library prepared a special guide to the collection, pointing up the nature of the papers acquired and their nobility of purpose. The underground press, according to the authors of the guide, filled a distinctive "need," for after all, the "daily papers today are not fit for the cat's box, or cabinet liners, or fireplaces." Such lesser and more unfit newspapers—which, incidentally, included the *Chicago Tribune* and the *New York Times*—were read only by ordinary people. That obviously amounted to an indictment.

Furthermore, according to the authors of the guide, it could be assumed that the political situation was the "raison d'etre of virtually all underground newspapers." In the convoluted prose of the 1960s these 100 newspapers, which apparently *had* usage in the fireplace or the cat's box, were purposeful and necessary. Some of them had circulations at one time of over 50,000. Most popular of the sheets was *It,* with some 50,000 subscribers; *Georgia Straight* with a circulation of 15,000; and *Door to Liberation,* which claimed a total of 10,000 subscribers.[1]

125

But all underground papers in the Sixties were not alike. Some were polemic in character, with little real news and much radical theory. Others were "youth culture" in style, and included features on astrology, recordings, rock groups, drugs and entertainment. Others were racist in nature, while some were strictly devoted to the feminist movement. A few were ecological in approach and some were devoted to gay liberation. There were even some which seemed to have the single purpose of undermining the morale of the U.S. Army during the Vietnam War.

It is really necessary to understand that the underground papers of the Sixties were not completely American in origin. Some of the larger and more powerful papers were published in Britain and Canada. These few, incidentally, were also better written. Few if any of the underground papers completely shunned the notion of profit, however. Almost all of them sold space—and that was true of international underground papers as well as those in American locations.

There were a number of common denominators to all, or virtually all, of the underground presses. Most of them appropriated material from other underground sources, in many cases without giving credit. Virtually all of the papers—perhaps 99.9 percent of them—were anti-Johnson and anti-Nixon. Many of them were basically anti-American in the sense of calling for the actual collapse of American power. Most of the papers subscribed to news services of one kind or another. Early on in the history of the movement, various centralized liberal and radical news services were organized. A partial list of such agencies would include the following:

Anarchist Press Movement
Africa Research Movement
American Revolutionary Media
Chevron International Media
China News Service
College Press Service
Canadian Press Service
Free Ranger Intertribal News Service
Free Ranger News Service
Intergalactic World Brain
Liberation News Service
Latin Revolutionary News Service
Prensa Latina
United Native Americans Liberation News Service
Underground Press Syndicate
United States Student Press Association
Youth International Party News Service[2]

Though most of the underground newspapers are dated as beginning in 1970, the late arrivals were merely spinoffs of previously established publications. The *Catholic Radical,* featuring articles by Father Daniel Berrigan and published in Milwaukee, was started in 1968. So was *Counterpoint,* another Wisconsin publication located at Stevens Point. *Guardian,* out of New York, was begun in 1968, as was the *Los Angeles Free Press. Peace News* of London, England, had a 1967 beginning and placed most of its stress on American Indians, South Africa, and Libya. The *Spark,* a feminist publication from Chicago, originated in 1967. *Veterans Stars & Stripes For Peace* was also started in Illinois in the same year. *It,* the highly successful London publication, dated from 1966. The *Village Voice,* which some radical papers refused to accept as underground enough, was started in 1958. Other papers of a socialist nature were also begun in that general period.[3]

What is surprising is the widespread character of the underground phenomenon. Canada had a number of such publications, including the *Georgia Straight* of Vancouver. *Sanity,* previously mentioned as an early "peace" paper, was also published in Canada and had a large reading public in the United States. Ireland had an underground paper entitled *The United Irishman,* a throwaway undoubtedly named in a fit of Celtic enthusiasm. Germany and Holland had some wild radical papers, and so did Belgium, of all places. Even Lebanon had an underground paper called *Fateh.*

One reaches a number of tentative conclusions when reading most American or Canadian underground papers. First of all, there seemed to be an outsize representation of Jews on the various editorial staffs— especially in the middle Sixties. Almost all underground publications, in their beginning issues, tended to be mild. After four or five issues, however, they tended to become far more vitriolic and aggressive. Thirdly, the attitudes of pre-Vietnam War papers were virtually the same as those of the later period. *Sanity,* for instance, was exhibiting the "peace" symbol on its masthead in 1963. And lastly, nearly every underground newspaper eventually got around to the practice of printing maudlin and generally bad poetry.[4]

Study of American and international underground papers also leads to more basic and lasting conclusions. Virtually all underground papers—as well as many university and college publications—eventually exhibited the paranoid style by 1970. The phraseology of the prose was similar from one paper to the next. In an odd way, perhaps the most used word by most of the underground press *was* "paranoid." It was applied to anyone who opposed the movement. It was used to describe presidents and prime ministers. It was hurled at big business, at the older generation, at almost anybody.

Likewise the phrase "standing ovation" gained widespread usage.

That compliment was always given to those who supported the movement, and the occurrence was invariably reported, whether engaged in by ten or ten thousand. But there were other words as well. Almost every underground paper had favorite "political prisoners" which it tended to publicize. Furthermore, everything Chinese—mainland Chinese, that is—was good. The *Berkeley Barb* of February 11, 1966, was even constrained to point out that the Chinese People's Army had "liberated" Tibet, described as one of the most "repressive regimes in the world."[5]

Cuba—Castro's Cuba—always received favorable treatment in the radical underground press. The earliest of such publications tended to portray President Eisenhower as a traducer of Cuban liberties (and also Puerto Rican liberties), and later issues reflected almost every Cuban propaganda charge about the United States. One such Cuban-originated propaganda item, accepted by almost every American underground paper, had seventeen million Americans on the verge of death by starvation.

Underground papers of the later Sixties invariably followed a common approach to law enforcement authorities. Police, or any law enforcement agents in uniform, were always referred to as "pigs." Those in mufti were sometimes called "narcs." In any police-radical confrontation, the police were the aggressors. No self-respecting underground publication could ever allow itself any other interpretation.

The great majority of underground papers were quite badly written and composed, a condition which was occasionally recognized by the best of such publications. As *Resurrection*, an underground paper, put it in 1970, too many radical papers contained a surplus of "mouthing and empty rhetoric. . . ." Some underground sheets, like *Vortex* of Lawrence, Kansas, were not only poorly written but were laced with vulgarities of the worst nature. The same could be said for many radical university newspapers which, though not underground in a sense, did much to emulate the radical press. Samuel Gould, the former chancellor of State University of New York, when asked what he missed most about his work, replied: "The brilliant prose styles of student newspaper columnists and editorial writers as they skillfully improvise on four-letter words, making every verb irregular, every tense imperfect, every noun peculiarly singular and possessive, and always arriving at amazingly erotic and unlikely conjunctions."[6]

Most underground newspapers operated on a basis of exchange; that is, numbers of copies were traded for issues of other papers. This undoubtedly accounts for similarities in word usage, as well as the pirating of information from one paper to the next. *Vortex*, an extremely radical paper, carried a column entitled "Bitteroot." At

Western Illinois University the group responsible for the publication of the radical student paper there called itself "Bitter Carrot." In a great many of the papers there was also a similarity in what were reputed to be letters to the editor, leading one to conclude that such items were less letters than they were adaptations of concepts derived from other publications.

Besides "repression," "oppression," "pigs," and other standard words, there was a tendency to write of "consciousness" in one form or another. Paper after paper freely used such phrases as "permeating our consciousness" or "the rape of our consciousness." Far more pronounced, however, was the use of the shock word "blood." It had application everywhere, and underground writers were obsessed with the visual imagery connected with it. The *Berkeley Barb,* for example, printed a poem in 1967 which included the words "bright in a gore-stricken jungle. . . . ," a phrase which reached the level of cant in those Vietnam War days. *Buffalo Chips* (Omaha), in 1967, printed this: "I find myself daily upon that box soap screaming through that can with four drops of blood on my hands. There are stains of wars of civil strife of auto aspirations of my own clawing fingers. People come from miles around beating their breasts and screaming. . . ." All of this may have been the "flower pangs of hedonism," as a writer for *Berkeley Barb* once put it, but it still fitted the broad conception of the paranoid style as described by the historian Hofstadter.[7]

Of course there were some differences in the underground press. Some laid stress upon one theme, others upon something else. But all in all there were far more similarities than exceptions. Furthermore, each paper could and did shift its ground whenever necessary. President Kennedy, for example, was out of favor with the radical press in 1963. In 1964 he was generally considered to have been a victim of demoniac forces by most underground writers. In the case of the Vietnam War, both domestic and foreign underground papers took the same stand. In Canada, where the war had essentially little effect, the "foreign" correspondent of the Boston paper *Avatar* reported that Canadian college students were "more determined than their American brethren" in bringing the war to a pro-Viet Cong conclusion.[8]

There is no evidence that there existed a tight organization, nationally speaking, within the underground press. But they were tied together into an extraordinarily effective loose alliance. When *Berkeley Barb* called for a "Vietnam Day" in 1965, correspondence was received from underground sources in Los Angeles, New York, Chicago, Philadelphia, Detroit, Portland, London, Buenos Aires, Tokyo, Montevideo, and Vancouver. Virtually all underground papers had access to so-called clearing houses designed for the exchange of information. One such arrangement was located in Urbana, Illinois, another in Hartford, Connecticut. A third—the Repression News Service—was located in Pittsburgh.[9]

Thus it was that the whole loose conglomeration of the underground press might direct its efforts against specific fronts. All such papers were opposed to U.S. participation in the Vietnam War, so there was no difficulty in pressing the cause in that respect. In other efforts the organization of united effort might have been different without the tentacles of organization. In one month, as an example, there was a spate of similarly worded articles on Bernadette Devlin, the Irish revolutionary. An enormous amount of material on Richard M. Nixon was borrowed from one paper to the next—as had been true of his predecessor. The information published in various papers about "political prisoners" likewise bore startling resemblance.[10]

Yet most papers kept up a varied barrage relating to issues involving the "establishment." *Vortex* of Kansas was an excellent example of typical underground reporting. Poorly written, wordy, repetitious, it ran the gamut of subject matter. One issue might call upon soldiers in nearby army camps to desert. Another laid heavy stress upon "our black brothers," and still another might deal with the feminist movement and gay liberation.

Occasionally the ecological theme crept into most underground papers, but one might suspect that it was used mainly as a holding point until other issues were provided. This was obviously true in the period just prior to the Cambodian invasion of 1970, when for a short period many underground presses dealt broadly with the declining quality of life. Other holding points—in lieu of more emotional issues —included a heavy sexual emphasis, counterculture undertones, the drug craze and the communal movement.

In regard to underground material upon the drug issue, it might be pointed out that such emphasis was laid upon this theme that one could arrive at the conclusion that the old American business ethic was in good health. There were always passing references to new and novel drug practices; in fact some papers spent a good deal of space in the Sixties upon methods of injecting peanut butter into the blood stream or on the reputed power of bananas. But drugs seemed basic to some underground papers. *Vortex* kept its readers informed on the price of drugs—acid at two dollars a hit, psilocibin the same price, mescaline, "really good dope," going at two dollars, and marijuana, "lots of it," at fifteen dollars a lid. *The Rag* of Austin, Texas, informed its readers in January 1970 that one could boost the power of marijuana by working isopropyl alcohol into it. *Georgia Straight* of Vancouver laid out instructions as early as 1967 on how marijuana could be grown at home.[11]

Along with these advices were found suggestions as to how to achieve sexual happiness. The frequency at which such articles were printed was some indication of the many maladjustments existing in this strangely hedonistic society. *Berkeley Barb* in 1966 cried out "hooray for orgies," and argued the values of nude dancing. There were, so said the paper, unexpected pleasures of "polygamous" matriarchal living (whatever that is), and in "sensuality as a way to the World of Love."[12]

Most of the underground press pushed what it considered to be the "new" art of living. If one belonged to the movement he was a "digger" who, at the age of eighteen or nineteen, had discovered the new Shangri-la. In truth there was less fiction than fact in a portion of that claim, for there was indeed an Oriental overtone in the whole movement. *The Buddhist Oracle*, an underground paper, advertised in 1967 that readers might obtain a new book entitled *The Tibetan Book of the Dead*, proclaimed by some in the movement to be the most influential publication in America since "Tom Paine's Common Sence [sic]." In many areas underground newspapers were given substantial advertising copy by new stores which specialized in the Oriental theme. One could buy incense in odors ranging through rose, jasmine, musk, sandalwood, Mysore, blend, pine, lavender, and Morgra. There was Japanese Kabuki incense, as well as frankincense, myrrh, sandalwood chips, Chinese strobe candles, Indian brass bells, Chinese brass bells, Japanese toothpicks, Zodiac pendants, and sandalwood soap.[13]

There was, throughout the underground press, an amazing dexterity in playing with the facts of history. Hofstadter, in describing the paranoid style, pointed out that the true paranoid sees within those demoniac forces which he imagines to be in operation against him, a "special technique for seduction. . . ." In *Berkeley Barb* in March 1966 one may find a perfect illustration of the perversion and traducing of fact. Dylan Thomas, the Welsh poet, did not die simply from alcoholism; he died because subtle forces in the United States led him to drink too much. Similar implications could be read into underground explanations of the deaths of rock stars Jimi Hendrix and Janis Joplin.

Hofstadter further described the paranoid style as including "fantastic conclusions" which are not argued "along factual lines." *Berkeley Barb* in April 1966 included the following words: "Three American presidents had been gunned down, and attempts made on the lives of four more (Jackson, both Roosevelts, and Truman; in FDR's case, two attempts). No European nation of the last century and a half can match that record." The writer's conclusion—America is a land of pure violence.[14]

In actuality four presidents have been assassinated—Lincoln, Garfield, McKinley and Kennedy. Theodore Roosevelt was not in the presidency when an attempt was made on his life. The try on Truman's life was made by Puerto Rican nationalists, which effort, incidentally, the *Barb* might have viewed with some pro-Latino-anti-American warmth. Jackson was wounded in a duel, and later shot at by an individual who was strictly psychotic. Disturbed individuals were also responsible for the deaths of Garfield, McKinley, and Kennedy.

Insofar as Europe is concerned, the *Barb* writer had stacked his facts to fit his conclusions. Tsars were blown up and machine-gunned in Russia; millions of people were put to death in Russia, Germany, China, and Cuba; and leaders were assassinated in a score of places.[15]

Hofstadter further argued that the true paranoid occasionally manufactures facts—that he has a curious ability to leap from one hastily studied observation to seemingly unavoidable conclusions. *Berkeley Barb* in 1967 printed one observer's reactions to the migrant problem in California. Hundreds of these workers, said the writer, had been forced to wait for hours in order to obtain treatment at various county hospitals in the state. Disregarding the obvious truth that lots of people from all classes wait for many hours in a great many hospitals, the writer vaulted to his conclusion. "There were lots of people starving," he wrote—in fact, "thousands" faced starvation. He didn't know of "any dying . . . [but] a lot of men were very ill." Not a single hard fact is offered in substantiation of the claim.[16]

Part of the same characteristic—that is, of the paranoid style—is applicable to the technique of retreating from whatever assertions are proven to be untrue. *Berkeley Barb* in 1966 carried a column in which the writer claimed that Adolf Hitler had become the Chancellor of Germany through popular election. Called to account on this fact, the writer admitted his error with the statement: "Blame it on hasty writing, and the intent to get as much into restricted space as possible. But the fact I had in mind still stands, the Nazis made it into power through an election that gave them a large majority."

The *Barb*'s contributor had covered up one terrible mistake with another perversion of history. Not once, in any *free* election in Germany, did Adolf Hitler get a "large majority."[17]

Consider the following historical mistakes as evidence of the paranoid stacking of facts. *Red Eye* of San Jose, in May 1970, offered a writer's observation that the Maginot Line was overrun in 1940 by German tanks. This was not true, of course, for the German invasion struck through Belgium, Holland, and the Ardennes Forest, where the Maginot Line was not constructed. *Rising Up Angry* of Chicago, which considered itself part of a "revolutionary organization dedicated to building a new man, a new woman, and a new world," offered its views on American history in 1970. "Italians like Sacco and Vanzetti were executed because they were revolutionaries," claimed a writer for the paper. Immigrants, so went the interpretation, have always had to live under unbearable oppressions laid upon their backs by capitalism. Parents are only the products of a "reactionary" educational system which is controlled by the "ruling class."[18]

Sacco and Vanzetti were executed because of the considerable evidence that they were guilty of murder. It was at the high tide of capitalism that most immigrants came to this country. Did they willingly come to be oppressed? Insofar as the educational system is concerned, one might add that not only did it produce parents but the children as well.

There are scores of illustrations of Hofstadter's paranoid style in the underground papers of the Sixties. Heroes and heroines of the movement demolish their enemies with a barrage of facts and a display of talent. *The Militant* of London rhapsodized over singer Eartha Kitt's distasteful performance at the White House during the Johnson administration. Miss Kitt was described as a woman of rare intellectual abilities; the *Militant* claimed that she could speak several languages. Furthermore, Miss Kitt, according to the *Militant*, had flattened the President's wife with that unanswerable blast on the condition of America. "No wonder the kids rebel and take pot," she was quoted as saying, "and Mrs. Johnson, if you don't understand the lingo, that's marijuana."[19]

On the issue of Vietnam the underground press forded the river of history by leaping from one unstable log to another. In 1967 a great segment of the movement press laid heavy stress upon American bombings in North Vietnam, and especially upon the alleged destruction of hospitals. So much was this theme stressed, and so often, that one would have to come to a conclusion that there could be no more buildings left standing in the entire country. At the same time, movement leaders who were visiting North Vietnam reported upon the cleanliness and serenity of the cities. It was a strange contradiction.

One writer for *Berkeley Barb* saw the North Vietnamese and the Viet Cong as the heroes of a world movement. They were the true "freedom fighters" of 1967. *Nashville Breakdown* offered its version of the truth about South Vietnam. "Basically it gets down to the fact that the NLF expresses the will of the majority of the people of South Vietnam," claimed the paper. "It already controls 80 percent of the country." The Kissinger settlement of 1973 dispelled that contention.

On the issue of "atrocities," every underground paper avoided the logical argument that they were probably carried out by both sides in Vietnam. In the Tet offensive of January 1968, some 3,000 inhabitants of Hue were put to death by North Vietnamese and Viet Cong battalions. Despite all evidence pointing to Communist responsibility for the deaths, many underground papers sought to turn the story around. *Vortex* printed one version in 1970 which claimed that the 3,000 trussed bodies of the Hue victims were actually killed by American bombs. "It took three weeks for the Americans to 'liberate' Hue," said the paper, "and it's hardly surprising that their bombs took several thousand lives in that time." The original version of this particular bombing story had its origins on Hanoi radio. *Vortex* failed to question the veracity of the North Vietnamese broadcasters, and not once did it raise the important question as to why the victims were bound and gagged.[20]

There was much marshalling of facts and argumentation by the radical left during the wild days of the spring of 1970. Especially was much of the rhetoric directed against the reputed evils of American capitalism. Indeed there were times when many of the movement's conclusions seemed to have had their beginnings in an opium pipe. *Red Eye* in California printed a statement to the effect that American capitalism had drained most of the world's underdeveloped countries of their wealth—and that the "poor peasant worker" is tired of seeing wealthy people eat and drink in MacDonald's hamburger stands. A contributor to *Resurrection*, an organ of the radical John Brown Society of Tucson, argued in 1970 that the black and brown people of "capitalist" America had been forced into drug addiction so that they could forget the conditions in which they lived. Whenever urban riots occurred, the paper argued, "the man" sent drugs into the ghettoes. After all, the drug pushers were really "pig" capitalists.[21]

There were times in 1970 when, as Hofstadter had described in his piece on paranoia, the "central image" of the underground press was that of a "vast and sinister conspiracy" which was determined to "undermine and destroy a way of life."[22] Unanchored in validation, facts were flung against the readers' wills with such abandon that effect was unavoidable. The burden of proof was left to those timorous enough to question assertion. *Space City* of Houston implied that the General Electric Company had accomplished terrible deeds of imperialism in Africa, India, and Asia with the help of "nazi" buddies. *The Rag* of Austin, Texas, listed by the Northwestern University Library as a paper which stressed "chicanos, women's liberation, comix, the Aquarian kitchen," said of General Electric: "One of the biggest reasons GE can use against its workers is the US government. . . . GE workers face the government policy of engineering a recession, a conscious plan to increase unemployment and reduce consumer demand."[23]

Vortex tossed out so many accusations in the early months of 1970 that they seemed to make no pattern whatsoever. Perhaps that was the point of it all. At any rate a writer for the paper claimed Vietnam to be the "cornerstone" of "money hungry" American corporations, including Foremost Dairies and the First National City Bank of New York. But that wasn't all that *Vortex* was worked up about. Indonesia had a new "CIA sponsored" government which, of course, was being manipulated by American capitalism. Furthermore, the paper stated, President Nixon was cutting "back on military and defense-related manpower," thus turning out 1,250,000 new unemployed. Once again, none of this seemed to be logical, and apparently it was not supposed to be.[24]

So it went, with the underground press in continuous struggle with the vague and insidious "enemy" which defied description. *Space City* saw a "direct link between the existence of ROTC and the future possibilities of American military aggression in the Third World countries." The destruction of ROTC, concluded the writer, would "be a blow for oppressed peoples throughout the world fighting for their liberation."[25]

Everywhere, as ever in the paranoid style, there were the exaggerated statements of doom and gloom blended together with the romantic notion of community. Each worked warp and woof with the other. The *New York High School Free Press* (yes, Virginia, there was such a paper) presented the "now" generation's concept of life as it was in 1970. The author, who one must assume was of high school age, seemed to have traveled much for his tender age—to such far flung places as Georgia and the Midwest. Like grandpa on the front porch, he portrayed the good old days before his "youthful hope and naivete [sic]" had turned into fear and cynicism. His love of freedom had been converted into a "fight against authority"; his love of life into a "fight for survival." His very life was "threatened," and he had grown "bitter and resentful" in his late years. Yet a tight bond had been formed with others and, as he put it, "we are forming a community around us." It was true, he said—this New York City boy—that he could no longer go to the park and find minnows and fish in the pond. "My throat is red and raspy from the riot-gas of the Illinois National Guard," he wrote. "My head is swollen from the 'Sons of Liberty' who beat me up because I'm a 'hippy-Jew'.... I no longer give a shit if anyone understands."[26]

(These sad-faced, humorless children of the urban middle class are really incipient George Apleys of the future. One can see them now—telling their children about those hard days of the 1960s.)

A contributor to *The Paper* of Mendocino, California, saw visions of the apocalypse, writing: "One of the problems . . . that will have to be faced by those few who remain here after the haulicost [sic] will be obtaining food. . . . The hunter of tomorrow will not only have to contend with a supply of game . . . but will have to determine also which rabbit is too radioactive to eat. . . ." The *Mother Earth News* seemed to be stressing the same point when it quoted excerpts from a recently published book to the effect that it did no good to build costly and crowded cities when they could be wiped out overnight. It was all slightly contradictory, it seemed. The ghettoes needed new housing, but it must not be built because it would be destroyed anyway.[27]

The sense of the paranoid community found strongest expression in those underground papers devoted to black and other ethnic aims. A writer to *Vortex* called upon the "brothers and sisters" to "take one weeks [sic] pay check and bury it, make a collage out of it . . . use it for toliet [sic] paper . . . but don't spend it." Another writer to the same paper discovered an empathy with the movement while traveling through the Berkshire Mountains. Hearing of the 1970 racial riots in Lawrence, Kansas, he wrote that he was immensely proud of "all you river city people and pretty soon I'll be back out there fighting for what's ours alongside you." Another writer for *Vortex* might have just returned from an exhibition of Delacroix and David when he wrote:

> Upon discovering that their community was about to be occupied and restricted by the enemy, the people organized a spontaneous community meeting . . . during a three day siege in which the people were outnumbered and out armed, men and women took to their streets despite the technology of death and attacked the enemy on all fronts. in [sic] an increasingly effective and sophisticated manner . . . sniping from roofs and bushes, burning the means of capitalistic production, constructing barricades to thwart and deter the pigmobiles, running the pig ragged by employing diversionary tactics. . . .[28]

He never explained how one could organize a "spontaneous community meeting," nor did he ever indicate how streets in Lawrence had become the property of a segment of society.

Hofstadter's description of the paranoid style is one in which the view of history becomes an almost personal one. The "enemy," forever repressive, attempts to control the press; he has "unlimited funds," and he creates a "new secret for influencing the mind." Slowly but surely he is gaining a stranglehold upon the educational system.[29]

The very use of the word "repression" became a kind of chant in the Sixties. It was applicable to everything—race, religion, politics, food, the media—everything. It implied, among other things, the supermind which exercised a finite and subtle control over all mankind. "Women are controlled by the media . . . ," a writer for *Vocations for Social Change* was constrained to write. But there were others who were guilty of repression as well, including "Uncle Sam and also some of the men that some of us live with. . . ." *Quicksilver Times*, an early anti-male chauvinist publication, claimed that women were slowly being isolated with babies, bottles, roaches, rats, and "houses often not fit to live in. . . ." The plot was a far-reaching one. "Women should not have to soothe tired souls so men can return to that disgusting corporate world the next day," the writer concluded.

The rise of the issue of repression as seen by the underground press is an interesting object for consideration—not just in terms of phraseology used, but in the timing and the origin of statements about it. In the late stages of the Johnson administration the underground press turned up the heat on the notion of repression, especially on the East and West coasts. The change could also be noted in the international underground press. *Avatar* of Boston warned in 1967: "An atmosphere is being erected by the mass media and precedents are being established by the police that threaten everyone—black and white—who has an independent mind and whose humanity impels him to speak out against the insane policies of the establishment." *Berkeley Barb*, on the other side of the nation, filled its June 30, 1967, issue with so many horror stories that one could conclude that the police had not left an uncracked head in California.[30]

The international underground press trumpeted the same theme. In February 1967 the *International Times* of London reported gory stories about head beatings by Munich police. Several months later the German "correspondent" of the *International Times* claimed of Germany that "there is a circle of panic and paranoia which is hard to break once it has been put into action." Repression from Bonn was on its way, was the conclusion. In August, the same paper happily reported that repression had hit England. A certain Michael X, a local black rights spokesman, had discovered the London police to be both oppressive and discriminatory.[31]

The procession of events in 1970 brought "repression" into full focus, and the underground press turned to the subject with vengeance. A veritable litany of stories worked their way through the radical press of the nation. A Liberation News Service dispatch appeared to be the opening gun. "Many hard-nosed Washington officials," it stated, "have privately given up hope that the press will be sufficiently censored by late 1970 to put across a big lie and they are already seeking ways to insure that they will not be sacrificed when the lottery hoax comes too late." *Vortex* cut loose at almost the same time upon the issue of repression. Its early February 1970 issue carried notice of a location in which students might meet without the "usual repressive destruction" created by the "cryptonazis." The same paper printed an implication that the U.S. was on the verge of emulating Nazi Germany, and a week later a writer in *Vortex* cried out that there was "repression, oppression, and suppression inherent in white, middle-class society which prevent lives of openness and freedom, which keeps us isolated from others and insulated from the injustices which are taking place."[32]

In that February 18, 1970, issue of *Vortex* another writer expressed thoughts about "black and brown and yellow and red brothers—subjugated by societal *oppression;* that is, they find themselves bound up in a complex network of economic and political structures which continually binds them in unliveable life-negating conditions." It was a mind-boggling sentence. But wait! the article continued by charging that the middle class was "subjected to a variety of forms of cultural *suppression,* and 'we' have been the victims of 'sensual repression within our personal, interpersonal, and sexual existences.'" The logic was incomprehensible.

Soon every phase of the movement was in full hue and cry over "repression." Jerry Rubin, bearded spokesman for the "Yippies," was quoted as saying to the students of Kent State University:

> Until you people are prepared to kill your parents you aren't ready for the revolution. . . . The American school system will be ended in two years. We are going to bring it down. Quit being students. Become criminals. We have to disrupt every institution and break every law. . . . Do you people want a diploma or to take this school over and use it for your own purposes?[33]

In May, the Reverend Ralph Abernathy attempted to pump up a sagging civil rights movement by announcing a 100-mile march through Georgia. The procession was to mark the "growing repression" which Abernathy claimed was afflicting the country. The march got underway from Perry, Georgia, on May 19 with about 600 people. During the course of the first day's events telegrams of support were received from a number of prominent Americans including Senator Muskie of Maine. Apparently encouraged by such high level backing for his procession, Abernathy then announced that the "repression" which existed in America was also aimed at the "Christian church, Catholic, Protestant as well as to the Jewish synagogues and to anyone else who dares stand up against the power structure."[34]

After the Kent State and the Jackson State confrontations, the paranoia on the left touched the perimeter of gibberish. *Red Eye* in California printed a report on a speech recently given by William M. Kunstler, a prominent lawyer for liberal causes. According to the almost incomprehensible review of the speech, Kunstler stated that the "country is now similar to Germany in 1932, just after Hitler took office." Either Kunstler or *Red Eye* was wrong, of course: Hitler became the chancellor of Germany on January 30, 1933. The piece also made wild predictions that the economic structure was about to fail, and that the transportation system of the country was about to collapse. Again, those forecasts might have been made by Kunstler—or possibly the reporter. At any rate, it does seem that the liberal-minded lawyer did make some statements about "repression" in the United States.

How strange it was that neither *Red Eye* nor Kunstler had anything to say about what seemed to be going on in the People's Republic of China in those early months of 1970. There, according to the *New York Times*, edicts had been issued against the "criminal opposition" found among some Chinese youth. Laws and actions were also being directed against "class enemies" who were trying to win people over to anti-Communist causes. Not a word of reproach on this situation was to be heard from Kunstler, Abernathy, or any of the underground papers.[35]

Rather were the latter inclined to reporting incidents or alleged incidents which might serve to whip their readers into a frenzy. Everywhere there was a similarity in phrasing—on "political prisoners," the Klan, "pigs," and Black Panthers. *Space City* of Houston saw the Klan behind every tree and bush. "An army of pigs, largely deputized Klansmen," claimed *Space City*, "have been robbing, beating, and busting not only those they catch with dope, but people at home." *Nashville Breakdown*, like most underground papers of the time, pressed the issue of the "murder of twenty-six Black Panthers."[36]

Undoubtedly there will be historical revisionism written about the Sixties. Americans some thirty years hence might read that nothing really happened during the decade; that the period was one of genuine reform rooted in the principles of American democracy. The truth now, however, is that the underground papers, many of which expressed the philosophy of violent revolution, had a certain and real effect on many of the young. A study by Urban Research which was completed in the middle of 1970 indicated, for instance, that a common thread was running through the national university community. It was that the United States should release all "political prisoners."

The truth, as Douglas Kneeland saw it in the *New York Times* in 1970, was that students were "more paranoid." They were buying guns, learning to use them in self-defense, so that when the "pigs" broke down the doors, they might fire back. The Reverend Malcolm Boyd, an Episcopalian priest, also quoted in the *Times*, found students who talked paranoically about the "hopelessness" of American society, the coming of the end for the earth, and the short time left "for any kind of viable human life. . . ." Boyd's own conclusion was equally doomridden.

> The Goliath of institutional violence looms over us. To counter it simplistically with the tyranny of violence can become a sordid, ugly, viciously inhuman act in itself, destroying people as well as the very heart of the revolution. . . .[37]

Everywhere the movement seemed to be moving in the same direction—a well orchestrated outcry against the establishment. "Repression" as an issue spanned the globe. Major British newspapers such as the *Times* and *The Guardian* appeared to swallow the notion of repression in America. French students, more hardened at playing the game, argued that everything was going well because prisons really hardened and educated militants, thus ensuring revolution in the United States.

Out in the heartland of America, at the University of Wisconsin, noted for its historical liberalism, Rena Steinzor of the *Daily Cardinal* gave her impressions of the plight of the country. "Time is running out for the American student," she wrote. "Each of us is up against the wall of his own morality and a desperate need for social change in this country."

But the *Cardinal* writer had more to say. There was Steinzor on student violence: "We are in the streets because we are attacking our own mother country—attacking it at one of its wells of lifeblood: the great research source that is the university." Steinzor on the rationalization for violence: "The buildings we burn are not our own. Nor are they the American people's, even though the American people pay for them. They belong to the Pentagon. . . ." And there was Steinzor, writing much like *Pravda*, presenting her views on society in the United States: "Life in America to us is kill or be killed in a jungle, make money and buy, succeed or be branded an outcast."[38]

Like eddies in a stream, the movement produced organization after organization, spinoff from spinoff. Tom Hayden, on the "op ed" page of the *New York Times*, had given the word that socialism was the answer and that the American "empire . . . must be dismantled." Though Hayden may have described himself as a member of "the Red Family," the relatives of the movement were striking off in all directions. *Red Eye*, providing a description of a near riot attending a visit to California by President Nixon, listed the participatory organizations. They included the Peace and Freedom Party, the Revolutionary Union, the United Farm Workers, the Iranian Students Association, the San Jose Liberation Front, the Mothers for Peace, Chicanos, blacks, Indians, and the unemployed. Because of "repression" by the police, these people had rightfully pounded upon cars and had thrown rocks at the President.[39]

From 1969 onward, the movement took varying positions on how to fight what it thought to be a "growing repression." *Berkeley Barb* advised that "intelligent persons" should seek to "free themselves of all forms of values. . . ." Down in Houston a "People's Party" was organized.

There were almost endless numbers of aberrations as the movement coursed through the fading years and months of the 1960s. *Geor-*

gia Straight of Vancouver gave instructions—little advices on how to defy repression at home and at school. "Insist that schools be kept open at night so you can have a place to sleep in case home conditions become unbearable," the paper said. Meanwhile the publishers of *Georgia Straight* arranged a little demonstration to illustrate the extent of repression in Canada. A nude was sent into the streets of Vancouver in broad daylight.[40]

Most interestingly the movement began to turn upon the very institutions that had stimulated and protected it during the early stages. From the original "free speech" episode at Berkeley in the middle 1960s, the crusade had only sporadically smoked away at universities and colleges. A quick charge was made in 1967 and 1968, and beachheads were established in what were euphemistically called "black studies." In other episodes the movement had managed to drive more moderate or conservative professors to cover.[41]

In 1970, however, *Berkeley Barb* began to raise the issue as to whether or not the administration of the University of California was really an able one. It was the opening gun in the assault against the administrative establishment of the whole American university community. "Cal was not a great university," commented a writer for the *Barb,* in fact, he continued, "no amount of Noble [sic] prize-winners or new buildings or long-range planning could conceal that fact."

By May it was obvious that the movement was manipulating the issue of repression into a general campaign aimed at controlling part or all of the American university structure. Hadn't Jerry Rubin intimated as much in a speech at Kent State University in Ohio? The entire grading system must be changed, it seemed. Courses should be made more entertaining—and, incidentally, easier. *Space City* in Houston made a head-on attack against Rice University, one of the better schools in America. It was too "damnably hard," students had to live "miserable lives," and the "mania for rationality" was almost "bizarre." The writer seemed to echo *Barb*'s assault on the California system:

> We do not have a community of scholars at Rice. We have, rather, a group of "highly select" students fighting it out, under the tutelage of highly select faculty, to be tops in their highly select courses. The whole circus is financed by Big Business and Big Government. . . . And, as becomes crystal clear during the Affairs, it is the good ol' American businessman on the Board of Trustees who calls the shots.[42]

Now it was a fight against the "repressive" attitudes of university administrations and faculties, and it took the form of demanding the institution of pass-fail courses and a greater role in the selection and evaluation of teachers. A reading of underground university papers in the months of 1970 does seem to indicate the importance to the movement of getting a whip hand over each and every faculty member.

Most university administrations, as they had done throughout the Sixties, caved in quickly on the pass-fail change. But on the hiring and firing of faculty members it was a different case—for here, administrators were quick to divine that victories for the movement here might lead the issue right up to the administrative level itself. Furthermore, faculty members were becoming ever more wary of changes which might affect the bread and butter aspects of their careers. Slowly but surely the American Association of University Professors began to dig in against its more radical membership, and union membership for faculty members held less distaste in the face of student threats.

Nevertheless, academic freedom of teachers in classrooms, on which point radicals had held their positions during the early 1960s, seemed to be in serious danger. Fred Hechinger of the *New York Times* was one of those who viewed the situation thusly in May 1970 when he wrote: "Radicals see this (whether or not an institution such as a university can be an instrument for change) as the only legitimate course, and the extremist fringe among the radicals would gladly destroy the university that refuses the role of revolutionary activism."[43]

The assault against the national educational system by the underground press simmered on the front burner all the way to the end of 1970. *Space City* listed its demands upon the school system. The article called for the elimination of the entire grading system, for it hindered the "development of the ability to know one's self, to enter into serious mindbending conversation, to think independently, to relate knowledge to obligation and so on. . . ." The grading system, according to the writer, established the notion that private reward should come at the expense of another. It is the war mentality of the "big competitive world," with self-interest groups "pitted rifle-barrel to rifle-barrel." What should replace the grading system? *Space City*'s answer: "orally given insights about their personal progress in an area. . . ."[44]

Resurrection of Tucson opened a new phase of the campaign against educational repression in the fall of 1970. Like most issues raised by segments of the underground press, the point was to gain a measure of recognition throughout the entire movement media. Children should be liberated from "repression," said *Resurrection*. After all, they had to bear many of the same indignities as women and blacks. Children should be born free so that they might be used in the coming revolution. "They will oppose all forces which hinder their development as full human beings," so the writer stated. "Given the sense that all human beings are worthy, they will also oppose the oppression

142

of other peoples." The movement had indeed come a long way from that moment in 1967—that ineffable breathless moment when Allen Ginsberg, the poet laureate of the movement, was quoted as saying that old people didn't deserve any respect at all.[45]

All in all, two of the more interesting ventures of the underground press into the dark world of paranoia involved so-called "secret plots." Demoniac controls and secret manipulations are, after all, a part of the main diet of paranoia. The first such instance occurred in 1967 when a goodly portion of the movement press discovered a fearsome plot on the part of the national government to build concentration camps for dissenters. The details of this nefarious plan involved the construction of six detention centers surrounded by barbed wire. *Berkeley Barb*, hot after the issue, claimed a real source for the story— a San Francisco minister who had heard the story from a man looking for a contractor to build the installations. "Barb doesn't know which of these versions is true . . . ," stated the writer. "It is possible that the contractor is a plant, or a dupe. The story may be an administration trial balloon or a device to create panic in conjunction with the 'report' from high Washington sources of an impending invasion of North Vietnam and declaration of war." It is interesting here to note that the writer failed to mention a last possibility—that the entire story was a hoax on the part of the underground press.

The tale did seem to have a beginning. There had been a small pamphlet published late in the Sixties entitled "Concentration Camps, U.S.A.," and written by one Charles R. Allen. Allen claimed that the Federal Bureau of Investigation had a plan tagged with the code name of "Operation Dragnet" and that some 500,000 names had been listed on "master pick-up" lists. There was never any real factual substantiation for the story other than Allen's original contribution, but that did not stop militant revolutionaries from promoting the scare.[46]

One other bit of ephemera which was caused by the underground papers of the 1960s was that of a plot or cabal connected with the assassination of President John Kennedy. Spurred by Mark Lane's *Rush to Judgment*, the movement not only managed to produce a scurrilous play entitled *MacBird*, but it echoed and reechoed the implications of base conspiracy. It should be remembered that the underground press was never enamored of President Kennedy during his lifetime, but with the assassination the movement discovered another lever with which to pry at public opinion.

Through 1967 Mark Lane was widely quoted in movement media, and he was furthermore utilized as another one of those peripatetic campus lecturers. *Berkeley Barb* in April 1967 quoted Lane as saying that "when the American people learn for the first time who planned the events . . . , they are going to be absolutely outraged and shocked and stunned." A Texas editor, Penn Jones, became an instant hero when he was quoted as predicting that the New Orleans figure, Clay Shaw, would die before his trial on charges of conspiracy in the Kennedy affair. The New Orleans District Attorney, James Garrison, drew the attention of *The Fifth Estate* of Detroit when he reputedly said that fascism had arrived in this country, presumably because of the alleged suppression of evidence on the Dallas assassination. "I don't say that President Johnson is involved in the assassination," Garrison was quoted as saying. "But wouldn't it be nice to know it?"[47]

None of the Lane-Garrison-Jones charges really worked out, of course, but they were widely disseminated by the movement press. And they fitted in so well with the conspiracy notions so prevalent in those years of paranoia. In the end some similar charges were made about President Nixon. One such story which passed through some faculties and underground papers of the early 1970s had Nixon, along with members of the Mafia, engineering the assassinations of the two Kennedy brothers. It was, the story went, the only way in which Nixon could manage entry to the White House. The logic was completely awry. If Nixon had been so close to the Mafia, then most certainly he could have managed the election of 1960, which he lost by an eyelash.

But logic is not in the paranoid style.

7

Two Presidents and Middle America

The 1960s certainly saw a plumbing of new depths in the matter of political innuendo. The American political scene was, as Lord James Bryce had noted some sixty years previously, particularly marked by this characteristic—but the new era brought greater debasement in an already debased art. During President Eisenhower's last four years, mudslingers charged that he no longer controlled the presidency in an effective way, that he was no longer capable of meeting the tremendous physical demands of the office, and that he had brought the nation to the brink of ruin by allowing it to fall behind in the international arms race. None of the charges was really true, and yet the intellectual-media segment of American society tended to accept them as so without question.

During President Kennedy's short time in office, he, too, was the target of some vilification. It was argued that the "Irish Mafia," a group of close advisers which interpreted Kennedy to the press, had grown far too powerful for the national good. The underground press of the radical movement, just beginning to pick up steam, was never sold on the famed Kennedy mystique and it inferred that the President was a war lover who doted on such books as Barbara Tuchmann's *The Guns of August*. Furthermore, the radical press pointed out, Kennedy loved the blood and gore of Ian Fleming's novels. *Sanity,* the Canadian publication, argued that such a choice of reading materials put Kennedy into the same classification as generals and bankers— men who looked upon others as nothing more than blockheads. Within a few years, a decade perhaps, the same underground press was to charge that President Nixon had surrounded himself with White House assistants with Germanic names and that the President had an abnormal liking for the motion picture *Patton.* These charges were likewise part of the general observation that Nixon was a "war lover."[1]

Only a few in the literary world saw some danger in the misdirection and sometimes deliberate misinterpretations brought on by unbridled mudslinging. David Lawrence of *U.S. News and World Report* was one of those who understood the pitfalls of extremity. Writing perhaps out of pique at the defeat of Senator Barry Goldwater in the 1964 presidential race, he offered some bitter lessons on how to succeed in American politics: be sure to call your opponent "heartless"; reiterate such claims so extensively that your opponent makes little headway when he protests about misrepresentation and distortion; charge your opponent with being "unstable"; and complain that he has no convictions. All of these techniques, said Lawrence, had already become the hallmark of the "liberal" or "radical liberal" media in the United States.[2]

When Senator Goldwater was the target of unprincipled psychiatric allegations of madness, it all seemed very well and appropriate and President Johnson possibly benefited from such allegations in the 1964 campaign. Yet, within a few years the gun was turned about and Lyndon Johnson was forced to run a gauntlet of distortions. In fact, the turnabout occurred almost immediately within the underground press. Within months it was echoed that Johnson had obliterated the two-party system, that he was in the way of becoming a dictator, that minorities had been "emasculated," and that his victory had made the establishment stronger than before.[3]

By 1967, when the Vietnam War was beginning to go sour, Johnson was the recipient of the full impact of paranoic mudslinging on the left. After all, one of the symptoms of paranoia is that victims rarely see it in themselves; paranoia afflicts only the enemy. *Berkeley Barb,* as early as 1967, accused the President of suffering from paranoia, and the charge was taken up by other papers. As in the case of President Nixon three years later, the attacks from the left became personal and filthy in character. *The Fifth Estate,* an underground paper, carried advertisements in 1967 for "Impeach President Johnson Kits," each kit including twenty "impeach 'bomber' Johnson" stickers and buttons, and ten bumper stickers with the same slogan.[4]

When it was all over for a harried Johnson in 1969, he had suffered much from the slings and arrows of an ungrateful political left. The liberal and Eastern press had very much left his side in the years of the Vietnam struggle, and it too served to keep pressure on the distraught Johnson. From campus to campus, mainly through the underground press, were passed the most vicious tales, some concerning sexual misconduct and others relating to the President's personal behavior. *Red Eye* of San Jose, recalling some of those stories a few years later, cited a Liberation News Service item that the President "yearned to tell people that their destiny was to do evil." The newspaper recounted that Johnson "conducted government business while defecating," and that he "tortured his beagle in public." The *Haight-Ashbury Tribune*, quoting from another underground paper, made reference to President Johnson's "madness" and his "nicotine-stained hands . . . his alcohol breath [which] speaks death." *East Village Other* printed a charge in 1967 that Johnson was "swacked out of his head on his usual drug, bourbon," during a White House performance by the Boston Light Opera Company. The President, so claimed the writer, seemed to be obsessed with danger and had ordered a full search by the FBI of the room in which the concert was held.[5]

The crescendo of the attack upon Lyndon Johnson was long, sustained, and relentless. In 1966 a play written by one Barbara Garson began showing upon American university campuses. Called *MacBird*, its characters included the Egg of Head, the Earl of Warren, the Wayne of Morse, Ken O'Dunc, MacBird and Lady MacBird. During the course of the performance the author has her three witches proclaim: "When shall we three meet again? In riot, strike, or stopping train? When the hurlyburly's done? When the race is lost or won? Out on the convention floor, or in some hotel corridor?"

No stretching of the imagination is needed to understand that MacBird is Johnson, and that he had achieved high position by a planned assassination. It is interesting to note that, in the spring of 1967, Berkeley students were able to see an "explosive" antiwar film called *Sons and Daughters*, a one-hour film of comedian Lenny Bruce's last performance, and *MacBird* all in the same evening.[6]

By June of 1967 the assault against President Johnson reached new heights. *Berkeley Barb* began a series of articles upon supposed concentration camps in which antiwar protesters were to be imprisoned. The implication was that the notion of executive oppression originated solely in the White House. "Highly informed sources told BARB this week," proclaimed the West Coast paper, "that on June 24, the day LBJ is scheduled to officially declare war on North Vietnam, a mass round-up of more than 35,000 'radicals and hippies' will begin all over the country."[7]

147

The concentration camp hoax, which is what it was, was skillfully designed to exploit student fears, and to promote a huge counterdemonstration to the President's scheduled June 23 appearance in Los Angeles. The *Los Angeles Free Press*, passing along the news of the planned demonstration to the faithful, quoted a "spokesman for the cadres" to the effect that those who wished to show their displeasure with Johnson would have plenty to do. Diversionary tactics would keep the police busy—so busy that the welcoming dinner for the President would have to be cancelled. "In any case," stated the spokesman, "that war criminal had better think twice before he shows his face in this part of the country or tries to campaign here."[8]

The pace of the anti-Johnson preparations appeared to operate upon a well planned schedule. "Juli," a writer to the *Berkeley Barb*, passed the word to underground groups operating in the San Francisco area. "When Johnson declares war . . . ," she wrote, "you will be the first to go. . . . Hide your files. Don't let them get the names of any more of you than they already have." All radicals, hippies and blacks had to unite, she argued—"so we can carry on underground resistance." About those concentration camps: They were "purposely located in out-of-the-way places like Tule Lake, California, and in the wastes of Utah. . . . If anyone does go there, they will be turned away by barbed wire fences and guards. . . ."[9]

Almost to the very instant of President Johnson's arrival in California, the beat of propaganda was insistent and effective. *Berkeley Barb*, on June 23, offered an article by Norman Potter, "Acting Northern California Director for Vietnam Summer." Potter pointed out that the Johnson dinner was a $1,000 a plate meal, and was to be held on the "same date as the rumor has for declaration of war." In a manner which augured later charges against President Nixon, Potter argued that Johnson had developed an aversion to public appearances. His long and garbled polemic against the President was summed up with the provocative question: "What will you do when the round-up begins?"[10]

The charge of repression was echoed throughout the underground press in the fading days of the Johnson administration. In the exact manner that the movement was to claim that President Nixon had inspired the supposed police war against Black Panthers in 1970, the underground press charged Johnson with the repression of black liberation movements in 1967. The "liberator movement, root and branch," wrote the *Berkeley Barb*, was the target of the national administration and of the "establishment." One writer for the *Barb*—apparently in deadly seriousness—proposed that Johnson was about to throw Roy Wilkins, Whitney Young and James Farmer, all black leaders, in jail.[11]

The attacks against Johnson were most vitriolic along the coastlines of the nation. *Avatar* in Boston argued the potentiality of real violence against the President and Mrs. Johnson. *Berkeley Barb* rather snidely compared Johnson to terrible dictators of the past, one of its writers saying: "When a country's leader makes public appearances only in a bullet-proof limousine surrounded by cadres of armed guards, it makes no difference whether he is called dictator of Haiti or President of the United States." The U.S. was, according to that writer, very simply a "police state," and Johnson was its "dictator." Four years later the same elements were to refer to "King Nixon" and his inaccessibility, and to the regime of repression which they claimed to exist.[12]

The gradual substitution of President Nixon for President Johnson in the scenario of the leftist attack upon American institutions extended from the inauguration of 1969 through the early 1970s. In almost every instance, the leftist and underground press exceeded or preceded the liberal establishment press in the nature of the assault. As the last vehicle in the inauguration parade disappeared in the distance, the underground press began to tie the new President to the Vietnam War. Only a few months after that, the more liberal commentators of press and television began the general substitution of the phrase "Nixon's War" for "Johnson's War."

While the underground attacks against Johnson were vicious, the crusade against the Nixon administration was beyond anything seen since the Civil War period. *Space City*, in January 1970, carried a news item concerning a Christmas "greeting" prepared by the editors of one underground paper. The illustration on the greeting was that of a couple making love. Below was a list of names including those of Nixon, Lawrence Welk, Art Linkletter, J. Edgar Hoover and the "silent majority." The bottom of the greeting was adorned with the single sentence: "From our family to yours . . . have a ball!"[13]

By the spring of 1970, the underground press began to draw invidious comparisons between Adolf Hitler and Richard Nixon. It was all part of the radical left's strange fascination with the German dictator. Quite wrongfully, for instance, the underground press cited Hitler as saying: "The streets of our country are in turmoil. The universities are filled with students rebelling and rioting." It was totally and factually in error. Much of the Nazi movement was given impetus by silent and tacit consent and support of the university community. Nevertheless, *Rising Up Angry* of Chicago blissfully used the quote to charge Nixon with turning the United States into a "fascist state." Shortly thereafter, the underground press began to push the rumor that Nixon, in the manner of Hitler, would abrogate the 1972 election.[14] A Liberation News Service item reprinted in much of the radical press gleefully quoted the *Wall Street Journal* to the effect that the

149

rumor was "hard to spike." The same underground paper proceeded to point out that Hitler had "burned down the legislature (the Reichstag)" in order to consolidate his power. As usual, the underground press ignored more recent historical findings which indicated that the Reichstag had truly been burned by a feeble-minded Hollander— though rather conveniently for Hitler.[15]

The hounds of the left were in full cry in pursuit of Nixon throughout the spring of 1970. *Off Our Backs*, a feminist publication, described the President as a "helpless frightened man" who was unable to use his "impotent technological muscle." *Rising Up Angry* filled its early summer issue with maudlin sentimentalities and vicious charges against the President. The lives of the young were "increasingly more miserable"—"we might be living a hard life"—"we might be barely surviving," were the commiserations of one writer. Who was to blame for all of this? The "super pigs," President Nixon and Governor Wallace of Alabama, of course. "Humanity won't be satisfied until the last pig is hung with the guts of the last capitalist," concluded the writer. *Red Eye* happily added its bit, quoting Dick Gregory, the black comedian, to the effect that "this is the most morally polluted, insane nation on the face of the earth. . . ."[16]

On April 29, 1970, American troops were ordered by President Nixon to invade the fringes of Cambodia. In the following weeks there was almost a marriage of convenience between the underground press and the liberal establishment media. The temporary union occurred against the backdrop of campus violence—riots against the ROTC, the trashing of off-campus stores, and the attempted firebombing of campus buildings. DePauw, Hobart, the University of Arkansas, Stanford, St. Norbert, Kent State, the University of California at Berkeley, Wisconsin, Washington at St. Louis, Kentucky, and dozens of other campuses were scenes of reported or unreported violence. Shots were fired into buildings or into the homes of instructors, fire bombs were exploded, buildings were set on fire, and riots and demonstrations were organized against specific targets.

Radical ethnic groups struck at the colleges and universities as well. Forty Puerto Ricans locked the head of Brooklyn College in his office. In New Haven, a huge student-Black Panther demonstration was planned to coincide with the opening of the trial of Bobby Seale, a Panther leader. Members of the "Venceremos Brigade," a group of student revolutionaries just returned from Cuba, were on hand to aid in the organization of the New Haven demonstration. Student activists everywhere saw the big moment at hand. In the garment district of New York, radicals called for an end to "racism and repression." Dave Dellinger, the aging paladin of the left, appeared almost everywhere—at one place crying that the "government's hands are dripping with the blood of Panthers and black people," at another saying: "Vietnamization is a fraud. . . . Nixon's plan to end the war is so secret that he doesn't even know it."[17]

The *New York Times* report of the New Haven antiwar and pro-Panther demonstrations were indicative of how far the establishment press was moving in the direction of its underground counterpart. The May 2 issue of the *Times* presented an account of the proceedings: the reporter insistently claimed that at no time in the ceremonies was there any "call to violence." Yet the same column described a student demonstration which mocked the "paranoia" of New Haven, a flag-pole at the Center Church from which flew the "yippie" flag (black for anarchy, green for marijuana), and the persistent chant of the street people:

> Guns and bombs and insurrection,
> We will take a new direction,
> We won't wait for evolution,
> We will make a revolution.

The *Times* account of the New Haven happenings was colorful, if nothing else. It portrayed a picaresque scene of strolling Black Panthers and radical sympathizers. One student commune passed out samples of its favorite natural foods recipe, consisting of peanuts, prunes, raisins, corn flakes, and fat-free milk—only to have the Panthers declare it as "sub-poverty level" food. Groups roamed up and down the streets, all the while taunting the police with cries of "pigs." Fires were set in the business area. Panther haranguers demanded that the crowd should "pick up guns" in response to aggression, and that the mob should send some buildings "to the moon." Yet, as the *Times* story persisted, there was "no call to violence."[18]

The media's contributions to the general unrest of those "days of rage" were substantial indeed. Much was made of President Nixon's off-the-cuff reference to the disturbances during a visit to the Pentagon. Directional microphones had picked up distinct references by the President to "these bums" who were "blowing up campuses." In no way had Nixon called students—all students—"bums." Yet, before the day was finished, the left and liberal press, in concert, seemed intent upon perverting Nixon's words into a condemnation of all students.[19]

Now there was a full scale attack by both underground and over-ground presses against the President. It was the Verdun of 1970. The *New York Times* editorialized on the Cambodian invasion, calling it an escalation of the Vietnam War and claiming that the President's argument that it would shorten the war had an "unconvincing ring" to it. Senators who opposed the invasion received more than adequate space in the *Times* and other antiwar papers. Cooper of

Kentucky saw a risk of prolonging the war; Metcalf of Montana, Hatfield of Oregon, Harris of Oklahoma, and Brooke of Massachusetts—all were duly cited by the *Times*. Javits, one of New York's own senators, was quoted as saying that Cambodia was pulling the U.S. "in deeper." And day by day, the *Times* posted a running account of college demonstrations. On May 4 the paper carried an advertisement for a national student strike at all universities and colleges.

Other newspapers took similar positions. The *New York Post*, whose historic tradition is somewhere in the area between the left field line and the dugout, called the Cambodian invasion "another dead-end road." *Newsday*, rapidly becoming one of the influential suburban papers in the East, called the invasion "utterly pointless." The *Cleveland Plain Dealer*, a big paper on the Kent State campus, called the President's speech concerning the invasion a "maudlin" and "offensive" demonstration. And on the Kent State campus proper, the various apparati of the left began to crank up tensions with attacks upon the ROTC building and nearby stores.

There is little question that the underground press as well as more leftist university newspapers received a shot of adrenalin by the accommodation of the establishment press to the antiwar movement. The most immediate reaction by underground editors was to move more to the left in order to provide elbow room for the converts. The *Roosevelt Torch*, a university-aligned paper, offered up one writer's charge that Cambodia was a cloak for "class domination," a "super-exploitation" of the blacks, and an anti-Communist crusade on the part of the Nixon administration. Other radical papers followed the same line.[20]

The tragic events at Kent State in Ohio, and at Jackson State in Mississippi, seemed to occur at the very moment when the polarization of America had reached the extremities. The movement seemed to sense a collapsing of all opposition. Middle America, on the other hand, seemed to have reached the limit of its tolerance for riots and demonstrations. It was almost as if Middle America and the movement had come eyeball to eyeball, and it was the latter which was to blink first. Spitting and hissing, the movement pulled back, and so did the liberal establishment. James Reston, writing for the *Times*, laid the mantle of blame upon the President. He appeared to offer as evidence the charge that Nixon had called students "bums," and he asserted that "the only people who can save him (Nixon) from the consequence of his violence are the students who are now so angry that they want to concentrate on more counterviolence."

Reston had misread the signs of the times. He had blundered down a trail which led nowhere. Following him through the briars and brambles were such writers as Tom Wicker, who used such terms as "obtuse and heartless" in reference to the President. Wicker seemed to be implying that the radicals' bombs and violence had begun *after* Nixon's misquoted statement concerning students. Pete Hamill of the *New York Post* seemed to infer that the President was a madman—and that the President was as "responsible for the Kent State slaughter as he and the rest of his bloodless gang of corporation men were for the anti-integration violence in Lamar, and for the pillage and murder that is taking place in the name of democracy in Cambodia."

The word "paranoid" now blossomed in the underground and liberal press. But who, at this moment, was really paranoid? On May 8 the *New York Times* questioned and probed the possibility that this nation would "slide the whole way and become like the raving brown-shirted plague that plunged the world into the depths of hell?" The president of Villanova University student body was given space in the *Times*, where he stated: "As President, the wanton slaying at Kent State and strife on many other campuses must lie on your conscience." The *Roosevelt Torch* referred to the Ohio National Guard as the "Ohio SS," and it claimed that Ohio "pig life" was reflected in its "Gestapo-like Ohio Highway Patrol." Once again reflecting the movement's fascination with Nazism, the *Torch* concluded that Ohio's "colleges are run like concentration camps."[21]

While the underground press now revived the old rumor that Nixon was about to "cancel" the 1972 election, the liberal establishment media continued to heap blame upon the President. Anthony Lewis of the *Times* implied in his column that Nixon had deliberately chosen to inflame the divisions among the American people. Joseph Rhodes, a black student appointed by Nixon to the President's Commission on Student Violence, was now widely quoted as lamenting that "almost no one in America was happy." But Hubert Humphrey, the dean of an outmoded liberalism, saw fit to lay a few things on the line. Liberals must stop defending campus violence, he said. Liberal credibility had suffered immensely from a covert and overt approval of the defiance of law and order. "The time has come for liberals to stop saying 'well-meaning' for those who use violence and disobedience of the law," Humphrey argued. "I say they are not well-meaning." Humphrey was running for office.[22]

The underground press, heedless of any damage it might be doing to the causes of true liberalism, continued to move further left in its attacks upon the administration. A writer for the *Trumpet*, a California paper, tied four of the movement's major issues in one sweeping statement: "Have you had enough of all of this organized insanity—the bloodbath in Indochina; the vicious destruction of our environment; the brutal oppression of the minorities; the rapid decay not only of our cities but our society itself?" *Resurrection*, the rancid Tucson paper, called the American Constitution a "piece of toilet paper to clean the filth from the bodies of those murderers who sit their lily white behinds on the White House rocking chairs. . . ." The same paper later ran a three frame cartoon which illustrated the mutation of Nixon into Frankenstein.[23] And later, the *Black Panther* presented a piece analyzing the organization of American society. At the apex, the writer stated, were the "most fiendishly diabolical paranoid, power-crazed and murderous beasts assembled in the annals of history . . . [men] who had surpassed the wildest dreams that ever danced in the depraved mind of Adolf Hitler."

Below these, in the structure of American society, *Black Panther* saw a layer of "vampires . . . disguised as human beings." They were experts in "merciless plunder, ruthless exploitation, vile treachery and deceit and the shameless enslavement of entire nations. . . ." The "beasts" and the "vampires" were united in one goal—to achieve "world military and economic domination." In all of this President Nixon was regarded as an insignificant "flunky" whose "policy making power is relegated to domestic affairs."

The phantasies of *Black Panther* ranged through an illogical sequence of reasoning. "John F. Kennedy was assassinated by the CIA because he attempted to exercise too much power over foreign affairs," the *Panther* writer stated. It is amusing that some years later, Norman Mailer, in his book *Marilyn*, was to attribute similarly strange aims to the CIA. In 1970, however, *Black Panther* saw almost everything in terms of "repression." The Pentagon was shooting blacks down on the street, fascism had become a reality, and to be black in America was to be guilty of a crime punishable by death. Through all of these errors in fact and fancy, the paper topped it all off by referring to George Santayana as a "Spanish philosopher."[24]

There were times, now, when the underground press tripped over the folds of its own logic. *Rolling Stone*, which might better be described as establishment underground in character, managed such a feat in its issue of June 11, 1970. A series of interesting reports drew the following picture: the American eagle was a helpless "giant"; everybody seemed to be on the verge of paranoia; and President Nixon had appeared on occasion to be incoherent and dazed. Yet, deeper in the pages of the paper was a listing of major events in 1970; that is, in the eyes of the editors. Though all the while the underground press, including the *Rolling Stone*, had been blasting Nixon for his "bums" speech—claiming it to have precipitated polarization—the list told a different story:[25]

Jan. 15: Leonard Bernstein and 90 cocktail guests entertain members of the Black Panthers.

154

Feb. 4: National Guardsmen removed 100 demonstrators from a university student union building, and students demonstrated against recruiters from General Motors, Standard Oil, and Chrysler.

Feb. 13: a mob of 2,000 smashed windows on the Univ. of Wisconsin campus and overturned a car.

Feb. 16: Park Police station in San Francisco is bombed.

Feb. 25: students smash and burn the Bank of America's Isla Vista branch —a total loss of $350,000.

Mar. 6: Diana Oughton and two others die in an explosion of an underground bomb factory in Greenwich Village.

Mar. 10: Denver reports 24 fires and explosions in a space of 45 days.

Mar. 12: Time bombs explode in New York City—at the IBM, General Motors and Socony Mobil buildings.

Mar. 27: another bomb factory explosion killing one and wounding another.

Mar. 31: students break glass in Palo Alto, with $5,000 in glass damages.

April 2: demonstrations and damage at Stanford University.

April 17: 500 students fight with police at Santa Barbara. One student is killed and 2,500 students inflict the most "wanton destruction in UC's history."

April 21: Yale goes on strike.

April 24: Yale's President Brewster states that he is "skeptical of the ability of a black revolutionary to achieve a fair trial anywhere in the US."

April 29: rioting at Ohio State with 300 arrested.

April 30: major riot at Columbus, Ohio, with 73 injured, 100 arrested. Marines flown to New Haven, Conn., in connection with Bobby Seale demonstration.

May 1-3: Kent State students set bonfires on streets, break bank windows, and burn down the ROTC building.

The ensuing events at Kent State and Jackson State slowly began to turn things about. Jerry Rubin's advice to the Kent State students, given prior to the deadly National Guard-student confrontation, now received wide distribution. Rubin had said that Ohio students should be prepared to "kill" their parents. Other important signs were to be seen. Faculty liberals, caught between their desires to support the movement and their desire to be paid, began to choose the latter. Schisms between establishment or faculty liberals and the movement were now most evident. There was a wild meeting at Roosevelt University in Chicago. One faculty member, striking the heroic pose, asked the students to make "direct battle" with President Nixon. After all, the President was a "jackass . . . or some kind of animal," or so said the political science instructor. But despite the wild rantings, plus the student support from Gay Lib and the Young Socialist Alliance, not enough money could be raised among the Roosevelt College faculty to send out a printed strike call.[26]

John Roche, who had been in President Johnson's inner circle and who was in 1970 at Brandeis University, offered up a brilliant study of faculty action at that institution. There was a meeting almost like a gathering at the river—a "seemingly endless stream of Pentecostal witnesses" rising to "affirm their guilt and their salvation." In the end there was a 127 to 3 vote to announce "fervent opposition" to the Cambodian venture, plus a 123 to 22 vote against "repression in the United States."

All of this was in the end a playing of games. Few faculty members really wanted to stand to the cross and await the nails. Repelled by their instructors' consistent refusal to walk arm in arm against Middle America, students bitterly disassociated themselves from what they called "fraudulent liberals." Slowly but positively the movement began to turn in upon itself. *Resurrection* of Tucson was given with the sudden revelation that "the people" were really a segment of American society with which they were unacquainted. The "people" were really those individuals who arose in the morning hours before movement members did, and they were the ones who worked long and hard to keep the country viable. "All power to the Lumpenproletariat," now cried *Resurrection*.[27]

Though much space was still to be given to "repression," the tone of many underground papers now became more subdued. *Vortex* of Lawrence, Kansas, was even reduced to advising its readers not to shoplift at Dillons, a local store. There was danger in being busted there—after all, the store managers and clerks "never consider the different situations people come from." Other papers laid a heavier stress upon escape from reality by means of drugs.[28]

The liberal establishment media continued throughout midsummer and early fall to harp upon the single theme of the "depressing" state of the nation. Tom Wicker of the *Times* found a good deal to be depressed about in the upcoming November elections. It was "the most depressing election campaign of recent times. . . ." The *Times* op ed and editorial pages continued to purvey doom and gloom. One writer announced that the Nixon Vietnamization policy would inevitably get the U.S. into further and deeper conflict, and would result in confrontation with the Soviets. Douglas Kneeland, writing on the college mood of December 1970, painted a sad picture of gloom upon the university and college campuses. Mary McGrory, in her syndicated column for the first week of November, managed an amazing contortion in logic. The antiwar movement, she said, had been taken over by the obscenity shouters—and all of this was the President's fault. Obviously she hadn't read *Rolling Stone*'s list of most important events in 1970.[29]

Apparently it was Middle America that had turned almost everything about, though nobody could really quite manage an adequate definition of that segment of national life. The nature of Middle America seemed to depend upon the individual who was attempting to define its parameters. A Super Bowl game between Kansas City and Minnesota in 1970 was turned by an announcer's definition into a victory for "Middle America." It was most true, of course, to limn Middle America as a variety of tastes, types, and classes. Peter Lisagor, writing for the *Chicago Daily News*, was probably closest to the mark when he declared that Middle America was everywhere. As if to scold intellectuals living in the East, Lisagor wrote: "The point here is that to treat Middle America as a regional entity, as congenial, hot-dog-and-beer terrain inhabited by folks who resent even a President delaying a baseball game, is politically self-deluding and risky."

The true Middle American, said Lisagor, is much like people anywhere, and he "understands as much, if not more, about the forces that govern his life as the Eastern liberal intellectuals so thoroughly detested by administration ideologues." That definition, at least, was a long way from television's Archie Bunker.[30]

For a great many years it was customary in theatrical centers of the East to portray sneeringly the fate of one night stands in Peoria or Dubuque. Many theatrical or acting careers have been launched from the simple revue skit of the country bumpkin in the big city. As the famed writer Mark Sullivan once wrote, even the great George M. Cohan "shared and fostered a characteristic New York City attitude toward that part of America lying west and south of the Hudson River." Not a few of Cohan's songs contained allusions to "hicks," "jays," and "one night stands."[31]

It seemed obvious in 1970 that few members of the Eastern intellectual establishment knew or understood the temper of Middle America. In fact, even when that great middle section of American society began to stir against the irresponsibilities of the radical left, not a few Eastern intellectuals immediately associated the reaction with WASP-populated areas in the Midwest. Peter Schrag, whose hangup about WASPs eventually led to a book on their supposed decline, took on the task of dissecting Mason City, Iowa, for the *Saturday Review*. The piece indicates a considerable concern that the Jewish population of Mason City is down some forty families from a previous period. Schrag also seemed worked up over the fact that there were no Jewish members in the Mason City Euchre and Cycle Club, and that the local NAACP was having difficulties keeping its membership up.[32]

Though the hard hat-college demonstrator confrontation and the housing authority-Forest Hills Jewish community fight would illustrate that the sense of Middle America extended beyond the WASPs, the

Saturday Review plowed on. In March 1970, it presented an analysis of Winnetka, Illinois, written by Wallace Roberts. Once again it was emphasized that here was a Midwestern city with few Jews and blacks. Roberts saw the young people of the town as restrained, "not from a Waspish sense," but by a "gut feeling. . . ." How Roberts could comprehend what constituted a "gut feeling," no one bothered to explain. Yet, just a few months later, the *Saturday Review* was at it again—this time with an article by Peter Schrag entitled "Out of Place in America." Before Schrag had gotten off the first page he had twice used the acronym WASP.[33]

What seemed to escape many interpreters of Middle America was that the realities of American life were far different from what they really wanted to think them to be. WASPs, if one chooses to call them that, were not recipients of the highest per capita income in the nation. The expanding suburbs of New York, Detroit, or Chicago were crammed not just with WASPs, but with Catholics and Jews. The proof lay in the simple fact that both inner-city Catholic churches and Jewish synagogues were being stranded by fleeing congregations. Archie Bunker, in other words, could be city bred or country born; Protestant, Jewish, or Catholic; and he could be any one of a dozen different ethnic extractions.

But still the Eastern media plowed on. In June 1970, the American Broadcasting Company began a series of specially prepared pieces on small towns in America. The *New York Times* got into the act with a detailed report on a demonstration of Italian ethnics in Columbus Circle. There, the *Times* reported, Adam Clayton Powell cried out to the crowd: "This nation is for all, not just the Wasps." The words were greeted by boos and catcalls from the crowd. Italians, like Poles and Portuguese, liked to think of themselves as in the mainstream of American life.[34]

There was little question on the part of most thinking Americans that the attempt by some Eastern liberals to associate intolerance and Protestantism with Middle America was nothing more than cant. It ignored the historical tradition that Protestants, as well as Jews and Catholics, have been in the forefront of equalitarian movements everywhere. It denied the truth that, during the American Civil War, for instance, Jews and Catholics fought alongside Protestants in the Confederate Army. Yet, the thought of WASP intolerance had become almost ritualistic. With apparent surprise, the *New York Times* reported that the state of Iowa had chosen a black for the Miss America contest. It was duly noted that the young lady was "indeed surprised that Iowa, with its conservative traditions, Silent Majority and small black population . . . was the first state to pick a black girl as its representative." Someone had failed to inform the *Times* reporter that the University of Illinois, almost a decade before, had picked a black girl as its homecoming queen.[35]

The hardening of middle-class American attitudes at the point of the Kent State confrontations spawned a new rash of "insight" articles concerning Middle America. Salinas, Kansas, was examined by *Time* in July—and again the peculiar Eastern syndrome appeared in full bloom. Salinas, it was finally admitted, could not *accurately* be called Middle America. Why? Well, according to a Salinas newspaperman, most of the people there tried to be "fair." Furthermore, the town had a black mayor and a hippie boutique.[36]

In the same month the *New York Times* looked at the Midwest with an article entitled "Culture Bubbles to the Surface in Chicago." Those words alone should have been a clue as to what the piece contained. Chicago, which might possibly be America's most vital city, was "struggling towards respectability," according to the *Times* writer. Chicago's "North Shore Wasp Culture" was working hard to raise money to continue the city's traditional outdoor music festivals. The old myth was truly dying hard, and perhaps it was *Time* magazine which first recognized its decline. Suburbia, *Time* concluded, was "something more than the stereotype of buttoned down Wasp commuters and wives who slurp 'tee many martoonis' at the country club." Richard Scammon, the political demographer, was trotted out by *Time* to prove its point. Gary, Indiana, said Scammon, was as much a suburb of Chicago as was Evanston, Illinois—and Gary was blue-collar black and blue-collar white, and hardly WASP in character.[37]

Stereotypes or no, the blue-collar white middle-class America which Scammon had come to know so well was becoming politically concerned. The hard-hat assault on New York demonstrators was only one aspect of the evidence of a sense of anger within Middle America. Joseph Kraft saw this in July 1970, writing that there was a "resentment of the blacks and the educated elite." Kraft did blame the Republican Party for taking advantage of this—something the Democrats had done for years—but the truth is that those resentments were there. *Newsweek* noted the same tide of sentiment at almost the exact moment in which Kraft had received his revelation. The surge of feeling within Middle America was in full flood, rich and pulsing with the frustrations of ten years. It was all "nonestablishment, nonintellectual, not very liberal and not at all sophisticated," so said *Newsweek;* and the people who composed Middle America were ultrapatriots. They took their July Fourths quite seriously. *Newsweek* summarized:

> The anger of these people will certainly be a major political factor to reckon with, if this country suffers an unconcealable defeat in Vietnam.

It seems likely to take the form of a ferocious, radical reaction against the whole liberal establishment.[38]

While liberals had prated about the frustrations and the pent-up angers of the young, they had failed to notice the extent of Middle-American disgust. On July 4, 1970, a relatively unsuccessful "Honor America Day" was held in Washington, and a scant 25,000 showed up for the ceremonies. But this was only the first part of the program. Later that night a crowd estimated by some at 350,000 turned out for the fireworks displays. On both occasions, antiwar dissenters antagonized the crowds by flaunting Viet Cong flags and shouting obscenities.

Two days later, on July 6, President Nixon broadened his appeal to Middle America by speaking in St. Louis. There he asked "What is right about America?," and with that he struck a strong responsive chord. Quite banally, and yet quite appropriately, he advised his audience to "love America . . . because America is a good country and we are going to make her better." Politically, at least for Nixon, no better position could have been taken. The evidence lay in the enormous and rapidly increasing sale of American flags.[39]

Not for a long time had so much attention been paid to Middle America. As Joseph Kraft had written in July, this segment of the public was now up for grabs. The Democrats had owned the blue-collar class for years, but now Governor Wallace of Alabama was rapidly gaining support while the President yearned to win its votes for 1972. Television was now devoting time to probings of its desires. The *New York Times* in early July discovered Iowa and Montana, and viewed them far less condescendingly than before. Iowa, it turned out, was a delightfully clean state with a low crime rate. It was found to be filled with hard-working people who liked living in the Midwest. To the correspondent's great surprise, everything seemed up to date in Oskaloosa—Iowa women had been wearing blue jeans for years. Great Falls, Montana, another *Times* writer declared, had changed so little that its July 4 celebration "could all have happened 30 years ago." How could she have known?[40]

By the end of the summer a new book confirmed the political changes in Middle America. Richard M. Scammon and Ben J. Wattenberg, in *The Real Majority*, saw America's greatest concerns as radicalism, crime, student disruption, drugs, pornography, morals, school integration, and noisy dissent. Quite rightly as it turned out, the two authors warned the Democrats against forming a coalition of socially alienated leftist elements, minority groups and intellectuals. In the end—that is, in 1972—this is exactly what occurred at the Democratic National Convention, and what resulted was almost catastrophic for the Democratic Party.[41]

In spite of the evidence that Middle America was not WASP, or rural, or made up of aged and crotchety bigots, it seemed to appear as if some in the Eastern media were not ready to believe otherwise. In fact, some coastal writers appeared to resent the relative stability and complacency of the small town. James Reston, whose background as a student at the University of Illinois should have given him some insight into Middle America, was overcome with doom and gloom. "The filthy sprawl of the cities is so overwhelming that nobody quite knows whom to blame," Reston wrote in October. The columnist did find something of a scapegoat in the form of the President who, Reston seemed to imply, had allowed unemployment rolls to go two million higher than they were in 1969.[42]

Reston's trek through the preelection months of 1970 was marked with depression and concern. "There is a sense of loneliness in the country," he wrote, "even of helplessness and doubt about the fidelity of our institutions. This is something new in our national life—something very dangerous to the American institutions. . . ." By November he was slightly more hopeful, claiming that the President had managed by ineptitude to "bring a divided, insolvent and confused Democratic Party back from the grave." Two days after the 1970 elections, in which the Democrats did quite well, he saw the results as a rejection of Nixon. Now there was indeed something good in Middle America. There was redemption in the knowledge that the people were "allergic to big ideas, big shots, and big mouths . . ."; the people were "fair and sensible." They had recognized the "squalid" aspects of President Nixon's campaign and that the Democratic Party had a "proper concern for the unemployed, the poor, the blacks and the young. . . ."[43]

Only in a vague way did Reston really comprehend the developments in New York proper. Middle America was right at Reston's back door. There had been a Communist Party candidate for the governorship, and he had received 7,760 votes. In 1942 a Communist candidate for the same post had gotten 45,220 votes. But the winning senatorial candidate in New York was James L. Buckley of the Conservative Party. He piled up 2,179,640 votes in a state which had one of the largest blocs of black and Puerto Rican voters in the nation.

What had separated America's intellectual community from Middle America was difficult to explain. Quite obviously most intellectuals had lost touch with the deep rationalism in American society. Claiming to be liberal, they had seen only that which they had wanted to see. They were alienated, and as Lewis Feuer of the University of Toronto explained it, "alienated intellectuals suffer from the ailment that they have ideas but no power . . . they regard themselves as an elite, fit to rule. It is an alienation stemming from the obstructed will to rule."[44]

Throughout 1970 and the years which followed, many American intellectuals continued to flicker in and out of touch with reality. They

161

would not understand, as former NBC commentator Chet Huntley had pointed out in November 1970, that America was sickened by slogans and obscenities and violence. From their pens came an undammed torrent of commentary which was guided only by their own willful codes. A professor of law at Northwestern University noted in December that the Supreme Court had lost its way. Chief Justice Warren Burger was too Middle American: he was "middle-class, middle-aged, middle-of-the-road, Middle Western," as James Reston might have phrased it. The legal expert never once touched upon the evils connected with being associated with the middle-of-the-road, or whether that was exactly where judges were supposed to be. But on the other hand, the law professor stated, Thurgood Marshall, the black justice, was just right: he was "genial . . . disarming . . . penetrating . . . [and] a poor man's champion." It was only proof, concluded the Northwestern professor, that there were too many WASPs on the Court.[45]

Down to the bitter conclusion in November 1972, and even to Inauguration Day of 1973, some in the intellectual community simply could not understand the essence of the country. Norman Mailer, for instance, rode into the New Year as if he were a minuteman urging people to the cause. The WASPs, said Mailer, were the "most Faustian, barbaric, draconian, progress-oriented and root-destroying people on earth. . . ." The "*real* mission of the Wasp in history was not, say, to create capitalism, or to disseminate Christianity into backward countries," proclaimed Mailer. It was to get the United States flag on the moon. Then, in one death-defying flight of imagination and evidence, Mailer outlined the WASP mind: it "bears more resemblance to the himself extraordinary distances through a narrow path. . . ."[46] Directed toward other elements of American society, such a generalization might have been the essence of racism.

8

Rhetoric and Causes in the Sixties

The decade of the Sixties was marked by a myriad of causes, some symbiotic in nature, some seemingly out of context with the others. They are important, because in greater or lesser ways they represented the meaningful aspirations or admirable goals of specific elements of American society. Few could deny the nobility of the aims of moderate civil rights groups. Nor were many Americans really out of sympathy with the goals of sensible ecologists. A great many people in the United States also saw fit to support the feminist movement during the decade.

In every case, however, the radical movement of the 1960s found fertile soil in which to flourish. And in virtually every instance, the aim of the movement was not so much to achieve the actual goals of each cause but to use each cause for the success of the movement. The rhetoricians of the left were quick to seize upon the sympathies generated within each lesser cause in the hope of adding to the totality of the entire crusade, and to the effectiveness of the movement inside of American society. Thus, in a sense, the movement only operated outside of the establishment on the very fringe of its radical left; its bomber left, so to speak. The major operation of the movement was to use the nobility of each greater or lesser cause for the sole purpose of persuading the establishment to turn itself over.

163

In the instance of the civil rights movement, the magnitude of that particular crusade was to have an enormous impact upon the establishment. As the march toward racial equality began to pick up steam in the early 1960s, the movement was able to seize upon it and establish a precedent necessary to the success of the revolution. That was, in essence, the public acceptance of the principle of legal nullification by means of moral sanction.

In the late 1950s and the early 1960s, it truly did seem necessary for civil rightists to break the law by opposing state and local statutes—in Southern cafes and restaurants, as instances. Once having succeeded here, the same civil rights crusaders moved to attack almost every law which could be levered by the principle of morality. In time, of course, the actions took upon themselves the coloration of sheer indiscipline. No matter how much of a sense of morality might be applied to the savage urban riots of the 1960s, the great bulk of American society saw them as incursions of mobocracy against the rights and property of others.

Long after the great Washington civil rights demonstrations of 1963 had passed into history, long after Martin Luther King had been buried, the civil rights movement began to reflect the general paranoia of the entire radical movement. King, in 1963, had described his dream: a society in which the "sons of former slave owners and slaves will be able to sit down together at the table of brotherhood." Three years later, the American educated (but not U.S. born) Stokely Carmichael laid out the philosophy of "black power." Blacks, he said, have never been allowed to organize—which was not true, incidentally—therefore, such organizations as SNCC should be "black-staffed, black-controlled, and black-financed." No longer were blacks to be used and manipulated by white liberals, Carmichael contended. Whites, including all white liberals, were to be viewed as a totality; that is, as "180 million racists." Thus, when SNCC became "all black," and the Carmichael principle was adopted by other black militants of the Sixties, the whole theme of King's brotherhood temporarily fell into obscurity.[1]

Building upon the Carmichael argument, such organizations as the Black Panthers sought to exploit both white liberals and the white liberal sense of guilt. The Black Panther platform, created in Oakland by Huey Newton and Bobby Seale, consisted of ten major points, several of them built upon the black paranoia that emerged in the middle Sixties. The most pertinent of these called for black control of black destiny, the end "to the robbery by the white man of our black community," the exemption of blacks from military service, and the institution of the principle of black judges and black juries in cases involving blacks.[2]

The mentality operating behind such organizations as the Black Panthers was dangerous, self-intoxicating, and deceptive. While posing as ghetto heroes, the Panthers, as described by Don A. Schanche in the *Atlantic*, selectively borrowed doctrines of death and disruption from other "isms." The atmosphere surrounding the organization was paramilitary. Its concept of power from the end of a gun was taken from Maoism, its notion of attacking capitalism was borrowed from Marx, its call for "more Vietnams" came from Che Guevara, and its general policies of terror and disruption were drawn from Al Fatah, the Arab terrorist organization.

Exaggerated rhetoric was a strain which ran throughout the black militant phase of the movement. Schanche, interviewing Eldridge Cleaver in Algeria, heard the black expatriate tick off an enemies list. He wished to "wring" President Nixon's neck; he wanted to "take off" the head of Senator McClellan, the Arkansas Democrat; he wanted to "aim at and pull the trigger" on Mayors Daley and Alioto (of Chicago and San Francisco, respectively), and he talked of a dim future for "Jewish slumlords" and Jewish capitalists. Schanche's conclusion was a description of almost pure paranoia: the Black Panthers and other allies had gone over the brink. There was a "madness" in the Panthers which could not be solved by simplistic liberal remedies.[3]

The liberal solution, in any case, rarely involves the factor of time. And time does, as the old cliché reads, heal a great many wounds. In the realm of wild and uncontrolled black rhetoric, it would necessarily be a slow process indeed. By 1970, the extremities of such rhetoric, fed by ever-increasing dosages of white guilt, had left King's notions of brotherhood so far behind as to seem almost unrelated.

Actually, of course, the militants had begun their assaults on the white establishment and the moderate civil rights crusade before King's tragic demise in Memphis. The Black Panther platform as it was originally prescribed set up a shocking list of proposals and it delineated a perverted view of history. Black people, said the initial platform, had been promised forty acres and a mule; the racist governments which followed Lincoln's death had denied that promise. Deception had been the keyword of white over black. Stokely Carmichael, for instance, argued in 1966 that the vote "ain't nothing but a honky's trick. . . ." The same Carmichael, in August of that year, contended that the ancestors of the American black man "were the greatest warriors on the face of this earth—Africans, Africans, Africans."[4] Such a statement covered a lot of literate history, including Genghis Khan, Tamerlaine, and Julius Caesar, and all who fought with them.

So blatant was the rewriting of history by some militant black organizations that the process shocked even the comprehension and understanding of the most masochistic white liberals. It seemed as if no one could agree on the amount of time during which blacks had been enslaved by the terrible WASPs of North America. Early in the 1960s it appeared customary to argue the civil rights cause by preluding every statement with "300 years of black bondage." As the decade progressed, so did the number of years of servitude grow. By 1965 it had expanded to 400 years. A year later Carmichael had it pinned down at 413 years. That would have dated the beginnings of black oppression at the year 1553: over a half-century before those historically famous WASPs landed at Jamestown. By the end of the decade it was not uncommon to hear white liberals in the national university community refer to 600 years of black oppression. Not once was it ever recalled that whites too had been oppressed; that the very word "slave" is derived from captive Slavs enslaved by Roman centurions.[5]

Hofstadter's early 1960s description of the paranoid style appropriately noted such historical flights of fancy. In 1966, some three years after Hofstadter had written his essay, Stokely Carmichael presented his views of American history—at least its beginnings:

> Let's examine history some more. People say it is a horrible thing to say that white people would think about committing genocide against black people. Let us check our history out. It is a fact that we built this country, nobody else. I'll explain that to you. When this country started, economically it was an agricultural country. The cash crop on the world market was cotton. WE PICKED THE COTTON! We picked the cotton. We did it. So it is *we* who built this country. It is we who have fought in the wars of this country.[6]

As Hofstadter wrote: "One should not be misled by the fantastic conclusions that are so characteristic of this political style into imagining that it is not, so to speak, argued out along factual lines." Paranoid judgments spring from certain "defensible judgments," and they are capable of a "curious leap in imagination that is made at some critical point in the recital of events."[7] In Carmichael's recitation of history is offered the notion that cotton was the principal staple of British colonial capitalism. Of course this is not so, for what saved the early American southern settlements was tobacco—and white indentured servants along with some blacks picked that crop. Now one approaches the "curious leap in imagination." Cotton built the country, blacks picked the cotton—so blacks built the country and fought the wars of the country. Neither of those two conclusions have a major justification.

But now Carmichael leaps to his crowning effort. The nation has become so "technological" that the black is no longer needed. Thus genocide is in the offing—the *man* "will consciously wipe us out." Imagining upon imagining is thus piled up, the result being a history that never was. That was Carmichael's way, one may suppose. A year later, as quoted by UNS from London, he was predicting his own death. "The CIA killed Malcolm X, and they probably will kill me," he stated. At this writing Carmichael is still alive, and of course Malcolm X was killed in a Black Moslem factional fight.[8]

By the end of 1967 the black militant movement had taken up the "repression" theme with vengeance. Hofstadter had argued at the beginning of the decade that the thwarted goals of the paranoic lead him to the point of view that there is a "world of power" beyond his imagining: power that is at once "omnipotent, sinister, and malicious. . . ." Such feelings generally crystallize into pure hate. White radicals were quick to seize upon these tendencies within black militancy, and they exploited them to their own advantage. *Nashville Breakdown* illustrated this quite adequately in a call to violence:

I HATE America. . . . I HATE the white folks who love the black folks who hate themselves. . . . I HATE "My Country 'Tis of Thee". . . . I HATE the good folks and the bad folks who hate me. . . . I HATE the politicians and the righteous and the press and the people who tell me what to think. . . . I'm going to kill America. . . . I'm GOING to take back my beautiful womanhood and let it tower over the stench of the American savage. . . . I GOING to wring your neck America. I'm GOING to wring your neck America. I'm GOING to twist it and turn it just to the popping point. . . .[9]

The ubiquitous Jerry Rubin, as quoted by *The Militant* in London in 1968, further indicated the willingness of the radical left to tie black militants into the movement. "We did not build CBS," he stated, "the Democratic Party, the Catholic Church, and we want no place in them. Vietnam is a case of the past trying to suppress the future. The American economy has rendered white middle-class youth and black working-class youth useless, because we are not needed to make the economy run."[10]

The black militant campaign against "repression" was opened by the radical George Forman in January of 1968. Other black militants and their white radical allies followed suit; the beginning of a campaign which achieved considerable success. Forman was able to gain financial commitments from several churches in the New York area, and was even able to enlist the aid of the Roman Catholic pastor of the Church of the Resurrection in Harlem. The priest accused his own church of sanctioning certain iniquitous conditions and of standing silent in the "face of injustice." Until the Catholic Church understood that "gospels demand freedom and the elimination of injustice, oppression and exploitation for all the victimized, including black people," he concluded, "then it will not ring true to the black people in America."

In 1970, Vincent Harding, the director of the Institute of the Black

World, and his associate William Strickland, listed a series of iniquities which composed part of the repression of blacks:

1. Abandonment of blacks by both political parties.
2. The "insane, wasteful, imperialistic war" in Vietnam.
3. The "arrogant national support of antiliberation forces across the Third World."
4. The "persecution and assassination of our young people."
5. The "deterioration and poisoning of the urban centers."
6. The "educational genocide practiced against inner-city children."
7. The economic depression of black America.
8. The "token desegregation" which is used to destroy black control of public education.[11]

Thus did "repression" and "genocide" become the themes of the black militant attack of the late Sixties. Much of the argumentation and rhetoric was aimed specifically against the police and the penal system. And some of it, incidentally, fringed upon the ridiculous more than the sublime. Ron Dellums, a candidate for the city council of Berkeley and later a member of Congress, offered up a prime sample of illogicality in the late 1960s, saying: "I don't like the idea of more police protection. If we put more police in South Berkeley, many minority youth will not be able to get employment because of arrest records."[12]

But fanaticism has no room for a sense of humor. It calls for serious attention to all the claims of the cause. So it was with the black militants and their white radical supporters. *Rising Up Angry,* a Chicago-based underground paper, straightfacedly stated in 1970 that there were 600 "political prisoners" in San Quentin—and that these represented only the tip of the iceberg. *The Rag* of Austin, Texas, contributed its own bit to the paranoia of the times with a quote from the aging leftist Dave Dellinger, who left prophecies of doom wherever he could find a paying college audience: "When imperialism is defeated abroad," said Dellinger, "it must either withdraw or institute fascism in this country. It doesn't happen all at once, but it has already been imposed on the black liberation movement, with a systematic attempt to wipe out the Black Panthers. . . ."[13]

The fantastic hoax concerning an alleged war by the police against Black Panthers fitted well into the general theme of repression. *Rising Up Angry* used the Panther extermination issue in midwinter of 1970 to substantiate the radical claim that it was time "to bring the mother [the U.S.] down." Dr. Benjamin Spock added the voice of ultra-liberalism later in that same year, claiming that the New Haven trial of Black Panthers was "part of an attack on black militants" by a government that "has gone berserk." A writer for *Resurrection* threw the feminist movement into the general melee by demanding freedom not only for Bobby Seale but for all imprisoned women. "Women in prisons are our sisters," the statement read. "People in prison for 'common' crimes should receive our support just as much as 'political prisoners' do. . . . All women prisoners should be freed."[14]

Keyed by the *Guardian* and the *London Times,* the radical underground press of Britain went all out on the "repression" of American black militants. *Red Notes,* reaching a hysterical tone during the case of the so-called Soledad Brothers, claimed: "Today the world is witness to the mass murder of thousands of Black, Brown and Yellow peoples. From age 1 to 80 these brothers and sisters are filling the graves of the Third World. In the struggle against repression to death as it makes no difference to the hired assassins of imperialism." Soon *Red Notes* was drawing analogies between "black repression" in America and the Irish issue, stating: "We now recognize that our racism and national chauvanism [sic] has retarded our support of the Irish people's struggle."[15]

Almost everywhere, the movement supported black militancy by an unbridled assault upon the police. *Red Notes* in Britain printed a series of reports—AGITPROP INFORMATION, they were called. They were descriptions of confrontations between London bobbies and blacks, done appropriately in three- and four-letter words. In Chicago at almost exactly the same time, *Rising Up Angry* gloated about the killing of "pigs" in the Cabrini-Green housing area. Throughout all of the movement, there was an apparent rationalization for violence. One black leader went so far as to blame whites for the destruction caused by black ghetto gangs; the whites "wanted" the gangs to perform in this manner. In Lawrence, Kansas, *Vortex* printed one writer's explanation of heavy property damage in the racial explosion in that city in 1970 by saying: "We don't give a goddamn about his union, his constitution, his police, his momma, his pay-the-proper-respect-to-life-rights-and-property of others argument."[16] It was simply a falling back upon violence as a means of achieving an end.

When not pushing the virtue of rightful vengeance against "repression," the movement pressed the alternate charge of "genocide." Arnold Beichman later destroyed this contention in his 1972 book, *Nine Lies About America,* but prior to that the flak flew hot and heavy. The key seems to have been the Black Panther effort to set a background for forthcoming trials of certain leaders of the organization and to win important support for a favorable verdict. *Rising Up Angry* dutifully parroted the charge, one contributor stating: "The U.S. ruling class is committing genocide on black people in general and the Black Panther Party in particular. The black community is the pig's target and the Black Panther Party is the bulls-eye."

The Black Panther "Message to America," quoted in *Resurrection in July,* continued attacks against "open fascism" and an "Archeo-

Colonialist" policy by the United States. There was a calculated "Fascist Genocidal conspiracy," a "barbaric organization controlled and operated by avaricious, sadistic, blood-thirsty thieves." It was an "inhuman capitalist system" designed as "the number one exploiter and oppressor of the peoples of the whole world." The system was about to engage in "shameless slaughter of the people of the world."[17]

The chorus was echoed widely. Many underground papers ran H. Rap Brown's 1967 warning that the government had prepared some twenty-four concentration camps for dissenting blacks, with a capacity of 500,000. The theme had willing and ready believers: one black woman said in May that "we blacks had better look out for the gas ovens."[18]

Leftist Tod Gitlin's contribution to *Motive* in November 1970 included the genocide argument inside of a long and rambling and fatuous piece entitled "The Dynamics of the New Left." There was genocide in Vietnam, Gitlin argued, and a "decorous fascism at home." Almost jubilantly did the writer exude the domino theory that when Vietnam fell, America could be driven from its position in Indonesia. The American scene was blanketed by the curtains of repression. "The paper tiger has real teeth," he stated. "The police state is in prospect." Furthermore, there were thousands of political prisoners in America—it "can no longer be doubted." The police were "nazis" who were engaged in "political assassinations" of Black Panthers. On the far right Gitlin could discern a "paramilitary" structure—Minutemen and others—stockpiling arms and intelligence. Radicals should move cautiously. Dangers existed in the "revolts in a majority of high schools, which should accelerate and sharpen the growing weight of the heavy hand. . . ."[19]

Most skillfully, the movement sought to assimilate minority and ethnic elements into the grand crusade. The establishment was almost always assumed to be the "anglos," which seemed to include virtually everybody whose ancestors came from Europe, including elements of the American Jewish community. Outsiders awaiting acceptance into American society included American Indians, Chicanos, and Puerto Ricans—though on occasions these three were grouped together as "Indians" or "Third World People." There was seldom any distinction made by radicals on the exact meaning of Chicano, though in theory it is generally applied to those native-born Americans of Mexican ancestry. Rarely, if ever, did the radicals approach the issue of illegal immigration or the fact that many included in the "deprived Chicano" classification were really unlawfully in the United States. In 1969, for instance, the Immigration and Naturalization Service reported some 74,272 "deportable" aliens, mostly of Mexican descent, living in Southern California alone. Nor was it commonly admitted by radicals that most Spanish-Americans residing in the mainland United States had voluntarily come to this country.[20]

Rather the words "genocide," "poverty," and "repression" were applied to almost all ethnic elements without discrimination. Stokely Carmichael, drawing upon his questionable knowledge of American Indians, claimed in 1966: "In order for this country to come about, the honky had to completely exterminate the red man, and *he did it.* . . . And he did it where he doesn't even feel sorry but he romanticizes it by putting it on television with cowboys and indians [sic], cowboys and indians."

In this same general period of time Carmichael had proclaimed that blacks had built the nation virtually by themselves.[21] His adherence to historical fact once again left much to be desired. The American Indian, poverty stricken as he was in some areas of the country, was far from extermination—many authorities believe that there are more Indians now than in 1607. Furthermore, it might have been added by Carmichael that American whites had done away with far more of their own numbers—in the Civil War, for instance—than of Indians and other ethnic and racial elements combined.

From time to time some radicals attempted to classify Chicanos and Indians together, as one ethnic element, so to speak. *Resurrection* in 1970 carried an article claiming that Chicanos were Indians who had come from the "northern land of Aztlan" and that those areas, now part of the United States, would be "fought for and defended." The Liberation News Service promoted the same argument, saying that Chicanos had engaged in a 120-year fight for land. "There is a long, hard political and economic struggle in these beautiful mountains," stated the LNS correspondent, but in the end land and justice would be achieved.[22]

Almost quite as often were the Indian and Chicano themes tied to the "third world" concept—a notion which was basically antiwhite and anti-American in theme. A Weatherman statement in 1969, written by such individuals as Mark Rudd and Bernadine Dohrn, both presently being sought by authorities, saw all such peoples as responsible for the "relative affluence of the United States." Even Angola, according to the Weathermen, had contributed to the American living standard. *Space City* tied the entire black, brown, and third world together with the words of a Rice University student of 1970: "As long as U.S. imperialism is able to wage large-scale wars," it was written, "it will use this ability to defend reactionary cliques in the Third World and suppress Black and Brown rebellions at home."[23]

All of this represented a grand attempt to coalesce and unite disparate elements on the left. The feminist movement, with its correspondingly appealing rhetoric—sexism, male chauvinism, etc.—found an almost natural home in the movement. With women's lib, as it came to be called, was added more distinctive marks of the movement: the bra-less look (some companies began making brassieres designed to provide such an illusion), large spectacles, hair parted and combed down from the middle, and a noticeable paucity of a sense of humor.

Also present was that peculiar perversion of history and knowledge, the stacking of unrelated and sometimes false data in order to reach a desired conclusion. One woman, writing for *Resurrection* in 1970, produced an interesting scenario for the feminist revolution. Girls, it was stated, should not be allowed to play with dolls, wear frilly dresses, or be told to pull down their dresses. In a grand spasm of illogic she concluded, "Our history has been stolen from us. Our heroes died in childbirth, from peritonitis, and overwork [doubtlessly she meant heroines]. . . . Our geniuses were never taught to read or write. We must invent a past adequate to our ambitions."[24] Obviously the writer had never read up much on Boadicea, Saint Joan, Golda Meir, or Indira Gandhi, all of whom added something to the zest of history. Neither did she understand that it was puerperal fever and not peritonitis that wiped out women in childbirth up to the middle of the Victorian period, when two men, Baron Joseph Lister and Oliver Wendell Holmes, helped to clear up that scourge. And lastly, she obviously had never contemplated the dangers of "inventing" history: in one paragraph she had already done it.

By 1970 numerous feminist liberation "underground" papers were in operation, as well as some tightly knit local and national action groups. Some of those last were grimly managed operations indeed. Among them were SCUM (the Society for Cutting Up Men), WITCH (the Women's International Terrorist Conspiracy from Hell), and NOW (the National Organization for Women). Among both underground papers and the organizations there was a liberal rationing of female chauvinism. *Off Our Backs*, in November 1970, offered one woman's complaints that she was tired of being "co-opted, exploited, ripped-off, patronized, seduced and raped." "I say if we want to be liberated," she concluded, "we must pick up the gun and turn it on the men who are issuing all these orders, the very men who are telling us that we must follow them . . . in order to get our liberation."[25]

Not infrequently did the feminist movement touch upon the extreme limits of rhetoric. A woman writing for *Resurrection* in 1970 indicated that she often had the desire to drive men to the ground and defecate upon them. She hated businessmen with smooth voices, pretty boys who analyzed her problems, construction workers and "freaks." Once women had thrown off this horrible oppression, they could accept "the love of a man wo [sic] will recognize us for what we truly are."[26]

Feminist Robin Morgan, writing for the *New York Times* in 1970, tied the womens' liberation movement into the grand revolutionary crusade of the decade. Even the *Times,* which was giving her space for her argumentation, was dominated by "rich white heterosexual males." Others—the poor, the nonwhite, homosexuals, and "especially females"—were "less than human. . . ." There was growing repression, Ms. Morgan added, and a growing "white male imperialism" which sought to keep "those people" from rebellion. All forms of media were male dominated but Ms. Morgan saw a new day coming. Even the *Times* might be liberated by a "revolutionary woman's collective. . . ." In any case, Robin Morgan's complaints may well have been welcomed by some of the *Times* staffers—those concerned about the heterosexuality of their colleagues.[27]

Almost to the last rule in the book did the feminist movement conform to the revolutionary pattern of the decade. Hypocrisy in American society? There was plenty of it, according to an article in *Off Our Backs.* So bad was the condition of American society, the writer claimed, that women should have a Lysistrata day—no sexual relationships with men until the importance of womanhood was recognized. The movement even had some folk heroes—Elizabeth Gurley Flynn, Angelina Grimke, "Mother" Jones, and Harriet Tubman.[28] And there should be women's studies in college curricula, a demand unbelievably acceded to by many history departments.

Were there contemporary heroes who exemplified radical zeal? *Off Our Backs* provided the name of Bernadette Devlin, the Ulster MP.[29] The terrible effects of capitalism? *Off Our Backs* proclaimed in 1970: "Who is the enemy? Is it men, the system, capitalism . . .? The system is the enemy, and in that men set it up, they are the enemy. But, men are the enemy only if we let them be."[30] The paranoia was obvious, even if the logic was less than stunning.

Inevitably did the theme of oppression creep into the feminist movement. A contributor to *Off Our Backs* wrote in 1970:

> Since women have been oppressed longer than any other group in history, men have a very heavy investment in continuing to oppress us. Their very sense of "manhood" is defined by their continuing to oppress. As a result, such a movement will be attacked viciously from both the right and the left, and attempts at subversion will continue. . . .[31]

One contributor to *Off Our Backs* saw oppression as the inability of women to have control over their own bodies. They were sexual objects—"pleasure machines to be victimized by unsafe and unresearched birth control." Of course the argument missed the point that the best birth control was a woman's own regulation of her emotions: and that each woman was free to do.

Some feminist rhetoric was almost beyond the comprehension of the stable mind. *Resurrection,* providing comment from the "Minister of Women" of the John Brown Party, claimed that "Our sisters are dying, Our daughters are dying." Oppression was everywhere—"Free Erika Huggins, Free Our Panther Sisters, Free all Women Prisoners, Free all political prisoners."[32]

In 1970 a writer for *Off Our Backs* contended that prostitutes should be considered political prisoners, an argument which might have raised a few eyebrows among the madams of that profession. Finally, and almost incredibly, "genocide" was offered as an example of some of the goals of contemporary American society. Poor people, claimed a contributor to *Off Our Backs,* were being forced to take birth control pills. This was a form of "genocide" as applied to women, and the practice of such techniques caused great suffering. It was a strange claim to come from a movement which quite generally supported free abortions, and which more often than not argued the values of love without marriage.[33]

It is proper to say that each action in society tends to create counter-action. In the instance of the feminist movement, the full development of a male liberation movement seemed far in the distance by 1973. There were some acerbic complaints on the college campuses of the country—especially as salary increase monies were increasingly used to correct alleged inequalities between men and women teachers. In the case of black militancy, however, the reaction of white society was intense and immediate. Even in 1964, when black militancy was becoming strident, a *New York Times* poll elicited some interesting opinions. The survey found that a little over 10 percent of the people of New York City saw the black civil rights movement to be appropriate. Slightly less than a quarter of the interviewees thought the movement excessive in its demands.

Six years later, Daniel Patrick Moynihan saw an improvement in black-white relationships. Citing samplings taken by the University of Michigan Survey Research Center, he pointed to an increase in the number of whites favoring desegregation. Moynihan's conclusions seemed to have been slightly premature, however. Two years later the state of Michigan gave Governor George Wallace an astounding victory in the Democratic primaries. The Southerner's victory was a crushing one and was widespread throughout the state, excepting those areas populated heavily by blacks.[34]

While few college-educated Americans were willing to accept the claims of Shockley and Jensen—two researchers who inferred or claimed inherent racial disparities—there was throughout the 1960s a hardening of white attitudes on the race issue. Samuel Lubell in a 1970 study of New York City uncovered quickening resentments among all types of white residents. In that city, which some had claimed as the most bias-free in the country, Lubell found that the "polarization of racial feeling [had] become probably the strongest political force agitating New York City's voters." Yet, at the same time, article after article in the *Times* and other Eastern-based publications continued to stress the antiblack sentiments supposedly existing in Middle America.[35]

By the summer of 1970 there was a high level of tension to be found in areas of New York City in which, by tradition, it was not supposed to exist. These spots included the Williamsburg section of Brooklyn, where Jews and blacks engaged in street fights, and the Jewish Defense League patrolled specific streets in order to protect Jewish businessmen. It was a long way from the South and the Klan, and seemed truly strange to hear one resentful Jewish Defense League leader argue that "Jews can riot, too."[36]

Inevitably Italians and other ethnic groups sought to consolidate blocs of voters and ethnic activists. Italian-American Unity Day rallies were held in New York City, and Italian and black confrontations occurred with increasing frequency in parts of New York and New Jersey. One very eerie part of the developing pattern of racial and economic tension was the reaction of some black middle-class elements to racial changes. In the town of North Hempstead on Long Island, the opposition of blacks to a federal housing project in that community caused some consternation. In a vote taken to determine the sentiment of the town, most resident blacks indicated opposition to the new federal housing—the charge being that it would bring in undesirable elements. Black militants immediately labelled those blacks who opposed the project "racists."

In Cleveland, Ohio, Lt. General Benjamin Davis, a black who had been brought in as the top police official in the city, resigned because, as he put it, he could not get proper "law and order" support in the curbing of such black militants as the Panthers. Both the North Hempstead affair and Davis's fight against the Panthers fell into the category of events which radicals quickly sought to forget.[37]

Slowly but surely the rage for black studies in university curriculums, which in themselves were products of a kind of paranoia, began to lose impetus. Scholars such as Daniel Boorstin pointed up anomalies in the idea of creating large numbers of black studies experts. After all, what the country needed were blacks trained in medicine, dentistry, and law. And there seemed also to be a growing tendency for some scholars to examine the nature of black studies with closer scrutiny. Robert Claiborne, in his book *Climate, Man and History,* argued most strongly against one aspect of black studies; that is, the claim that Africa was *the* cradle of civilization. Claiborne wrote:

Black nationalists have begun referring to Africa as "The cradle of civilization." With all due respect, this just isn't so. . . . Egypt, to be sure, was *a* cradle of civilization, and one that subsequently exerted some influence on Europe to the north and much more on Black Africa to the south. But . . . Egypt . . . is culturally part of the Middle Eastern and Mediterranean world.[38]

It was in the white blue-collar class that black militancy rubbed the fur the wrong way, and nothing showed that more than Governor Wallace's growing popularity in the Northern industrial states. Getting at the real nature of the aroused white hostility became the goal of political pollsters and analysts—especially during the Middle-America syndrome of 1970. It was truly unfortunate in a sense that so much money and effort was expended along these lines, however. Eric Hoffer had expressed the prevailing white blue-collar sentiment as early as 1964 when he wrote: "We believe that the Negro should have every right we have: the right to vote, the right to join any union open to us, the right to live, work, study and play where he pleases. But he can have no special claims on us. . . . He has certainly not done our work for us. Our hands are more gnarled and work-broken than his, and our faces more lined and worn."[39] But Hoffer in the 1960s was satire material for many Eastern intellectuals: his sentiments were too simplified and direct. Surely there had to be more complicated explanations of white blue-collar opposition to black militancy.

Yet by 1973 the hardening of racial attitudes on the part of whites had extended to the college campus. Examples of the change were neither complicated nor confusing. Charges of racial discrimination against whites were raised at Cornell, the site of some of the more violent black militancy in the Sixties. White students at the Ithaca campus were charging that they were not allowed to enroll in black studies courses, that there was discrimination in the black dormitory and cultural center, and that there had been an unequal recruitment by the university of other ethnic groups. These arguments marked an abrupt change from the good-natured fun poked at black studies programs in the 1960s. At one time in that decade the students of Bradley University in Peoria, Illinois, had demanded that school be dismissed on St. Patrick's Day, that potatoes and corn beef be part of every university meal, and that due honor and respect be paid to the nation's heritage from Ireland.[40]

But now, in the 1970s, there were minor rumblings on the part of white students. At Princeton University it was discovered that every qualified black applicant for the class of 1975 had been admitted. Only one out of every four white applicants had been accepted. At Columbia University students noted that the Malcolm X Liberation Center, a campus sponsored and financed activity, was open to black students and their guests: a guest was defined as "someone who shares a common culture, heritage, color consciousness and is a son or daughter of Africa. . . ." At the University of Washington, a white law student saw his application to law school rejected, while black applicants

176

whose law board scores were lower than his were accepted. The resultant law case—DeFunis *v.* Odegaard—reached the Supreme Court in 1974, only to be dismissed by the court on the basis that the University of Washington had atoned for its sins by admitting DeFunis before the case reached the high bench. Despite the sigh of relief in many quarters, however, the failure of the court to deal with the problem only postponed the inevitable.[41]

While black, Chicano, feminist, and ethnic militancy tended to arouse greater or lesser countermovements during the Sixties and Seventies, the one crusade which found a general acceptance in both middle and radical America was that concerning ecology. Actually the ecological movement was not new; indeed the very word "ecology" is based upon a Greek derivative. Prior to 1960, the problem of man's relation to nature was generally discussed under the less charismatic phrase, the "balance of nature." The Progressive Era at the turn of the century had given due recognition to the impingement of industrial society upon the natural environment, and the national park system had been created. Even the Progressives were not the first environmentalists, however. Darwin had noticed and recorded the impact of smoke upon British insect life, and the great British poet, William Wordsworth, had written much about the conflict between good and industrial society. In the 1940s, just prior to the American entrance into World War II, Hollywood had created a most touching movie based upon the novel *How Green Was My Valley,* a semiautobiographical work by Richard Llewellyn. Both the movie and the novel emphasized the impact of industrialism upon Welsh family life.

Into the 1950s such magazines as *U.S. News and World Report, Time,* and *Newsweek* gave increasing attention to industrial pollution, in several instances pointing to breakdowns in sewage and filtering systems throughout the nation. The same could be said of dozens of the most important newspapers which gave space to the same issues. Through the writings of Rachel Carson, Barry Commoner, and Paul Ehrlich, ecology became a cause that impinged on even the most insensitive types. In the Sixties, both Carson and Ehrlich concluded that the insecticide DDT was enormously damaging to wildlife of all types, and possibly to human beings as well. Other writers increasingly stressed corporate greed, and blamed it for the devastation of huge tracts of land through strip mining.

Some of the criticisms were quite valid; others were questionable both on the basis of history and upon the real needs of what had become a highly complicated society. The call for the preservation of various species, though admirable in many instances, ofttimes lacked real balance in argumentation. Norman D. Newell, writing for *Scientific American* in 1963, pointed out that at one time there were some 2,000 families of animals roaming the earth. Most had become extinct long before man had become a factor in determining the nature of the environment. Some had evolved into other forms. One-third of those families were still in existence. Long before industrialization had become a factor—eons away, in fact—the dinosaur and sixteen other "superfamilies" had become extinct.[42] Approximately 450 species disappeared prior to man's super-ascendancy over the earth, and some seventy others had vanished in areas which had never been industrialized at all. There were once elephants and bears in the British Isles: now there are none, and neither are mourned. Of course this is not to say that the diminution of the remaining families of life should be accepted with grace.

By the mid-Sixties, ecology had become a marvelous holding ground for the radical movement. In between major confrontations—for example, in the hiatus before the Cambodian invasion—ecology was always and inevitably trotted out as an issue that had been discovered by the movement. Eventually, as paranoia invaded almost all aspects of the movement, ecology fell victim to overkill. It was not that everything that was written about ecology was wrong; it was that there entered into the movement's interpretation of ecological damage a new kind of fatalism. One magazine intoned that Lake Erie was dead. It really wasn't, of course, and in 1974 the fishing industry on that lake was showing a smart revival. Santa Barbara was drowning in oil due to a tragic fault in drilling operations. Sea life in the area was doomed—so said a great many ecological novitiates. Santa Barbara was not doomed, and by 1974 virtually every trace and effect of the catastrophe had disappeared.

Yet each claim had some element of truth in it; enough to cause some in the ecological movement to indulge in paranoic flights of fantasy. Sensible and sober C. L. Sulzberger, writing for the *New York Times* in 1970, saw a world "civilization . . . preoccupied with suicide." Russia was coating its lakes with garbage, French rivers were foaming with detergent, and the United States was suffocating under an avalanche of sludge.[43] Some scientists were revelling in the delicious possibility that the milk of American mothers contained more DDT than the milk from cows. Paradoxically, there were almost no complaints in the 1960s that New York City street cleaners had to contend with over 150 tons of dog droppings each day.

Concern in establishment journals over the ecological situation was centered upon a number of potential hazards. At the exact height of the college unrest of 1970, in May and June, much of the press devoted a great deal of space to the pollution of streams and highways. It was pointed out that government investigators had found high levels of mercury in numerous rivers and lakes. Among the last were Lakes Erie and Champlain, the St. Lawrence River, the Wisconsin River, the Mississippi, the Rio Grande, and scores of other freshwater spots. Federal warnings went out to the general public on the eating of fish caught in those lakes and waterways. Interior Secretary Walter J. Hickel called the mercury an "intolerable threat to the health and safety of Americans." The *New York Times* offered articles which pointed out the terrible consequences of too great an ingestion of mercury, and tendered the consoling advice that lesser amounts would cause only kidney and liver damage, diarrhea, tremors, dizziness, irritability, and depression. Though there were no reported cases of mercury poisoning in the United States from the eating of freshwater fish by that time, which was July 1970, the *National Observer* pointed out that between 1953 and 1960 some 110 Japanese citizens had been killed or disabled from eating fish taken near the outlet of a large plastics plant in Minamata, Japan.[44]

Time magazine enlarged upon the scare theme in late August by quoting HEW statistics that some 900,000 Americans were drinking water which contained arsenic, lead, selenium, and fecal bacteria. Vermont was singled out as one state which was deficient in water treatment services, and Cincinnati, Charleston, College Park (S.C.), Long Island, and portions of California were listed as urban areas which needed an upgrading of sewage treatment facilities.[45]

In that same dreadful summer of discontent, the establishment press rediscovered the dangers of polluted air. The *National Observer* carried the National Air Pollution Control listings, and pointed out that New York City air was high in sulphur oxide content which, it was added, has a facility for eating into clothing, buildings, and statues. Chicago, Pittsburgh, and a host of major and minor cities appeared to offer their own specialities in air pollution. At the same time, the *Observer* categorized smog as consisting of three types—photochemical smog, sulphur dioxide, and "just plain ashes and soot."[46]

Other bastions of the establishment press entered the ecological fray. The *Saturday Review* carried a piece on the erosion of "Eden," which seemed to build upon the notion that pollution was pushing Hawaii into the sea. *Look,* in the very same month, got into varying aspects of pollution and conservation with an article on the national park system. Vandalism, pilfering, overuse, and the presence of nature-loving junkies had almost eliminated the pleasure aspects of the national playgrounds.

On the issue of strip mining, which had so concerned much of the media over the previous ten years, it should be remembered that some areas that had been blitzed by the great earth movers did offer surprising financial and recreational gain in due time. In west central Illinois, for instance, some of the scarred land grew back as heavily populated game reserves. Great numbers of strip mining gouges were dammed at either end and became in time wonderful fishing spots, especially for largemouth bass and northern pike. In the early 1970s a unique experiment was underway, with the City of Chicago contracting with one county for the right to dump treated effluent on the mined-over land. One could say, as the decade reached near the halfway mark, that the land had become more fertile, more productive of game, and open to game fishing than it had been when occupied by the Peoria Indians.[47] Unfortunately these were developments never mentioned in the *National Observer*'s July 1970 blast against strip mining in Kentucky.

One of the more interesting pieces dealing with pollution appeared in the *New York Times* before the end of 1970. In an Op Ed article written by Dr. Edgar Berman, it was pointed out that there was a kind of people pollution:

> The ultimate necessity of legislation and guidelines for a strong population policy must be faced. Elected officials can no longer evade debating the ideologic issue of whether the individual right to procreate, to the detriment of society, is a basic human right and a fundamental freedom and whether it can be legally halted without damaging the fabric of freedom.[48]

The article was a kind of milestone in illustrating how far liberalism had come. Was the American left about to embrace the very essence of George Orwell's *1984* by advocating the federal limitation of families (and of procreation)?

Underground and radical papers were quick to seize upon every facet of the ecology issue, for of all of the decade's argumentation it alone seemed to draw wide support. The comedienne Carol Burnett closed many of her programs with an appeal for conservation and for the anti-pollution crusade. The media's talk-sit shows trotted out every wildlife expert who could be found. As with the other causes of the decade, the whole gamut of connective evils was trotted out—capitalism, genocide, death for the masses, doom, imperialism, the Third World, etc.

Most radical papers could, with little apparent effort, whip up highly documented though essentially slanted pieces upon the whole range of ecology. Few, if any, probed the real ecological situations that surrounded the lives of college newspaper editors and radical journalists, such as the overuse of automobiles by university students, the proliferation of hamburger joints and outdoor theaters over lush prairie lands, or the littering of college campuses with handbills and graffiti. In one instance a radical college newspaper in the Midwest flamed out its discontent about highway billboards—yet it remained editorially mute about the construction of a movie theater upon an idyllic piece of land. An underground paper in Texas raged mightily against those responsible for the gigantic oil spills of the 1960s and 1970s, without once referring to the economic benefits derived by a nearby university from oil royalties.

Ecology was, without question, one of the better issues for holding moderates to the radical left. A writer for the *Roosevelt Torch* in Chicago saw the ecology movement as a vast and subterranean conspiracy designed by the old to provide a "safe" issue for the young. Students and radicals would not be fooled, the writer added: they would not allow ecology to blunt the "attack that radical student groups like SDS are making against racism, imperialism, male chauvanism [sic] and the oppression of workers." But, the writer continued, the ecology movement offered radicalism a great opportunity; that of turning the country "against the polluters themselves."[49]

Other movement papers echoed the same argument. A writer for *Red Eye* of San Jose pointed out that "ecology is our newest issue." He then proclaimed: "politicians have discovered, from keeping their graspy fingers on the pulse of America, that we are poisoning our air and water, ripping the beauty from the land. . . . Ecology has even replaced Vietnam as our issue."

The same paper, a month later, offered the advice that the task for "ecological radicals" was to raise issues for "basic transformations." "This winter and spring," the writer claimed, "we can expect a series of radical ecological actions: the bombing of more corporate headquarters, sabotage to the industrial machinery that pollutes and obstruction at airports and other transportation centers."[50]

Space City of Houston presented an article which cleverly moved through word manipulation into the world of demonology. The country was being raped (a favorite word in the underground press)—"we are being murdered." Ecology proved that though man might be "manipulable," nature eventually canceled out all "human pretension to mastery over the earth." There then followed an awesome array of data about bilharzia, a disease and infestation of the body caused by bathing in the Nile. It was, somehow, all related to capitalism. The author's conclusion was forthright: "We want the World, and We Want it Now."

Bilharzia is, of course, a parasitic worm which inhabits shallow waters of the northern part of the Nile and it does bore into human skin with diresome consequences. But to connect bilharzia to American capitalism—or any capitalism—was a perfect illustration of the paranoid style. Those little worms had been in the Nile in the time of the pharoahs, and from that time to 1974 modern industrialism had truly touched Egypt but slightly.

Radical leaders were profoundly surprised by the appeal of the anti-pollution crusade. A writer for *Space City* announced his astonishment over the fact that "ecology freaks abound." It was a good holding issue, he stated, and he offered the news that "American river [sic] is polluted." Was he writing about an actual river, or all American rivers? At any rate he plodded onward in the hope of weaving ecology into the movement's goals. Ecology "enables us to locate bits and pieces of death and fit them together into a mosaic of destruction. . . ." It was suggested that smokestacks should be plugged with cement, and something should be done about the universities—those "laboratories of death technology. . . ."[51]

Later in 1970 a student writer for the *Roosevelt Torch* said ecology was only one of the major issues facing the nation. Revolution, argued the young radical, would have to be creative in its absorption of ecological problems. One method of meeting the pollution and ecology roadblocks was "to rid the earth of such folks as the Krupps and the Farbens (and the Rockefellers and the Fords) . . . remove from the earth the idea of profit from another man's labor." As to the true environmentalists—they were just laying down a liberal line: "Just because they say they're concerned about the ecology of the earth doesn't mean they really are."[52]

It was a tour de force in logic. Only within the movement was there the insight to discern the truth. Had the writer ever heard about the "Farben family"? The writer's final conclusion—that thousands of miners had been sent to their deaths by "filthy strip mines"—was sheer and consuming ignorance. The writer had obviously never seen a strip mine: work in those above-ground surroundings is relatively safe. Relatively safe, that is, by comparison to pit mines. But then who in the entire movement was there who had worked a pit mine? And what was the importance of fact?

Much of the underground and radical effort floundered wildly over the ecology movement—mainly because of a lack of real technical knowledge—and the result was to move quickly to plaintive cries of doom. *Roosevelt Torch* in April 1970 contained the pitiful whimper that "our food is poisoned—Our air is poisoned—Our water is poisoned. It is not a joke. It is nothing rhetorical. They are KILLING US."

Throughout the underground press the ecology issue was squeezed for every possible derivative value. *Motive* of Nashville pulled back the curtain on some gruesome possibilities for the future. "All sorts of things" could happen—coastal cities might have to be evacuated, and the entire food system could be disrupted. A writer for the *Rag* of Austin pointed out that five years hence (dating from January of 1970) "severe and permanent damage will gave [sic] occurred at the cost of millions of lives." It was predicted in the same newspaper some days later that the entire deer population was being wiped out by ecological change. This last was again a product of soaring and untutored minds. Deer were plentiful in most parts of the union and were, in fact, becoming a nuisance to Midwestern corn growers. In places like Minnesota the overabundance of deer was playing havoc with the food supply of other animals such as elk[53]

Underground commentary upon ecology ranged from the clever to the ridiculous. A writer to *Red Eye* in October—using the typical "they" in reference to the manipulative unseen enemy—saw the problem of mankind as resting in the greed of big "consumerists businesses." Ancient peoples were healthy until forced to big city life by rampant capitalism. *Vortex* of Lawrence, Kansas, became upset because the local authorities of Iola, a nearby town, had conducted a roundup of pests. Some 2,000 mice, 124 starlings, 38 rats, and 38 opossum (a word incidentally mispelled by the writer) had been brought in by one boy alone. *Vortex*'s contributor was distraught by the slaughter and closed with a call for "A PIG FOR GENOCIDE."[54]

One of the funniest events of the year occurred in San Jose, California. There, according to *Red Eye*, a highly instructive teach-in was held, with classes in the following subjects:

The Population Bomb
Black, Brown and White on Population
The Brown Man: A Man in Harmony With His Environment
Waste of Human Resources

Groups participating in the rites included the East Bay Sharks, Gay Liberation, Women's Liberation, Black Studies, Mexican-American Studies, and other ethnic entities. Along with the listing of the program *Red Eye* included the going prices on marijuana, acid, peyote, and hashish.

It appears to have been an exciting day. Groups of young people appeared in their shiny automobiles and participated in a ceremonial appropriately titled "The Procession and Burial of a 1970 Automobile." Once done, the students leaped into their chariots and flamed on to the next session, leaving the grounds strewn with beer cans. An "economics professor" was then heard presenting his views on the ecological problem. In an amazing display of ideological pyrotechnics he managed to tie the entire issue of pollution to the Civil War and the French Revolution. The Chavez boycott of grapes also found its way into his discourse as well as the strike of transit workers in New York City. BART, San Francisco's interesting experiment in urban transport, was then thrown into the pot along with Andrew Mellon and Lake Tahoe. The speech was concluded with a brilliant summation. "Capitalism," argued the "professor," "is a wonderland of contradictions. . . ."[55]

In all of this there was the danger of nullifying an excellent goal with sheer overstatement. Furthermore, despite all of the dangers that seemed apparent in the previous decades, there had been substantial advances for the betterment of mankind. With each step forward in Western man's attempts to lift himself from the level of mere existence, there had always been the doomsayer on hand to cry the inevitable wolf. In May 1872, for instance, *Scientific American* carried a piece on the deadly dangers present in the overuse of chemicals in water, paint, food, and enamels.[56]

Other examples of doomsaying were recorded. London newsmen complained in 1862 that the deadly and polluted rivers and skies of England would decimate the population of the country—yet London in 1973, a century later, was sparkling and bright. The terrible pollution of most major cities in the Victorian age from horse droppings may have been replaced by that of the automobile, but the drop in the cholera and typhoid rate was a happy one. In 1910 over 15,000 animal carcasses were hauled away by street cleaners in New York alone, only to be replaced by the junked automobile. Which was best for the people?

Despite the furious deluge of ecology articles in the Sixties, it was possible to say that the death rate among newborn children continued to decline in the United States. Milk was purer than it had been a hundred years before and, despite all of the inadequacies in sewage treatment, so was the water. There were atmospheric inversions in the 1960s, but these phenomena are not new. The Meuse Valley in Belgium had a terribly lethal smog in 1930 brought on by a combination of coal smoke and other factors; and Donora in Pennsylvania had experienced the exact same ordeal in 1948. St. Louis, Pittsburgh, and some other cities had, through the years, enacted some very tough laws concerning the burning of high sulphur-content coal, and all of them were infinitely cleaner as a result. Los Angeles, by banning local trash burning, had at least moved the problem of garbage from the city to the landfills.

The great hazard of doomsaying on the ecology issue was in backlash, of course. Unfortunately there was not only a great deal of sheer overstatement of environmental decay, but a substantial amount of hypocrisy. It was possible, for instance, to find more sympathy for the cracked shell of an eagle egg than for an aborted fetus of a human being—that is, in some circles. When the Eisenhower administration failed to provide aid to the Egyptians for the building of the Aswan Dam, the howl from the left was deafening. The Russians, on the other hand, were applauded for coming to the rescue and for helping in the creation of a dam which flooded some 5,000 square miles of land—an achievement which also changed the ecological structure of the Nile and which wiped out huge segments of Egyptian history. A similar act in this country would have aroused the furies.

The double standard was particularly obvious in the underground press. A Dutch tanker laden with oil and dashed against a reef off the British Isles never seemed as large as an American tanker guilty of the same navigational error. Local American industries which dumped wastes into the Great Lakes seemed far more guilty than were the scores of German or Norwegian ship captains who pumped out their ships' bilges into Lake Michigan. Perhaps it was some of these instances which brought the *New York Times* to a consideration of ecological backlash. That paper warned in 1970 that there was a "hysteria" within the ecology crusade which could possibly lead more to harm than to good.[57]

But there was hysteria everywhere in 1970, and the backlash to it would inevitably affect the believability of the environmentalists. The Santa Barbara oil spill, which came at the end of the 1960s, was pushed by the underground and overground media for all of its worth. In the end, when it was proven that little if any damage was done to the undersea life in the channel, the results probably hurt these respectable proponents of the ecology crusade. A similar scare was delivered from Alaska, where news bulletins pronounced the death of 86,000 birds from petroleum spillage. While some questioned just who in Alaska could count exactly 86,000 birds, others pushed an investigation to determine the exact nature of the causes of those deaths. Scientific investigation eventually proved that the birds had died from eating poisoned plankton. A twin incident had happened to birds in Oregon some days earlier. In both instances the blame immediately fell upon oil spills.[58]

As 1970 edged by, an increasing number of articles debunking ecological overstatement began to appear. The *National Observer* in July presented an article by a Rockhurst College professor in which it was argued that so-called population pollution was not the cause of crime, the high death rate, and foul air. Holland was adduced as a nation in which the density of population reached 1,000 people per square mile. The United States with a figure of 57 offered a startling contrast. Britain with its 50,000,000 people crowded into an area smaller than California was offered up as another example. Crime and pollution indicators seemed to prove that population—at least in Britain and Holland—did not stand as a single root to chaos.[59]

Senator Barry Goldwater followed this up with an article in the *New York Times* in December 1970, which in the main was a pitch for the passage of a bill to support the construction of the controversial supersonic air transport plane. Goldwater pointed to examples of doomsaying in the past—that an underwater A-bomb test at Bikini atoll would blow a hole in the surface of the earth, that a dam across the Colorado River would destroy Grand Canyon, and that H-bomb testing in the 1950s would lead to certain doom for humanity. Now, according to the senator, doomsayers were offering the same possibilities for the SST—that it would melt the ice caps at the poles, that all fish would be killed, that the ozone blanket around the earth would be weakened, and that SST emissions would cause skin cancer.[60]

What was needed, of course, was a sensible and rational approach to ecology. In some cases the ecological structure of the earth was actually being strengthened by scientific advances. By 1970, for instance, chinook salmon were beginning to swim once again from the Columbia River into the Willamette; the latter was a stream previously regarded as one of the nation's foulest waterways. Studies of the Connecticut River, and the effects of nuclear plant discharges into it, offered startling surprises. Despite the calefaction caused by hot water releases by the plant, in the first eleven months of its operation the river experienced increased varieties of plants and fish. Beetles, dragonflies, damselflies, and striped bass were appearing in ever increasing numbers, and some thirty-six species of fish were collected over a span of time. The only discernible negative effect of the power plant was upon catfish, which, because of the increase in the force of the river's current, were forced to swim faster and which became, as a result, smaller in size.

Studies of the Hudson River also began to turn up new developments. That river now seemed far cleaner than it had been in thirty years, and seemed to offer possibilities of complete restoration. Seventeen municipal sewage plants had been added to the megalopolitan area north along the Hudson's banks, twelve more were under construction, and thirty-three more were in the planning stage. Striped bass up to thirty pounds were being taken from the river, spot fish were showing up in larger numbers, shad and bluefish were back, weakfish were coming upstream and blue crabs had returned for several consecutive years. Some scientists were now arguing that a little sewage might be good for the Hudson—it caused the plankton to flourish and to build upon the ecological chain.[61]

The hysteria of the 1960s in respect to ecology had brought about negative as well as positive results. The enforcement of the DDT ban had worked to some degree. Bald eagles appeared at Kentucky Lake in the midlands for the first time in several years, and other elements in the bird population seemed to be coming back. One of the major reasons for the strengthening of species of certain birds was, of course, the concurrent increase in the food supply in the form of forest-killing insects. The tussock moth, now allowed to flourish unhandicapped by DDT, was wiping out huge sections of timberland in Oregon and Washington. The Douglas fir, along with White and

Grand firs, were especial targets for the tussocks. Once destroyed, the trees would require decades to replace.[62]

The truth was that by 1973 a great deal had been done to make the quality of life a little better in many places. There was actually more fresh water than ever before in history—one could see this from any low-flying plane. Public fishing lakes had doubled to twelve million acres between 1950 and 1970. Lake trout were back in Lake Michigan because of lamphrey killing techniques, and some of the best sport fishing anywhere could be found in harbor inlets of that great body of fresh water. Coho and chinook salmon had been successfully transplanted to numerous inland lakes, including Lake Michigan, and saltwater bass had been naturally reproduced in freshwater lakes in the Carolinas. Deer were a pestilence in some areas—and as for the wolf, he was alive and doing fairly well.

The United States, as it was in 1973 or 1974, was unquestionably a better place to live in than it had been in 1932. In fact, it exceeded most of the world in the proper adjustment between the quality of life and man's surroundings. In the ecological sense, what was truly needed was a rationality. Man is forced by his character to take from nature; the problem was that of balancing off man's necessities against the normal desire for affluence.

Epilogue

In the Fall of 1974 a 32-year-old "houseperson" wrote a letter to the *New York Times Magazine* in which she pointed out the gloom and doom that had prevailed over the previous decade. As she put it, first came the bomb, then cigarette smoking, the pill, auto exhaust fumes, dying oceans, fears about pollution and environment, and overpopulation. The seventies ushered in new fears—stolen A-bombs, asbestos, and the latest of terrors, the black holes in space. "Please," she begged, "next Sunday, some good news, some hope. *Please.*"

This sensitive New Jersey woman was merely illustrating one of the major problems of our days. As Daniel Boorstin wrote at the end of the Sixties, the "very instruments of education, of information and of 'progress' make it harder every day for us to keep our bearings in a larger universe." The people of the United States, partially through the increased influence of the hot medium, television, have lived in a crisis atmosphere for nearly two decades. The old arguments that a nation can become inured to such crises have not held water. Instead, the country has seen its nerve ends rubbed raw; its sensitivities so heightened that, without crisis at hand, the very moment of existence almost becomes purposeless. On these rare occasions of peace and tranquility, the usual charges from the omnipresent doomers and gloomers have been along the lines that the people have become "apathetic."

The major result of such dooming and glooming as well as the crisis atmosphere generated by the news media has been a heightened sense of national hypochondria. "The nation is sick" was the cry heard in the days following President Kennedy's assassination. "The nation is sick" was the clarion call of the reformers during the urban riots of the 1960s. The same such cries were heard during the various stages of the Vietnam War, the Kent State riots, and Watergate. Some of our public spokesmen had quite obviously lost what is absolutely necessary in the broader realm of common sense; that is, a sense of history. They had become awash in a sea of sentimental immediacy.

That is what makes the celebration of national life called the Bicentennial so very important. Americans, in general, are being encouraged to look back—not as did James Russell Lowell a century ago, when he suggested that our greatest mistake had been the American Revolution—but in the sense of attempting to understand how far the country had come since the days of its founding.

One may face the problem of escaping what Boorstin has called the "prison" of national hypochondria with several devices. That eminently fair historian has indicated the need to abandon the cult of youth—what he has called the "voguish reverence for youth and for the 'culturally deprived.'" Boorstin argues that the educational system must move away from the "relevant" and in the direction of the "cosmopolitanizing, the humanizing and the unfamiliar." He has further written: "To be really persuaded that things *can* be otherwise, we must look into the whole Historical Catalogue and see how and when and why they have actually *been* otherwise."

But a further modification of Boorstin's approach might also help. After all, the 1960s represented a giant Woodstock of doomsaying. I am quite sure that some of the people who were so eminently quotable in the Sixties would just as soon forget what they said or wrote. The greatest lesson in responsibility, however, is to be held responsible for one's statements.

In other words, Americans should not really try to forget the rhetoric and paranoia of the 1960s, but should disinter those words of doom and gloom and hold them up for spectrum analysis. Was America really sick in the 1960s? Was the country going quickly down the road to ruin? Had the nation been torn loose from its historical moorings?

The obvious answer to all three questions is, of course, that we are still here. The nation is still functioning, even after an unprecedented dismissal of both a president and a vice president. The country is still basically sound, perhaps not as sound as a dollar in the old sense of the word, but it is still mighty and prodigious. An enormous American middle class has emerged, and that in itself augurs well for future stability and development. The American laboring class—that is, the blue-collar class—has made enormous strides toward the national mean of American life. More Americans are engaged in more leisure-time activities than ever before, and that is a mark of achievement unmatched by any other nation past and present.

This does not mean that American society is without flaws, for every society has a few cracks in the plaster. The country still has its unemployed, though in that respect it is interesting to note that the estimated number of illegal immigrants now living in the U.S. almost exactly equals the unemployment percentages of 1974. The country still has its slums, but taking a realistic view one has to come to the conclusion that exact equality of wealth is really unattainable. By saying that, it is not meant that we should forget the unfortunate and the poorly educated: we must understand that the words "unfortunate" and "poorly educated" are words of comparison. Then too, the nation has still not solved the problem of the aged. Here, it is obvious that nursing homes are not the answer.

Henry L. Mencken used to argue that what any country needs is a good sense of humor. Maybe he was right, and perhaps we have lost that delightful sense of humor which used to run through our ranks. One thing is certain, however, and that is that we need far fewer doomers and gloomers. Perhaps that sounds a little presumptive, but it does seem that we need a great deal more of what the country used to call "good old American horse sense." After all, we are a free people, and it is well within our tradition to remain free. We are a virile nation who, as the French socialist Jean Revel has said, are meeting our problems head on. We are still here, which is of course the big thing—occupying some fifty states and territories—and I suspect that we will be here for a good time to come.

We have our history to tell us all of this. And we still have our history to help us when, sometime in the future, we will again hear those pitiful and self-serving cries that the world is coming to an end.

Notes

Chapter 1
Roots Far and Wide

1. More recent articles on returned American prisoners indicate that the real cultural shock over changes in American society took about three weeks to develop.

2. An interesting article reflecting a change or reversal in attitudes of former members of the movement is to be found in James Kunen's "The Rebels of '70," *New York Times Magazine*, 28 October 1973.

3. Late in 1973 there was an increasing tendency to attack the theme of "The Waltons," both in the *New York Times Magazine*, 3 October 1973, and by Pauline Kael in *The New Yorker*, 10 December 1973. Readers of the *Times Magazine* piece seemed to defend the show in the *Times Magazine* of 10 October.

4. Hugh D. Graham and Ted R. Gurr, *Violence in America: Historical and Comparative Perspectives* (New York: Bantam Books, 1969), p. 576.

5. William E. Leuchtenberg, *A Troubled Feast: American Society since 1945* (Boston: Little, Brown and Co., 1973), p. 173.

6. Representative Bella Abzug, Senator Frank Church, and Daniel Ellsberg, of "Pentagon Papers" fame, were all doves on Vietnam but strong for aid to Israel.

7. *The Manchester Guardian*, International Edition, 17 November 1973. It is titled in this manner as to differentiate it from an underground paper with a similar name.

8. Leuchtenberg, *A Troubled Feast*, p. 176.

9. Peter L. and Brigitte Berger, "The Blueing of America," *New Republic*, 3 April 1971.

10. *New York Times Magazine*, 25 October 1970.

11. John M. Blum, Edmund S. Morgan, Willie Lee Rose, Arthur M. Schlesinger, Jr., Kenneth M. Stampp, and C. Vann Woodward, *The National Experience: A History of the United States* (New York: Harcourt Brace Jovanovich, Inc., 1973). The 1968 election is discussed on p. 778; the "decade of violence" is discussed in pp. 781-89.

12. Eugene J. McCarthy, *Frontiers in American Democracy* (New York: World Publishing Co., 1960), pp. 63-70.

13. Paul Goodman's disillusionment, for example, was deep and profound. Prior to his death he wrote that he had "imagined that the world-wide protest had to do with changing political and moral institutions," but that he had come to realize the emergence of a "religious crisis of the magnitude of the Reformation in the fifteen-hundreds, when not only all institutions but all learning had been corrupted. . . ."

14. *International Herald-Tribune*, 1 June 1971.

15. Dumas Malone and Basil Rauch, *America and World Leadership, 1940-1965* (New York: Appleton-Century-Crofts, 1965), p. 262.

16. Norman Mailer, "Superman Comes to Supermarket," cited in *American Society since 1945*, ed. by William O'Neill (New York: Quadrangle, 1969), p. 21. *New York Times*, 10 January 1960.

17. Victor Navasky, "Notes on Cult," *New York Times Magazine*, 7 March 1966. Long before the appearance of Spiro Agnew on the national scene, Navasky details the existence of an "intellectual establishment."

18. "Suburbia: The New American Plurality," *Time*, 15 March 1971.

19. *U.S. News and World Report*, 4 January 1960; 26 October 1964.

20. An interesting note about university disturbances of 1970: In the early part of 1970 the Selective Service System fell 11,000 men behind in meeting draft needs, and it became obvious that the university pool of 52,000 college graduates was to be used. Many young men, especially in the "emerging universities," maintained a graduate school status in order to continue avoidance of the draft. Obviously the needs of Selective Service in 1970 had something to do with the general disturbance in the country.

21. *U.S. News and World Report*, 11 April 1960.

22. Arnold Beichman, *Nine Lies about America* (New York: Library Press, 1972).

23. *Sanity*, June, July, August, September, 1963.

24. *Ibid.*, June 1964; January 1965.

25. *U.S. News and World Report*, 21 December 1964. There is still no hard evidence of financial support to the movement from abroad.

26. *Ibid.*

27. *Ibid.*, 28 March 1960. For disturbances in New England, see same source, 9 November 1964.

28. *Ibid.*, 20 July 1970.

29. President Mathews' statement is in *National Observer*, 24 August 1970. President Miller Upton of Beloit held to his own line: "Although my own sentiments are basically with the young people, I must admit that there is a general pandering to the young at the present time that is both disgusting and irresponsible. . . ." See *U.S. News and World Report*, 15 June 1970.

30. *Saturday Review*, 10 January 1970. Miss Mead also stated: "Today, nowhere in the world are there elders who know what the children know, no matter how remote and simple the societies are in which the children live." It is a questionable statement. See also *Time*'s laudatory youth article, 17 August 1970, and its revised outlook on 17 September 1973—"The Graying of America."

31. *New York Times*, 11 October 1970.

32. Leuchtenberg's *A Troubled Feast* seems to zero in on weaknesses of college administrators during the decade.

33. *New York Times*, 11 October 1970.

34. Richard Hofstadter, *The Paranoid Style in American Politics and Other Essays* (New York: Vintage Books, 1965).

35. *Sanity*, March 1964.

36. Hofstadter, *The Paranoid Style*, p. 30.

37. *Candle*, Ann Arbor, Michigan, no. 1.

38. Hofstadter, pp. 30-32.

39. *East Village Other*, New York City, 1 May 1967.

40. Hofstadter, pp. 30-32.

41. *Connections*, Madison, Wisconsin, 1 November 1967.

42. Hofstadter, p. 4.

43. *Ibid.*, p. 38.

44. *East Village Other*, 1 September 1967.

45. *Free Student*, Los Angeles, 22 November 1967.

46. *Red Eye*, San Jose, California, 11 March 1970.

47. "Blood Echoes," *The Collected Artist's Worksheet* (Detroit: Workshop Press, 1967). The item is taken from Worksheet No. 1, originally published in 1965.

48. *The Buffalo Insighter*, Buffalo, New York, 20 November 1967. *Distant Drummer*, Philadelphia, November 1967. *Dallas Notes*, November 1967.

Chapter 2
The Ancient and Modern Art of Doomsaying

1. Daniel Leonard, *Massachusettenis* (1810), pp. 187-88, as cited in Thomas Bailey's *The American Spirit*, Vol. 1 (Lexington, Mass.: D. C. Heath and Company, 1973), p. 96.

2. Despite the rumors that the Bastille contained a great many political prisoners, the assault upon the prison produced seven inmates, two of whom were mental cases, four who were forgers, and one who, by some strange circumstance, was kept in the prison by his own family.

3. The Great Fear simply cannot be explained. It was possibly the result of literally thousands of rumors which created mass paranoia.

4. Much of the rhetoric of the French Revolution has a similarity to that of the 1960s. Saint-Just, describing the aims of the French Revolution, argued that "opulence" was a crime, that children should live together and on natural foods, and that communal living was idyllic.

5. Dexter Perkins, *The Monroe Doctrine, 1823-1826* (Cambridge, Mass.: Harvard University Press, 1927), p. 167.

6. John Graham Brooks, *As Others See Us* (New York: Macmillan, 1909), p. 31, pp. 310-15, p. 321.

7. *Edinburgh Review* 33 (1820): 78-80.

8. Quoted in Gerald E. Stearn's *Broken Image: Foreign Critiques of America* (New York: Random House, 1972), pp. 14-19.

9. Shortly after World War II, the Soviet Union reissued Dicken's *American Notes* for the Russian people.

10. Brooks, *op. cit.*, p. 241, p. 336.

11. Maxim Gorky, "The City of Mammon," *Appleton's Magazine* 8 (1906): 177-78. See also H. G. Wells, *The Future in America* (New York: Harper & Brothers, 1906). It is interesting to compare Jean Revel's *Without Marx or Jesus*, a more recent book on America by a foreign socialist.

12. Vincent Harding, "Black Radicalism: The Road from Montgomery," in *Dissent: Explorations in the History of American Radicalism*, ed. Alfred E. Young (DeKalb, Ill.: Northern Illinois University Press, 1968), p. 321.

13. Ernest van den Haag, "Mead, Another Man's Poison," *Atlantic Monthly* (June 1970), pp. 118-20.

14. From Emerson's *Complete Works*, Vol. 3 (1884), pp. 240-43.

15. *Harper's Weekly* 1 (1857), p. 642.

16. Quoted in Ari Hoogenboom, *Spoilsmen and Reformers. The Berkeley Series in American History* (Berkeley, Calif.: Rand McNally, 1964), pp. 49-50.

17. Dunne is cited in Mark Sullivan's *Our Times: Pre-War America, 1900-1925* (Chautauqua, N.Y.: Chautauqua Press, 1931), pp. 87, 93. See also Leland Baldwin, *The Flavor of the Past: Readings in American Social and Political Portraiture*, Vol. 2 (New York: American Book Company, 1969), pp. 141, 255. Walter Lippmann in the *New York Times*, 28 September 1973.

18. William L. Shirer, *The Collapse of the Third Republic* (New York: Simon and Schuster, 1969).

19. *Common Sense* 11 (May 1942), p. 160.

20. John Franklin Carter, "These Wild Young People," *Atlantic Monthly* (September 1920), pp. 301-4. T. S. Eliot is quoted in the *New York Times*, 30 March 1959.

21. Arthur Ponsonby, *Casual Observations* (London: G. Allen & Unwin, Ltd., 1930), p. 150.

22. T. Harry Williams, Richard Current, and Frank Friedel, *A History of the United States*, Vol. 2 (New York: Knopf, 1964), p. 540.

23. Rexford G. Tugwell, "The Responsibilities of Partnership," address before the Iowa State Bankers Association, Des Moines, 27 June 1934.

24. Herbert Hoover, *Campaign Speeches in 1932* (New York, 1933), pp. 191-2. See *Chicago Tribune*, 7 January 1940.

25. The quote is found in Williams, Current, and Friedel, *op. cit.*, p. 580.

26. Stevenson's acceptance speech, 1952.

27. Eisenhower was generally mocked from the left. Still, as in the case of other general-presidents in past U.S. history, the country did not fight any major wars in the Eisenhower administration.

28. There were strong attempts by educationists to throttle the Bestor book.

29. *Chicago Sunday Tribune Magazine*, 26 November 1972. See *Newsweek*, 1 March 1971; also *Time*, 10 April 1972, which points out that by 1965 Jewish families enjoyed incomes of $7,000 a year and that only 35 percent of all U.S. families were up to that level.

30. Norman Mailer, "The White Negro," in *Advertisements for Myself* (New York: G. P. Putnam, 1959), p. 312.

31. *New York Times*, 3, 4, 24 January 1960. The *Times* also predicted no big war.

32. Howard Zinn, *SNCC: The New Abolitionists* (New York: Knopf, 1965), p. 3. Quite a few entertainment figures tried to build the Chessman case into a version of the Sacco-Vanzetti affair.

33. *U.S. News and World Report*, 22 February 1960.

34. *New York Times*, 28 January 1960.

35. *Ibid.*, 23 January 1960.

36. *Ibid.*, 15, 17, 24 January 1960.

37. *Ibid.*, 6 February 1960. See also, Leuchtenburg, *A Troubled Feast*, p. 117.

38. *New York Times*, 16, 28 January 1960. *U.S. News and World Report*, 29 February 1960.

39. The Eisenhower address was delivered 18 January 1961, and is found in the *Congressional Record*, 16 February 1961, pp. 2210-11. Proxmire's statement is in the *Congressional Record*, 24 March 1969, pp. S3072-78.

40. Lord Clark's statement was printed in the *New York Times*, 7 October 1970. Clark also added that the "inheritors" of our "catastrophes look cheerful enough." He is obviously referring to the doomsayers of the 1960s.

Chapter 3
Rhetoric on the Campus

1. *New York Times*, 11 January 1971.

2. *U.S. News and World Report*, 1 February 1960.

3. *New York Times*, 11 January 1971.

4. *National Observer*, 20 July 1970.

5. *Ibid.*

6. Testimony of Bruno Bettelheim, Senate Committee on Government Operations 1969, Ninety-First Congress, First Session, *Hearings on Riots, Civil and Criminal Disorders* (Washington, D.C., 1969), pp. 3,039-3,079.

7. *New York Times*, 30 December 1970.

8. Peter Chew, "Black History or Black Mythology," *American Heritage*, August 1969.

9. Francis Russell, Tragedy in Dedham: The Story of the Sacco-Vanzetti Case (New York: McGraw-Hill, 1971).

10. Robert Maddox, *The New Left and the Origins of the Cold War* (Princeton: Princeton University Press, 1972).

11. For instance—the constant claim that George Orwell's *1984* was an anti-fascist book. Orwell wrote the book in the late stages of his life when he was a dedicated anti-Communist. The book is a statement against communism.

12. Carl Oglesby, "Cowboys and Indians," *Western Illinois Courier,* 9 October 1973. In this article Oglesby writes that Kennedy was murdered "in order to make the Vietnam War." Eight years earlier he had written: "The original commitment in Vietnam was made by President Truman. . . ."

13. Mitchell Cohen and Dennis Hale, *The New Student Left* (Boston: Beacon Press, 1966), pp. 9-13. Kirk's speech is in Charles Yost, *The Age of Triumph and Frustration: Modern Dialogues* (New York: R. Speller, 1964).

14. Joan Didier has described Berkeley in palmier days. See *Life,* 5 June 1970.

15. Carl Davidson, "The New Radicals and the Multiversity," reprinted in *The New Left: A Documentary History* (New York: The Bobbs-Merrill Company, 1969), pp. 323-335, passim. The last was edited by Massimo Teodori.

16. Dave Dellinger, *Revolutionary Nonviolence* (Garden City, N.Y.: Doubleday, 1971), p. 71.

17. Fred Hechinger in the *National Observer,* 14 July 1973.

18. Robert Conquest, "The American Psychodrama Called Everyone Hates Us," *New York Times Magazine,* 10 May 1970.

19. As quoted in Benjamin DeMott, *Surviving the 70s* (New York: E. P. Dutton & Company, 1971), pp. 75-77.

20. *Ibid.,* pp. 104-105. *The Trumpet,* Goleta, Cal., June 1970. On student left communications *New Left Notes* of Chicago indicated as early as 6 May 1966 that a grid of shortwave operators was being set up. *Saturday Review,* 30 May 1970 in "A Listening Ear" points out the existence of a "radio network" with stations at Brandeis, California, Western Reserve, Vanderbilt, and NYU.

21. *Studies on the Left,* II, 1.

22. *Beyond Berkeley,* ed. by Christopher G. Katope and Paul G. Zolbrod (New York: Harper & Row, 1966), p. 271.

23. *Sanity,* Toronto and Montreal, January, April, 1965; June 1964.

24. Oglesby's speech is reprinted in Teodori's book *The New Left,* pp. 182-188. The citations here are from pp. 185-187.

25. *New Left Notes,* Chicago, 4 March 1966. *The Fifth Estate,* Detroit, 14 November, 15 December 1966.

26. *Berkeley Barb,* 14 October, 18 November 1966.

27. *New Left Notes,* 18 February 1966. *Berkeley Barb,* 11 February 1966.

28. *Time,* 15 June 1970.

29. *The Fifth Estate,* 15 November 1966.

30. *The New Left,* Teodori, p. 68.

31. *East Village Other*, New York, 13 March 1967. This is a very interesting citation in view of the post-Watergate mood, when many underground and campus papers began to claim "see, we were right all along." *The Western Courier*, 14 January 1974, for instance, says: "Frank Zappa told us a long time ago about Suzie Creamcheese, the Brain police, centerville, plastic people. . . ."

32. Raymond Mungo, *Resist*, Palo Alto, Cal., April 1968. Teodori describes Mungo as a former student of Boston University, a founder of the Liberation News Service and a "draft resister."

33. Kenneth Keniston, "Morality, Violence, and Student Protest," *Motive*, Nashville, March 1970.

34. *New York Times*, 6 November 1970.

35. Lawrence J. Dessner, *Journal of Popular Culture*, Winter 1971, pp. 769-776.

36. *Red Eye*, San Jose, 4 June 1970.

37. *The Roosevelt Torch*, 18 May 1970.

38. *Vortex*, Lawrence, Kansas, 29 April, 12 May 1970.

39. *Space City*, Houston, 11 April, 24 April 1970.

40. *New York Times*, 8 October 1970. *The Courier*, Macomb, Ill., 27 May 1970.

41. *Red Mole*, London, March 1970.

42. As indicated in Beichman's *Nine Lies About America*, pp. 68-69.

43. *The Western Courier*, 27 May 1970.

44. *Knox Now*, February 1970.

45. *Red Eye*, 26 February 1970.

46. *New York Times*, 20 December 1970.

47. *Ibid.*, 27 June 1970.

48. Stone is quoted in *New York Times*, 23 May 1970. Reston is from the same paper shortly thereafter—31 May 1970.

49. *The Roosevelt Torch*, 23 February 1970. *Western Courier*, 27 May 1970.

50. *New York Times*, 7 June, 28 October 1970.

51. *Ibid.*, 7 June 1970.

52. *Ibid.*, 8 May 1970.

53. *Ibid.*, 8 October 1970. *Western Courier*, 27 May 1970. *Red Eye*, 4 June 1970.

54. *Southern Illinois University News to Alumni*, June 1970. *National Observer*, 31 August 1970.

55. Amitai Etzioni, "Lunch with 3 Prospective Bombers," *Wall Street Journal*, 27 October 1970. An interesting theory of Prof. Henry Silverman of Michigan State University suggests that tendencies to radicalism are often passed from generation to generation.

56. *Time*, 15 June 1970. Mrs. Smith had a tough time with the press thereafter and was beaten in her reelection bid in 1972.

57. *The Roosevelt Torch*, 23 February 1970. *New York Times*, 14 November, 28 October 1970.

58. *U.S. News and World Report*, 22 June 1970.

59. *New York Times*, 11 March 1970, 29 June 1970.

Chapter 4
The Education of the University Establishment

1. Cited in *Good Things About America Today*, published by *U.S. News and World Report*, Washington, D.C., pp. 55-81, passim.

2. *U.S. News and World Report*, 13 June 1960.

3. John K. Galbraith, *The New Industrial State* (New York: Houghton-Mifflin, 1967), pp. 282-292.

4. The word "Chicano" is usually applicable to individuals of Mexican origin who were born to parents having American citizenship.

5. Charles Palmer, as quoted in *U.S. News and World Report*, 15 June 1970, states: "The trouble seems to come from the in-between teachers who are trying to make a name for themselves." My own experience is that many of these people were not necessarily good teachers or researchers, but that they were extremely good politicians who hammered university administrators into concessions in terms of pay raises or promotions.

6. Buell G. Gallagher, quoted in *U.S. News and World Report*, 29 March 1965.

7. *New York Times*, 10 October 1970.

8. This is not to say that rationalism had completely disappeared. Sidney Hook and Daniel Boorstin were evidence that rationalism still existed on the university campus.

9. *U.S. News and World Report*, 15 June 1970.

10. Robert Nisbet, "Who Killed the Student Revolution?" *Encounter*, February 1970.

11. *Ibid.*, See also *National Observer*, 20 July 1970.

12. Richard Todd, "Voices of Harvard '70," *New York Times Magazine*, 7 June 1970, pp. 26-79, passim.

13. *New York Times*, 31 July 1970. *Chicago Tribune*, 11 December 1970. See also *New York Times* for 5 August 1970.

14. *Ibid.*, 5 May 1970.

15. *Ibid.*, 2 May 1970.

16. *The International Times*, 27 February 1967. *New York Times*, 31 December 1970.

17. The rumor was everywhere. Moynihan's discussion of it is in the *New York Times*, 7 June 1972.

18. *Ibid.*, 3 May 1970. It was strange indeed that when the Communist forces fired rockets indiscriminately into civilian areas, there was little or no condemnation of the act from the American left.

19. *Ibid.*, 8 May 1970. *The Roosevelt Torch*, 14 September 1970.

20. *New York Times*, 14 May 1970. *U.S. News and World Report*, 15 June 1970.

21. Most major universities had this problem. In Europe the same conditions seem to have existed as well. *The International Times*, 16 June 1967, reported on "Young kids fleeing approved schools, authoritarian parents, hanging around the Tube stations, seeking a place to sleep in empty rooms in condemned houses, some shooting Preludin, becoming physical wrecks." The reference was mainly to Scandinavia.

22. *Time*, 6 July 1970.

23. I heard this at the height of the 1970 troubles.

24. *Time*, 6 July 1970.

25. *Saturday Review*, 10 January 1970, contains an article entitled "Participation is Learning," by Robert S. Powell, Jr. He criticizes "uninspirable" teaching. Lewis Mayhew, Stanford, was quoted by *U.S. News and World Report*, 15 June 1970, as saying: "Too many faculty members have insisted on their own academic freedom but have been careless about the student's right to question, criticize or dissent." See also *The Roosevelt Torch*, 18 May 1970.

26. *U.S. News and World Report*, 15 June 1970; *Time*, 22 June 1970.

27. Rowland Evans and Robert Novak, "Campus Hysteria Wanes," *Peoria Journal-Star*, 28 September 1970.

28. *Newsweek*, 6 July 1970.

29. *New York Times*, 16 July 1970.

30. Interview with William Dyke, *U.S. News and World Report*, 5 October 1970.

31. *New York Times*, 17 October 1970.

32. *U.S. News and World Report*, 29 June 1970.

33. *Ibid.*, 22 June 1970; *New York Times*, 10 September 1970.

34. *Ibid.*, 6 October 1970.

35. See two articles appearing in *A.A.U.P. Bulletin*, December 1973. They are "On Institutional Neutrality Revisited," by John F. A. Taylor, and "The Undergraduate Curriculum: What Did We Do To It," by Ronald Wendling.

Chapter 5
The Intellectual-Media Establishment

1. Beers is cited in an editorial in the *National Observer*, 20 July 1970. The *Observer* further states: "Television has become a political power unto itself, a Fifth Estate that can influence public opinion as no other element in our society." I would like to add that any deep investigation of television corporate holdings would also indicate an enormous financial power as well. Dale Minor, in *The Information War*, published in 1970, gives the example of RCA which bought NBC in 1926, later purchased Random House (which had previously bought Alfred A. Knopf). CBS was the parent company to Holt, Rinehart and Winston, while ABC merged with ITT in 1967.

2. Quoted in *National Observer*, 20 July 1970.

3. Comment by Ralph Oder, New School for Social Research, *New York Times*, 25 January 1960.

4. Sidney Hyman, "The Failure of the Eisenhower Presidency," *The Progressive*, May 1960. Hyman appeared thirteen years later on an ABC "in depth" program, his comments sounding much like those of the earlier period. This time they were about the United States in 1973.

5. Hofstadter, *The Paranoid Style*, p. 7.

6. Quoted in *New York Times*, 28 September 1973. Lippmann's views had changed with the times. Regarding the relocation of Japanese-Americans

in 1942, Lippmann wrote: "Nobody's constitutional rights include the right to reside and do business on a battlefield. . . . There is plenty of room elsewhere for him to exercise his rights." This statement comes from Edward N. Barnhard and Floyd W. Matson, *Prejudice, War and the Constitution* (Berkeley: University of California Press, 1954), pp. 75, 77, 80, 86-87, 110, 350.

7. *U.S. News and World Report*, 8 February 1960. Nicola Chiaromonte, "The Will to Question," *Encounter*, 1953.

8. *U.S. News and World Report*, 2 May 1960.

9. *National Observer*, 29 December 1973.

10. *Time*, 8 June 1970.

11. Edward J. Epstein, "The Panthers and the Police: A Pattern of Genocide?" *New Yorker*, 13 February 1971.

12. Minor, *The Information War* (New York: Hawthorn Books, 1970), p. 154. Minor discusses a number of faked news items. James Keogh, *President Nixon and the Press* (New York: Funk and Wagnalls, 1972), also contains material of this type. I heard Sander Vanocur's comment and noted it instantly. The account of the Fort Worth case was broadcast on WBBM, Chicago, 5 September 1970.

13. Alan Adelson, "Too Big to Fight," *Saturday Review*, 14 March 1970. See also: *Time*, 8 June 1970, and *Newsweek*, 9 November 1970. *National Observer* covers topic on 6 July 1970.

14. Tom Wolfe's foreword is to Arnold Beichman's *Nine Lies About America* (New York: The Library Press, 1972).

15. *National Observer*, 6 October 1970.

16. *New York Times*, 2 June 1970.

17. *National Observer*, 20 July 1970. *Sanity*, June 1964.

18. Hirschman is quoted in *New York Times*, 8 October 1970. *Red Eye*, San Jose, Calif., 4 June 1970.

19. Up to August 1966 the total number of blacks killed in Vietnam amounted to 14 percent of all American dead. The total number of blacks in Vietnam in the same months was 21,519, considerably less than *Red Eye*'s 37 percent. See *U.S. News and World Report*, 15 August 1966.

20. Norman Cousins, "The Intermediate Battlefield," *Saturday Review*, 8 November 1969.

21. *Space City*, Houston, 11 April 1970.

22. *New York Times*, 2 May 1970.

23. *Ibid.*, 3 May 1970.

24. *Ibid.*, 5 May 1970. See also *Times*, 7 May 1970.

25. *Ibid.*, 7 May 1970.

26. *Ibid.*, 1, 8 May 1970.

27. *Ibid.*, 17 May 1970. On 10 May Reston seemed to be implying that some 17 million in the American university community were involved in the demonstrations.

28. *Ibid.*, 27 July 1970. Henry Steele Commager, "Is Freedom Dying in America?," *Look*, 14 July 1970. Commager was not optimistic.

29. This was an impression I received from watching Hugh Downs on his *Today* show, NBC, 30 July 1970. Hesburgh is quoted in *New York Times*, 9 May 1970.

30. *Ibid.*, 3 October 1970. See also *Times* for 6 December 1970.

31. Tom Wicker in *Times*, 6 October 1970. Green is quoted from *New York Times Magazine*, 18 October 1970.

32. *Ibid.*, 7 October 1970.

33. *Ibid.*, 25 December 1970. Wicker in the *Times*, 22 December 1970. See also *Motive*, Nashville, March 1970 for an interesting piece on poverty in America which has students grubbing through garbage cans for food.

34. Robert Conquest, "The American Psychodrama Called Everyone Hates Us," *New York Times Magazine*, 10 May 1970.

35. *Ibid.*, 17 May 1970.

36. Fred Hechinger in *National Observer*, 14 July 1973.

37. *Ibid.* I heard George Frazier on CBS Morning News, 28 September 1973.

38. Richard Goodwin, "Sources of the Public Unhappiness," *New Yorker*, 4 January 1969.

39. *New York Times*, 12 September 1973.

40. *Saturday Review*, 30 May 1970.

41. See "Campus Radicalism," *Christian Crusade*, 1 July 1970. *Times*, 6 July 1970.

42. Ayn Rand, quoted in *New York Times Magazine*, 17 May 1970.

43. Daniel Boorstin in *Newsweek*, 6 July 1970.

44. James A. Michener, *The Quality of Life* (New York: J. B. Lippincott, 1970).

45. Henry Fairlie, "Common Denominator, High and Low," *New York Times*, 31 December 1973.

46. *Ibid.*, 7 November 1970.

47. *Ibid.*, 13 July 1970. Dunne is quoted in Mark Sullivan's *Our Times: Pre-War America*, p. 429.

48. "Joe Kelly Has Reached His Boiling Point," *New York Times Magazine*, 28 June 1970.

Chapter 6
The Underground Press and Days of Doom

1. *Guide to Underground Newspapers in the Special Collections Department*, compiled by R. Siefer and J. Simmons (Evanston, Ill.: Northwestern University Library, 1971), pp. 9-10.

2. *Ibid.*, p. 15.

3. *Ibid.*, pp. 19-42, passim.

4. Jewish over-representation in the movement worried many leaders of that ethnic group in America.

5. *The Berkeley Barb*, 11 February 1966. Underground newspapers were always at a loss in dealing with Communist acts of repression. Rarely, if ever, did they refer to Communist slave camps, the Katyn Forest, or Solzhenitsyn.

6. *Resurrection*, Tucson, June 1970. The *New York Times*, 28 October 1970.

7. *Berkeley Barb*, 23 June 1967. *Buffalo Chips*, Omaha, 1 December 1967. See also *Berkeley Barb* for 16 October 1967.

8. *Avatar*, Boston, 7 July 1967.

9. *Berkeley Barb*, September (n.d.) 1965. Clearing houses were often listed in special underground papers such as *Vocations for Social Change*, Canyon, Calif.

10. Some special campaigns—the "free Angela Davis" crusade or the "free Joan Bird" campaign. A good example of this material can be found in the feminist publication, *Off Our Backs*, 30 May 1970.

11. *Vortex*, 29 April, 12 May, 1970. *The Rag*, Austin, 27 January 1970. *Georgia Straight*, 8 September 1967.

12. *Berkeley Barb*, 13 May 1966.

13. *The Buddhist Oracle* (n.d.), 1967.

14. *Berkeley Barb*, 11 March 1965, 15 April 1966.

15. Robert Conquest, the British writer, has estimated that twice as many people died in Russian prison camps than in Nazi concentration camps.

16. *Berkeley Barb*, 9 June 1967. Exaggeration was standard procedure in underground papers when referring to poverty in the United States.

17. *Berkeley Barb*, 19 August 1966.

18. *Red Eye*, San Jose, California, 21 May 1970. *Rising Up Angry*, Spring 1970.

19. *The Militant*, London, 29 January 1968.

20. *Berkeley Barb*, 12 May 1967. *Nashville Breakdown*, Vol. I, No. 2. *Vortex*, 4 February 1970.

21. *Red Eye*, 23 April 1970. *Resurrection*, Tucson, 31 August 1970.

22. Hofstadter, *The Paranoid Style in American Politics*, p. 29.

23. *Space City*, Houston, 20 December 1970. *The Rag*, Austin, Vol. 4, No. 9, quoting from *Dock of the Bay* and *Old Mole*.

24. *Vortex*, 18 February, 3 May 1970.

25. *Space City*, 14 February 1970.

26. *The New York High School Free Press*, as quoted by *Space City*, 14 February 1970.

27. *The Paper*, Mendocino, Calif., June 1966. *The Mother Earth News*, citing *The Freedom Way*, a publication written by Victor Croley, 1970.

28. *Vortex*, 15 April 1970. See same paper for issues: 29 April, 12 May 1970.

29. Hofstadter, *Paranoid Style*, p. 32. *Vocations for Social Change* (n.d.). *Quicksilver Times*, as quoted in *Nashville Breakdown*, Vol. I, No. 3.

30. *Avatar*, Boston, 21 July, 4 August 1967. *Berkeley Barb*, 30 June 1967.

31. *The International Times*, 27 February, 16 June 1967. Also 31 August 1967.

32. LNS dispatch to *Vortex*, 4 February 1970. See *Vortex*, 4, 18 February 1970.

33. *New York Times*, 23 May 1970.

34. *Ibid.*, 21 May 1970.

35. *Red Eye*, 4 June 1970. *New York Times*, 18 June 1970.

36. *Space City*, 6 June 1970. *Nashville Breakdown*, Vol. 1, No. 1. I do not recall seeing any recantation by any underground papers after Epstein's article.

37. *New York Times*, 24 June 1970. See *Times* also for 5, 20 December 1970.
38. *Ibid.*, 8 October, 10 November 1970.
39. *Ibid.*, 14 November 1970. *Red Eye*, 12 November 1970.
40. *Georgia Straight*, 8 September 1967.
41. *Berkeley Barb*, 27 January 1967.
42. *Space City*, 9 May 1970.
43. *New York Times*, 3 May 1970.
44. *Space City*, 14 February 1970, citing article from *The Open Door*.
45. *Resurrection*, 5 November 1970. *The International Times*, 30 January 1967.
46. *Berkeley Barb*, 16, 23 June 1967.
47. *Ibid.*, 7 April, 15 September 1967. *The Fifth Estate*, 15 December 1967.

Chapter 7
Two Presidents and Middle America

1. *Sanity*, October 1963.
2. *U.S. News and World Report*, 30 November 1964. Charges of psychological instability were leveled against Senator Goldwater in 1964. During the Watergate crisis of 1973 almost every action of President Nixon was scrutinized by some for signs of mental stress, and much was made by the press of the shoving of an aide by the President. Very little was written by the liberal press in regard to President Johnson's personal idiosyncrasies.
3. *Sanity*, December 1964.
4. *Berkeley Barb*, 2 June 1967. *The Fifth Estate*, 15 December 1967.
5. LNS report printed in *Red Eye*, 12 February 1970. *Haight-Ashbury Tribune* (Free Press), n.d. *East Village Other*, 1 May 1967.
6. A review of *MacBird* is found in *Berkeley Barb*, 18 March 1966. See also issues of same paper, 21, 27 April 1967. A similar instance emerged in the first years of the Nixon administration with the film *Millhouse*, a collection of film clips.
7. *Ibid.*, 9 June 1967.
8. *Ibid.*, quoting *Free Press*.
9. *Ibid.*
10. *Ibid.*, 23 June, 16 October 1967.
11. *Ibid.*, 7 July 1967.
12. *Avatar*, 21 July, 4 August 1967. *Berkeley Barb*, 7 July 1967.
13. *Space City*, 17 January 1970.
14. *Rising Up Angry*, Spring 1970.
15. LNS dispatch, printed in *Resurrection*, June 1970.
16. *Off Our Backs*, 19 March 1970. *Rising Up Angry*, Summer 1970. Dick Gregory is quoted in *Red Eye*, 12 March 1970.
17. Some of the violence of these days is cataloged in the *U.S. News and World Report*, 29 June 1970. Dellinger is quoted in *Western Courier*, Macomb, Illinois, 27 May 1970. See also *New York Times*, 1 May 1970.
18. *New York Times*, 2 May 1970.

19. The almost deliberate misquoting of President Nixon is handled in James Keogh's *President Nixon and the Press* (New York: Funk and Wagnalls, 1972), pp. 59-60.

20. The establishment newspapers are quoted by *New York Times*, 2 May 1970. See also *The Roosevelt Torch*, 18 May 1970.

21. *New York Times*, 6, 7, 8 May 1970. *The Roosevelt Torch*, 18 May 1970.

22. Anthony Lewis in the *New York Times*, 23 May 1970. Rhodes is quoted by same paper, 8 October 1970. *Chicago Tribune*, 17 August 1970.

23. *The Trumpet*, 4 July 1970. *Resurrection*, 5 November 1970. See also issue of last named paper, December (n.d.) 1970.

24. *The Black Panther*, as quoted in *Rising Up Angry*, Summer 1970.

25. The list is condensed from the *Rolling Stone*, 11 June 1970.

26. Rubin's statement is quoted in *New York Times*, 23 May 1970. *The Roosevelt Torch*, 11 May 1970.

27. John Roche, "On Being an Unfashionable Professor," *The New York Times Magazine*, 18 October 1970. *Resurrection*, 24 July 1970.

28. *Vortex*, December 1970.

29. *New York Times*, 3, 7, 20 November 1970. Mary McGrory's column appeared in the *Peoria Journal*, 8 November 1970.

30. *Chicago Daily News*, 20 July 1970.

31. Mark Sullivan, *Our Times: The United States, 1900-1925* (Chautauqua, N.Y.: The Chautauqua Press, 1931), p. 350.

32. Peter Schrag, "Is Main Street Still There?," *Saturday Review*, 17 January 1970, pp. 20-25.

33. Wallace Roberts, "No Place to Grow," *Saturday Review*, 21 March 1970; Peter Schrag, "Out of Place in America," *ibid.*, 9 May 1970, pp. 12-49.

34. *New York Times*, 30 June 1970.

35. *Ibid.*

36. *Time*, 13 June 1970.

37. *Ibid.*, 6 July 1970. *New York Times*, 3 July 1970. The *Times* could have mentioned that the Midwest has produced writers such as Willa Cather, Richard Wright, Wright Morris, J. F. Powers, Nelson Algren, Kurt Vonnegut, Jr., Tennessee Williams, Saul Bellows, Ernest Hemingway, and a host of others. Also that the Chicago Symphony Orchestra is probably the best in the world.

38. Kraft's column was syndicated and published in the week of 9 July 1970. See also *Newsweek*, 6 July 1970.

39. *National Observer*, 13 July 1970.

40. *New York Times*, 6 July 1970.

41. Richard M. Scammon and Ben J. Wattenberg, *The Real Majority: An Extraordinary Examination of the American Electorate* (New York: Coward-McCann, 1970).

42. *New York Times*, 4 October 1970. Actually unemployment in 1970 was far less than what it was during the Kennedy administration.

43. *Ibid.*, 28 October; 4, 5 November 1970.

44. As quoted by Jeffrey St. John in the *New York Times*, 10 October 1970.

45. Jon R. Waltz, "The Burger-Blackmun Court," *New York Times Magazine*, 6 December 1970.

46. Mailer is quoted in *Time*, 8 February 1971.

Chapter 8
Rhetoric and Causes in the Sixties

1. The quotation is from King's "I have a dream" speech made in Washington on 28 August 1963. Carmichael's quote is from an essay on "Black Power" printed in the *New York Times*, 5 August 1966.

2. A "platform" written in 1966 and which for years appeared in every issue of the organization newspaper.

3. Don A. Schanche, "Panthers Against the Wall," *The Atlantic*, May 1970, pp. 56-61.

4. *New York Times*, 5 August 1966.

5. *Ibid.* I once heard a university professor use the term "institutional slavery for 1,000 years" in relation to blacks in America.

6. *Ibid.*

7. Hofstadter, *Paranoid Style*, p. 37.

8. Carmichael is quoted by LNS in *Berkeley Barb*, 1 September 1967. As to black participation in military conflict engaged in by the U.S., the actual contribution of the race has varied according to the particular war. In every case it can be said that the black contribution was *not* the major one.

9. Hofstadter, *Paranoid Style*, pp. 31-32.

10. *The Militant*, London, 8 January 1968.

11. Forman is quoted in *The Militant*, 1 January 1968. The cleric was the Rev. Lawrence El Lucas, Church of the Resurrection in Harlem, quoted in *New York Times*, 22 December 1970. Harding and Strickland appear in the *Times*, 23 December 1970.

12. *Berkeley Barb*, 24 March 1967.

13. *Rising Up Angry*, Summer 1970. *The Rag*, n.d.

14. *Rising Up Angry*, Midwinter 1970. *New York Times*, 14 August 1970. *Resurrection*, 24 July 1970. A political prisoner seems to have been any black in prison.

15. *Red Notes*, May-June 1970. The leftist assault upon American "repression" was intense in European papers.

16. *Red Notes*, n.d., a flyer mailed to some 700 organizations and which was entitled AGITPROP INFORMATION. *Rising Up Angry*, Summer 1970. *Vortex*, 29 April 1970.

17. *Rising Up Angry*, Spring 1970. *Resurrection*, 7 July 1970.

18. Brown is quoted in LNS dispatch, *Avatar*, No. 14, 1967. *New York Times*, 8 May 1970.

19. Todd Gitlin, "The Dynamics of the New Left," *Motive*, November 1970.

20. The same can be said of other groups. Scores of Chinese enter the U.S. illegally every month. New York City's Hispanic-American population contains great numbers of illegally entered Trinidadians, Haitians, and Colombians. Chicago has large numbers of illegally entered Mexicans. See *U.S. News and World Report*, 13 July 1970.

21. *New York Times*, 5 August 1966.

22. *Resurrection*, 31 August 1970. *Vortex*, 18 February 1970.

23. The Weatherman statement was submitted to the SDS Convention in June 1969. It appeared in *New Left Notes*, Vol. IV, 18 June 1969. *Space*

City, 14 February 1970, contains relevant information on the subject. In an article entitled "No Mañanas for Today's Chicanos," *Saturday Review*, 14 March 1970, John Rechy writes feelingly of three dozen Mexican workers locked in a windowless truck, and of how some of them suffocated. One obtains the impression that this is all due to the "wave of official terror" unleashed by the Border Patrol. Actually these were illegal immigrants; they were *locked* in a windowless truck to avoid detection. See also *Resurrection*, 7 July 1970, which writes of Puerto Ricans being slaughtered in New York by capitalism.

24. *Resurrection*, 31 August 1970. Peritonitis may derive from puerpural fever, but it also can be sexually impartial, occasionally resulting from appendicitis.

25. *Off Our Backs*, 8 November 1970.

26. *Resurrection*, 24 July 1970.

27. *New York Times*, 22 December 1970.

28. *Off Our Backs*, 27 February 1970. I knew "Mother" Jones in the sense that I grew up near her home. From what I knew of her, she would have died a premature death laughing at certain aspects of women's liberation. Her consuming interest was in bettering the lot of American coal miners (all male).

29. *Ibid.*, 19 March 1970. Ms. Devlin, in receiving the key to New York City from Mayor Lindsay, had returned the key to the "people" to whom the city belonged—"the poor and the black. . . ." See also, *Off Our Backs*, 14 December 1970.

30. *Ibid.*, 8 November 1970.

31. *Ibid.*

32. *Ibid.*, 27 February 1970. *Resurrection*, 15 September 1970.

33. *Off Our Backs*, 31 July, 19 March 1970.

34. *New York Times*, cited in *U.S. News and World Report*, 5 October 1964.

35. An interesting article on Jensen appeared in *Life*, 12 June 1970. See also *New York Times*, 13 July 1970.

36. *Ibid.*, 30 June 1970. There had been earlier racial violence between Jews and blacks during the mid-1960s. Many Jewish-owned businesses and stores had been burned and sacked during the riots of the decade.

37. *New York Times*, 24 July 1970. *Chicago Tribune*, 24 July 1970. See also the *National Observer*, 13 July 1970.

38. Robert Claiborne, *Climate, Man, and History* (New York: W. W. Norton & Company, 1970).

39. *U.S. News and World Report*, 28 December 1964.

40. *New York Times*, 29 September 1973.

41. See *The Alternative*, March 1973.

42. Norman D. Newell, "Crises in the History of Life," *Scientific American*, February 1963. Reprint published by W. H. Freeman and Company, San Francisco, 1963.

43. *Saturday Review*, 3 January 1970, an article entitled "Priorities For the Seventies," pp. 17-19, 84. C. L. Sulzberger, "Foreign Affairs: The Logic of Destruction," *New York Times*, 10 May 1970.

44. *New York Times*, 9 July 1970. See same paper for 15 July, and the *National Observer*, 13 July 1970.

45. *Time*, 31 August 1970.

46. *National Observer*, 10, 3 August 1970.

47. "The Erosion of Eden," *Saturday Review*, 6 June 1970. "How to Wreck a National Park," *Look*, 16 June 1970. *National Observer*, 20 July 1970.

48. Edgar Berman, "We Must Limit Families by Law," *New York Times*, 15 December 1970.

49. *Roosevelt Torch*, 16 February 1970.

50. *Red Eye*, 29 January, 12 February 1970.

51. *Space City*, 17 January 1970.

52. *Roosevelt Torch*, 18 May 1970.

53. *Ibid.*, 20 April 1970. *Motive*, April 1970. *The Rag*, 27 January 1970.

54. *Red Eye*, 15 October 1970. *Vortex*, 4 February 1970.

55. *Red Eye*, 29 January, 26 February 1970.

56. *Scientific American*, May 1872.

57. Walsh McDermott, "Air Pollution and Public Health," *Scientific American*, October 1961. Reprint issued by W. H. Freeman and Company, San Francisco, 1961. See also the *New York Times*, 4 May 1970. One interesting comment not yet proven out: In 1973 the highly respected liberal David Lilienthal, on CBS's *Morning News*, indicated that he did not think Vietnam's productive capacity had been damaged by the American use of defoliants.

58. *New York Times*, 2 May 1970.

59. Thomas Jermann, "It's Time to Defuse Population Explosionists," *National Observer*, 27 July 1970.

60. On Op Ed page, *New York Times*, 16 December 1970.

61. *Ibid.* I sailed on the Ohio and Hudson Rivers in 1943 and 1944. Conditions are vastly improved now over what they were then.

62. *National Observer*, 15 September 1973.

Bibliography

Books

Bailey, Thomas. *The American Spirit*. Vols. I and II. Lexington, Mass.: D. C. Heath and Company, 1973.

Baldwin, Leland. *The Flavor of the Past: Reading in American Social and Political Portraiture*. Vols. I and II. New York: American Book Company, 1969.

Beichman, Arnold. *Nine Lies About America*. New York: Library Press, 1972.

Blum, John M.; Morgan, Edmund S.; Rose, Willie Dee; Schlesinger, Arthur M. Jr.; Stampp, Kenneth M.; Woodward, C. Vann. *The National Experience: A History of the United States*. New York: Harcourt Brace Jovanovich, 1973.

Brooks, John Graham. *As Others See Us*. New York: Macmillan, 1909.

Claiborne, Robert. *Climate, Man, and History*. New York: W. W. Norton and Company, 1970.

Cohen, Mitchell and Hale, Dennis. *The New Student Left*. Boston: Beacon Press, 1966.

Dellinger, Dave. *Revolutionary Nonviolence*. Garden City, N.Y.: Doubleday, 1971.

DeMott, Benjamin. *Surviving the Seventies*. New York: E. P. Dutton & Company, 1971.

Galbraith, John K. *The New Industrial State*. New York: Houghton Mifflin, 1967.

Good Things About the U.S. Today. Washington, D.C.: U.S. News and World Report, 1970.

Graham, Hugh D., and Gurr, Red R. *Violence in America: Historical and Comparative Perspectives*. New York: Bantam Books, 1969.

Hofstadter, Richard. *The Paranoid Style in American Politics and Other Essays*. New York: Vintage Books, 1965.

Hoogenboom, Ari. *Spoilsmen and Reformers: The Berkeley Series in American History*. Berkeley, Calif.: Rand McNally, 1964.

Katope, Christopher G., and Zolbrod, Paul G. *Beyond Berkeley*. New York: Harper & Row, 1966.

Kelman, Steven. *Push Comes to Shove: The Escalation of Student Protest*. Boston: Houghton Mifflin, 1970.

Keogh, James. *President Nixon and the Press*. New York: Funk & Wagnalls, 1972.

Leuchtenberg, William B. *A Troubled Feast: American Society Since 1945*. Boston: Little, Brown and Co., 1973.

Maddox, Robert. *The New Left and the Origins of the Cold War*. Princeton, N.J.: Princeton University Press, 1972.

Mailer, Norman. *"The White Negro": Advertisements for Myself*. New York: G. P. Putnam, 1959.

Malone, Dumas, and Rauch, Basil. *America and World Leadership, 1940-1965*. New York: Appleton-Century-Crofts, 1965.

McCarthy, Eugene J. *Frontiers in American Democracy*. New York: World Publishing Company, 1960.

Michener, James A. *The Quality of Life*. New York: J. B. Lippincott, 1970.

Minor, Dale. *The Information War*. New York: Hawthorn Books, 1970.

O'Neill, William. *American Society Since 1945*. New York: Quadrangle, 1969.

Perkins, Dexter. *The Monroe Doctrine, 1823-1826*. Cambridge, Mass.: Harvard University Press, 1927.

Ponsonby, Arthur. *Casual Observations*. London: G. Allen & Unwin Ltd., 1930.

Russell, Francis. *Tragedy in Dedham: The Story of the Sacco-Vanzetti Case*. New York: Random House, 1971.

Scammon, Richard M., and Wattenberg, Ben J. *The Real Majority: An Extraordinary Examination of the American Electorate*. New York: Coward-McCann, 1970.

Shirer, William L. *The Collapse of the Third Republic*. New York: Simon and Schuster, 1969.

Stearns, Gerald E. *Broken Image: Foreign Critiques of America*. New York: Random House, 1972.

Sullivan, Mark. *Our Times: Pre-War America, 1900-1925*. Chautauqua, N.Y.: The Chautauqua Press, 1931.

Tenbroek, Jacobus, and Matson, Floyd W. *Prejudice, War and the Constitution*. Berkeley: University of California, 1954.

Teodori, Massimo. Ed. *The New Left: A Documentary History*. New York: The Bobbs-Merrill Company, 1969.

Wells, H. G. *The Future in America*. New York: Harper & Brothers, 1906.

Williams, T. Harry; Current, Richard; and Friedel, Frank. *A History of the United States*. New York: A. A. Knopf, 1964.

Young, Alfred E., Ed. *Dissent: Explorations in the History of American Radicalism.* DeKalb, Ill.: Northern Illinois University Press, 1968.

Zinn, Howard. *SNCC: The New Abolitionists.* New York: Knopf, 1965.

Overground or Established Newspapers

Chicago Tribune
International Herald-Tribune
Manchester Guardian
New York Times
Peoria Journal-Star
Wall Street Journal

Underground and Campus or Off-campus Newspapers

Avatar (Boston)
Berkeley Barb
Blood Echoes: The Collected Artist's Worksheet (Detroit)
Buddhist Oracle (Cleveland)
Buffalo Chips (Omaha)
Candle (Ann Arbor)
Connections (Madison)
Dallas Notes
Distant Drummer (Philadelphia)
East Village Other (New York)
Fifth Estate (Detroit)
Free Student (Los Angeles)
Georgia Straight (Vancouver)
Haight-Ashbury Tribune (also *Free-Press*)
International Times (London)
Militant (London)
Nashville Breakdown
New Left Notes (Chicago)
New York High School Free Press
Off Our Backs (Washington, D.C.)
Paper (Mendocino, Calif.)
Rag (Austin, Texas)
Red Eye (San Jose, Calif.)
Red Mole (London)
Red Notes (London)
Resist (Palo Alto, Calif.)
Resurrection (Tucson, Ariz.)
Rising Up Angry (Chicago)
Rolling Stone (New York)
Roosevelt Torch (Chicago)
Sanity (Toronto and Montreal)
Space City (Houston)
Trumpet (Goleta, Calif.)
Vocations For Social Change (Canyon, Calif.)

Vortex (Lawrence, Kan.)
Western Illinois Courier: sometimes *The Courier* (Macomb, Ill.)

Weeklies, Magazines, Periodicals

Alternative
Atlantic Monthly
AAUP Bulletin
Appleton's Magazine
Common Sense
Chicago Tribune Sunday Magazine
Christian Crusade
Congressional Record
Edinburgh Review (1820)
Encounter
Harper's Weekly (1857)
Journal of Popular Culture
Knox Now, a publication of Knox College, Galesburg, Illinois
Life
Look
National Observer
New Republic
Newsweek
New York Times Magazine
Scientific American
Time
Saturday Review
Southern Illinois University News to Alumni
U.S. News and World Report

Special Articles in Periodicals and Newspapers

Adelson, Alan. "Too Big to Fight." *Saturday Review*, 14 March 1970.
Berger, Peter L. and Brigitte. "The Blueing of America." *New Republic*, 3 April 1971.
Carter, John Franklin. "The Wild Young People." *Atlantic Monthly*, September 1920.
Chew, Peter. "Black History and Black Mythology." *American Heritage*, August 1969.
Commager, Henry Steele. "Is Freedom Dying in America?" *Look*, 14 July 1970.
Conquest, Robert. "The American Psychodrama Called Everyone Hates Us." *New York Times Magazine*, 10 May 1970.
Cousins, Norman. "The Intermediate Battlefield." *Saturday Review*, 8 November 1969.
Epstein, Edward J. "The Panthers and the Police: A Pattern of Genocide?" *New Yorker*, 4 January 1971.
Etzioni, Amitai. "Lunch with 3 Prospective Bombers." *Wall Street Journal*, 27 October 1970.

211

Gitlin, Todd. "The Dynamics of the New Left." *Motive*, November 1970.

Goodwin, Richard. "Sources of Public Unhappiness." *New Yorker*, 4 January 1969.

Gorky, Maxim. "The City of Mammon." *Appleton's Magazine*, No. 8, 1906.

"How to Wreck a National Park." *Look*, 16 June 1970.

Hyman, Sidney. "The Failure of the Eisenhower Presidency." *The Progressive*, May 1960.

Jermann, Thomas. "It's Time to Defuse Population Explosionists." *National Observer*, 27 July 1970.

"Joe Kelly Has Reached His Breaking Point." *New York Times Magazine*, 28 June 1970.

Keniston, Kenneth. "Morality, Violence and Student Protest." *Motive*, March 1970.

Kunen, James. "The Rebels of '70." *New York Times Magazine*, 28 October 1973.

McDermott, Walsh. "Air Pollution and Public Health." *Scientific American*, October 1961.

Navasky, Victor. "Notes on Cult." *New York Times Magazine*, 7 March 1966.

Newell, Norman D. "Crises in the History of Life." *Scientific American*, February 1963.

"Priorities for the Seventies." *Saturday Review*, 3 January 1970.

Rechy, John. "No Mañanas for Today's Chicanos." *Saturday Review*, 14 March 1970.

Roberts, Wallace. "No Place to Grow." *Saturday Review*, 21 March 1970.

Roche, John. "On Being an Unfashionable Professor." *New York Times Magazine*, 18 October 1970.

Schanche, Don A. "Panthers Against the Wall." *Atlantic Monthly*, May 1970.

Schrag, Peter. "Is Main Street Still There?" *Saturday Review*, 17 January 1970.

Schrag, Peter. "Out of Place in America." *Saturday Review, 9 May 1970*.

"Suburbia: The New American Plurality." *Time*, 15 March 1971.

Sulzburger, C. L. "Foreign Affairs: The Logic of Destruction." *New York Times*, 10 May 1970.

"The Erosion of Eden." *Saturday Review*, 6 June 1970.

"The Graying of America." *Time*, 17 September 1973.

Todd, Richard. "Voices of Harvard '70." *New York Times Magazine*, 7 June 1970.

Van den Haag, Ernest, "Mead, Another Man's Poison." *Atlantic Monthly*, June 1970.

Waltz, Jon R. "The Burger-Blackmun Court." *New York Times Magazine*, 6 December 1970.

Index

ABC, 106
Abernathy, Rev. Ralph, 138, 139
Adler, Mortimer, 59-60
Affluence, age of, 12
AFL-CIO, 124
Africa Research Movement, 126
"Age of Rubbish, The," 96
Agitprop Information, 169
Agnew, Vice President Spiro, 108, 122
Al Fatah, 165
Alabama, 124; University of, 32
Alaska, 185
Aldridge, John, 72
Aldrin, Buzz, 109-10
Algeria, 165
Alien and Sedition laws, 43
Alioto, Mayor Joseph L., 165
Allen, Charles R., 143
American Association of University Professors, 142
American Broadcasting Company, 158
American Civil War, 46, 149, 158, 171
American Heritage, 67
American Historical Association, 67
American Notes, 44

"American Psychodrama Called Everyone Hates Us, The," 117
American Revolution, 41, 113, 189
American Revolutionary Media, 126
American University, 76
Amherst, Mass., 82
Amherst College, 72, 75
Anarchist Press Movement, 126
Anderson, Maxwell, 68
Anderson, Sherwood, 52
Angola, 171
Ann Arbor, Mich., 35
Apley, George, 135
Appalachia, 111
Argentina, 88
Arkansas, 121; University of, 55, 150
Arno Press, 67
Arthur, President Chester A., 56
Aswan Dam, 184
Atlanta, 24, 115
Atlantic, The, 92, 165
Atlantic Monthly, 47, 50
Attucks, Crispus, 67
Austin, Tex., 130, 134, 168, 182
Avatar (publication), 129, 137, 149

Babbitt, George, 53
Baez, Joan, 70, 76, 110, 111
Baker, Russell, 121, 122
Ball, George, 69
Banfield, Edward, 104
Bank of America, 155
Baraboo, Wis., 84
Bastille, 42
Beard, Charles, 53, 54
Beaujoir, Le Chevalier Felix de, 43
Beers, Samuel, 104
Beethoven, Ludwig van, 83
Beichman, Arnold, 27, 80, 169
Belafonte, Harry, 28
Belgium, 127, 132, 184
Bellow, Saul, 72, 115
Bellows, George, 52
Beloit College, 32, 97
Berger, Brigitte, 18
Berger, Paul L., 18
Berkeley, Calif., 71, 141, 168
Berkeley Barb (publication), 75, 128, 129,
    131, 132, 133, 137, 140, 141, 143-44, 146,
    147, 148, 149
Berle, Adolf, 74
Berlin, 48, 92
Berman, Dr. Edgar, 180
Bernstein, Mr. and Mrs. Leonard, 123,
    154
Berrigan, Father Daniel, 127
Best and the Brightest, The, 121
Bestor, Arthur, 57
Bettelheim, Bruno, 16, 17, 34, 66
"Beverly Hillbillies, The," 15
Bicentennial (national), 189
Bikini atoll, 185
Bilharzia, 181
Birmingham, Mich., 24
Black Moslems, 167
Black Panther (publication), 154
Black Panthers, 72, 79, 80, 93, 116, 119,
    123, 139, 148, 150, 151, 164, 165, 168,
    169, 170, 175
Black Power, 76
Black revolution, 21, 22, 23-24, 76, 167-71,
    174-77
Blackburn College, 101
Boadicea, 172
Bond, Julian, 76
Bonn, 137
Boorstin, Daniel J., 97, 123, 175, 188, 189
Boston, 74, 115, 129, 137, 149; Light Opera
    Company, 147; Massacre, 67; Tea
    Party, 67
Boston University, 95
Bourbons, 73
Boyd, Rev. Malcolm, 139
Boyle, Kay, 49

Bradley University, 176
Brandeis University, 75, 156
Brewster, Kingman, 155
Bridge at Arles, 52
Brigham Young University, 99
British Bomber Command, 74
British Empire, 47
Bronk, Detlev, 59-60
Brooke, Senator Edward W., 152
Brooklyn, 175
Brooklyn College, 150
Brooks, John, 22
Brooks, Van Wyck, 52, 53
Brown, H. Rap, 170
Brown University, 75
Bruce, Lenny, 23, 147
Bryan, William Jennings, 47, 53
Bryce, Lord James, 45, 46, 52, 145
Buckley, Senator James L., 161
Buckley, William, 99
Buddhist Oracle, The (publication), 131
Buenos Aires, 129
Buffalo, N.Y., 91
Buffalo Chips (publication), 129
Bundy, McGeorge, 121
Bunker, Archie, 25, 157, 158
Bunker, Ellsworth, 74
Burger, Chief Justice Warren, 162
Burke, Edmund, 44
Burnett, Carol, 180
Burns, Robert, 97
Burschenschaften crusades, 17
"But Britain Did Not Die at Yorktown,"
    121
Byron, George Gordon, Lord, 44

Caesar, Julius, 165
California, 20, 24, 70, 72, 89-91, 98, 132,
    134, 137, 138, 140, 148, 153, 170, 179,
    185
California, University of, 64, 98; at Berke-
    ley, 29-30, 33, 70, 71, 73, 75, 90, 91, 98,
    141, 150; Los Angeles, 101; San Diego,
    98; Santa Barbara, 155
Call, Harold, 60
Calvert, Gregory, 76
Cambodia, 72, 79, 82, 84, 93, 111, 112, 113,
    121, 122, 130, 150, 151-52, 153, 156, 178
Cambridge, Mass., 115
Canada, 27-29, 31, 35, 73, 88, 118, 126, 127,
    129, 146
Canadian Press Service, 126
Candle (publication), 35
Carmichael, Stokely, 164, 165, 166-67,
    171
Carson, Rachel, 177
Carter, John Franklin, 50-51
Castro, Fidel, 28, 59, 72, 73, 93, 128

214

Casual Observations, 51
Cather, Willa, 52
Catholic Radical (publication), 127
CBS, 67, 68, 108, 119, 167
Champlain, Lake, 178
Charles II, 38
Charleston, 179
Chase, Stuart, 50
Chavez, Cesar, 123, 183
Chessman, Carol, 59
Chevron International Media, 126
Chew, Peter, 67
Chiaromonte, Nicola, 107
Chicago, 24, 52, 59, 74, 79, 109, 118, 124,
  127, 129, 132, 149, 155, 158, 159, 165,
  168, 169, 179, 180, 181
Chicago, University of, 16, 92
Chicago Daily News, 157
Chicago Tribune, 54, 57, 125
China, 47; People's Republic of, 31, 38,
  123, 128, 132, 139
China News Service, 126
Chrysler Corporation, 155
Church of the Resurrection, 167
CIA, 135, 154, 167
Cicero, Ill., 24
Cincinnati, 179
Civil rights, 163, 164, 165, 166, 174
Civil War, U.S. *See* American Civil War
Claiborne, Robert, 175-76
Clark, Lord Kenneth, 63
Clark, Ramsey, 76
Cleaver, Eldridge, 165
Clemens, Diane Shaver, 68
Cleveland, 175
Cleveland Plain Dealer, 152
Clifford, Clark, 69
Climate, Man and History, 175-76
Cobden, Richard, 43
Cohan, George M., 157
Cold War, 68
Collapse of the Third Republic, The, 49
College Park, S.C., 179
College Press Service, 126
Colorado River, 185
Columbia River, 186
Columbia Spectator, 84
Columbia University, 70, 101; Malcolm
  X Liberation Center, 176
Columbus, Ohio, 155
Commager, Henry Steele, 72, 114
Commercial Associated Network
  (Great Britain), 60
Committee to Defend America by Aid-
  ing the Allies, 54-55
Common Cause, 114
Commoner, Barry, 177
"Concentration Camps, U.S.A.," 143

Connecticut, 24, 79; River, 186
Connections (publication), 36
Conquest, Robert, 117
Constitution, United States, 154
Cooper, Senator John Sherman, 151-52
Copernicus, 32
Copland, Aaron, 52
Cornell University, 71, 176
Cotton Bowl, 115
Counterpoint (publication), 127
Cousins, Norman, 60, 111-12
Crèvecoeur, Michel G.J. de, 43
Cuba, 28, 59, 61, 62, 73, 128, 132
"Culture Bubbles to the Surface in Chi-
  cago," 159
Cummings, E.E., 49
Czechoslovakia, 96

Dachau, 84
Daily Cardinal (publication), 140
Daley, Mayor Richard J., 124, 165
Dallas, 69, 144
Dane County (Wis.) Selective Service
  office, 84
Daniels, Jonathan, 52
Darwin, Charles, 177
David, Jacques L., 136
Davidson, Carl, 71, 75
Davis, Lt. Gen. Benjamin, 175
Davy, Sir Humphry, 44
DDT, 177, 178, 186
Declaration of Independence, 113
Defense, Department of, 57, 104
DeFunis, ——, 177
DeFunis *v.* Odegaard, 177
Delacroix, Ferdinand V.E., 136
Dellinger, Dave, 71, 150-51, 168
Dellums, Ron, 168
Denver, 155
DePauw University, 150
Des Moines, Iowa, 108
Detroit, 23-24, 38-39, 74, 129, 144, 158
Deutscher, Isaac, 71
Devlin, Bernadette, 130, 173
Dickens, Charles, 44-45
Dirksen, Senator Everett M., 77
Dohrn, Bernadine, 171
Dominican Republic, 73, 74
Donora, Pa., 184
"Dooley, Mr.," 48
Door to Liberation (publication), 125
Dos Passos, John, 49, 110
Douglas, Stephen A., 81
Downs, Hugh, 115
Dulles, John Foster, 54
Duncan, Isadora, 49
Dunne, Finley Peter, 48, 107, 124
"Dynamics of the New Left, The," 170

East Village Other (publication), 36, 37, 76, 147
"Eastern Establishment," 104, 108, 121
Ecology crusade, 177-87
Educational expansion, 22, 25-27, 88
Educational Testing Service, 32
Educational Wastelands, 57
Edwards, Jonathan, 41
Egypt, 175-76, 184
Ehrlich, Paul, 177
Eisenhower, President Dwight D., 20, 21, 22, 27, 55, 56-57, 58, 60, 61, 62, 63, 106, 128, 145, 184
Eliot, T.S., 51, 52
Ellsberg, Daniel, 122
Emerson, Ralph Waldo, 46-47
Emory University, 91
Encounter (British magazine), 91-92
England. *See* Great Britain
Enlightenment, the, 18
Epstein, Edward J., 80, 81, 116
Epstein, Joseph, 57
Erie, Lake, 178
Ervin, Senator Sam, 124
Essex, University of, 72
Etzioni, Amitai, 84-85
Evans, Rowland, 98
Evanston, Ill., 100, 159

Fair Play for Cuba Committee, 59
Fairlie, Henry, 123
Farmer, James, 148
Fateh (Lebanese publication), 127
Faulkner, William, 109
FBI. *See* Federal Bureau of Investigation
Federal Bureau of Investigation, 29, 75, 143, 147
Federalists, 43
Feiffer, Jules, 60
Feminist movement, 171-74
Feuer, Lewis, 161
Fifth Estate, The (publication), 74-75, 144, 146
Fink, Hans, 95
Finland, 54
First National City Bank of New York, 135
First Tuesday (program), 108-09
Fitch, Robert, 59-60
Fitzgerald, F. Scott, 49, 51, 52
Fleming, D.F., 68
Fleming, Ian, 146
Fleming, Robben, 66
Flexner Report, 57
Florida, 31
Flumenbaum, Martin, 84
Flynn, Elizabeth Gurley, 173
Fordham University, 94
Foremost Dairies, 135

Forman, George, 167
Fort Lauderdale, Fla., 31
Fort Worth, Tex., 109
Fortas, Abe, 74
Fountainhead, The, 122
Fox, Charles James, 44
France, 31, 42, 43, 47, 48-49, 52, 73, 88, 140, 178
Franklin, Benjamin, 44
Fraser, George, 119
Free Ranger Intertribal News Service, 126
Free Ranger News Service, 126
Free Student (publication), 38
Freeman, Roger A., 100
French Revolution, 42-43, 83
Froines, John, 80
Fuchs, Klaus, 55
Fulbright, Senator J.W., 55, 121, 122
Future in America, 45

Galbraith, John Kenneth, 60, 89, 104
Galesburg, Ill., 81
Gallagher, Dr. Buell, 91
Gandhi, Indira, 172
Gardner, John W., 114, 121, 122, 124
Garfield, President James, 131, 132
Garrison, James, 144
Garson, Barbara, 147
Gary, Ind., 23, 159
Gary, Romain, 123
Gay Lib, 155
General Electric Company, 134
General Motors Corporation, 155
George III, 73
Georgia, 138; University of, 115
Georgia Straight (Canadian publication), 125, 127, 130, 140-41
Germany, 49, 132, 137, 138; West, 31, 74, 87, 88, 127, 137
Gershwin, George, 52
Gettysburg Address, 83
Gilbert and Sullivan, 12
Ginsberg, Allen, 143
Gitlin, Tod, 170
Glazer, Prof. Nathan, 93
Godwin, Edwin Lawrence, 47
Goethe, Johann Wolfgang von, 17, 38, 72
Goldwater, Senator Barry, 17, 146, 185-86
Goodman, Paul, 18, 94
Goodwin, Richard, 120
Gorky, Maxim, 46
Gould, Dr. Samuel B., 102, 128
Graduate, The, 33
Grand Canyon, 185
Great Britain, 31, 43, 48, 49, 52, 54, 60, 80, 87, 88, 122, 126, 127, 137, 166, 169, 178, 184, 185

Great Falls, Mont., 160
Great Fear, 42
Greeley, Andrew M., 105
Green, Philip, 116
Green, Representative Edith, 95
Greene, Felix, 75
Greening of America, 17, 18-19
Greening of America, The, 118
Greenwich Village, 115
Gregory, Dick, 37, 74, 81, 150
Grey, Earl, 41
Grimke, Angelina, 173
Gross, Mason, 93
Gruening, Senator Ernest, 71
Grund, F.J., 43
Guardian (publication), 127
Guatamala, 73
Guevara, Che, 83, 165
Guggenheim, Mrs. Randolph, 123
Guns of August, The, 145

Hacker, Andrew, 97
Haight-Ashbury Tribune, 147
Haiti, 73, 149
Halberstam, David, 121
Hallett, Douglas, 95
Halley's Comet, 41
Hamill, Pete, 153
Hamilton, Alexander, 42, 47
Hampton, Fred, 80, 112
Handlin, Oscar, 67
Hanoi, 134
Harding, Vincent, 167-68
Harlem, 167
Harper's Magazine, 35
Harper's Weekly, 47
Harriman, Averell, 69
Harriman, Roland, 74
Harris, Louis, 24
Harris, Mrs. Comanche, 123, 124
Harris, Senator Fred R., 123, 152
Hartford, Conn., 130
Harvard Crimson, 83
Harvard University, 27, 33, 46, 58, 65, 66, 76, 85, 86, 89, 91, 93, 96, 98, 104
Hassam, Childe, 52
Hatfield, Senator Mark, 115, 152
"Have the News Media Become too Big to Fight," 109
Hawaii, 179
Hayakawa, S.I., 66, 92, 95
Hayden, Tom, 28, 79, 140
Health, Education and Welfare, Department of, 57, 103, 179
Hechinger, Fred, 71, 118-20, 142
Hedonism, 30-31, 48, 49
Hegel, Georg W.F., 38
Heller, Joseph, 64
Hemingway, Ernest, 49, 51, 52, 64

Hendrix, Jimi, 131
Henry, Patrick, 113
Herblock, 61
Hesburgh, Father Theodore, 99-100, 115
Hesse, Herman, 64
Hickel, Walter J., 113, 179
High Wycombe, England, 74
Hirschman, Martin, 80, 111
Hiss, Alger, 55, 60
Hitler, Adolf, 55, 132, 138, 149-50, 154
Hobart College, 150
Hoffer, Eric, 176
Hoffman, Abbie, 37
Hofstadter, Richard, 35, 36, 37, 77, 82, 96, 106, 110, 111, 129, 131, 132, 133, 134, 136, 166, 167
Holland, 127, 132, 185
Hollings, Senator Ernest F., 115
Hollywood, 60, 177
Holmes, Oliver Wendell, 172
"Honor America Day," 160
Hook, Sidney, 104, 123
Hoover, J. Edgar, 149
Hoover, President Herbert, 53-54
Hoover Institution on War, Revolution, and Peace, 100
Horowitz, David, 68
Horse, Perry, 123
Houston, 79, 112, 116, 134, 139, 140, 141, 181
How Green Was My Valley, 177
Howard University, 75
Howe, Irving, 120-21
Hudson River, 186
Hue massacre, 120, 133-34
Huggins, Erika, 174
Humphrey, Senator Hubert, 61, 97, 105, 108, 153
Huntley, Chet, 162
Hutchins, Robert M., 60
Hyman, Sidney, 106

IBM Corporation, 155
"I Can Hear It Now," 68
Illinois, 32, 44, 81, 96, 100, 101, 127, 179; Joint House-Senate Committee on Campus Unrest, 93; National Guard, 135
Illinois, University of, 101, 159, 161; Champaign-Urbana, 84; Chicago Circle Campus, 93
Immigration, 87-88, 123
Immigration and Naturalization Service, 170
"In the Nation: Further into the Quagmire," 113
Independent Socialist Club, 70
India, 38, 86, 134
Indiana, 62, 115

Indochina, 153
Indonesia, 135, 170
Institute of the Black World, 167-68
Intellectual-media community, 103-24
Intergalactic World Brain, 126
International Times (British publication), 137
Iola, Kan., 183
Iowa, 101, 108, 158, 160
Iranian Students Association, 140
Ireland, 43, 62, 127, 169, 176
"Is Freedom Dying in America?", 114
It (British publication), 125, 127
It Can't Happen Here, 54
Italian-American Unity Day, 175
Italy, 88
Ithaca, N.Y., 176

Jackson, President Andrew, 30, 131, 132
Jackson State College, 82, 84, 138, 152, 155
Jamestown, Va., 166
Japan, 20, 88, 116
Javits, Senator Jacob, 124, 152
Jefferson, Thomas, 42-43, 44, 113
Jensen, ——, 174
Jeremiads, 47
Jewish Defense League, 175
John Birch Society, 17
John Brown Society, 134, 174
John J. Pershing College, 101
Johns Hopkins University, 101
Johnson, Mrs. Lyndon B., 149
Johnson, President Andrew, 56
Johnson, President Lyndon B., 17, 21, 23, 27, 69, 73, 74, 75, 76, 77, 103, 104, 105, 126, 133, 137, 144, 146-49, 156
Jones, "Mother," 173
Jones, Penn, 144
Joplin, Janis, 131
Journey's End, 49
Joyce, James, 49, 64
"Juli," 148
Justice, Department of, 118

Kael, Pauline, 15
Kansas, 130
Keats, John, 112
Kelman, Stephen, 66
Kemble, Charles, 44
Keniston, Kenneth, 77
Kennedy, Mrs. Jacqueline, 75
Kennedy, President John F., 12, 21, 22, 23, 27-28, 33, 35, 37, 59, 60-61, 62, 63, 69, 75, 94, 104, 107-08, 121, 129, 131, 132, 143-44, 145-46, 154, 189
Kennedy, Senator Robert F., 12, 33, 69, 77, 94, 144

Kennedy, Senator Edward M., 66, 76, 124
Kent State University, 26, 66, 79, 82, 84, 85, 138, 141, 150, 152, 153, 155, 159, 189
Kentucky, 152, 180; University of, 150
Kentucky Lake, 186
Kerr, Clark, 90
Khan, Genghis, 165
King, Martin Luther, 12, 164, 165
Kirk, Grayson, 70
Kissinger, Henry, 133
Kitt, Eartha, 133
Kneeland, Douglas, 82, 139, 156
Knox College, 81, 101
Kolko, Gabriel, 68
Korean War, 27, 35
Kraft, Joseph, 159
Kristol, Irving, 104
Ku Klux Klan, 17, 139, 175
Kunstler, William M., 138-39

LaFarge, Rev. John, 59-60
Lakeland College, 101
Land, Mark, 74-75, 143-44
Latin America, 20, 76
Latin Revolutionary News Service, 126
Lawrence, David, 89, 107, 146
Lawrence, Kan., 79, 128, 136, 156, 169, 183
Leary, Timothy, 38
Lebanon, 127
Lenin, Nikolai, 78
Leninism, 80
Leonard, Daniel, 42
Leuchtenburg, William E., 15, 16, 17-18
Lewis, Anthony, 112, 121, 122, 153
Lewis, Lloyd, 52
Lewis, Sinclair, 49, 52, 53, 54
Liberation News Service, 126, 137, 147, 149, 171
Liberia, 108-09
Libya, 127
Lincoln, President Abraham, 81, 83, 131, 165
Lindsay, Mayor John V., 113-14
Linkletter, Art, 149
Lippmann, Walter, 47-48, 59, 62, 107
Lipset, Martin, 86
Lisagor, Peter, 157
Lister, Baron Joseph, 172
Llewellyn, Richard, 177
London, 38, 80, 127, 129, 133, 137, 167, 169, 184
London Times, 43, 140, 169
Long Island, N.Y., 175, 179
Long Island University, 94
Look (magazine), 114-15, 179
Los Angeles, 24, 38, 109, 129, 148, 184

218

Los Angeles Free Press, 127, 148
Lowell, James Russell, 47, 189
Lowell, Robert, 23
Lubell, Samuel, 119, 174-75
"Lunch With Three Prospective Bombers,"
84-85
Lynd, Staughton, 71
Lysistrata, 173

MacBird, 143, 147
McCarthy, Eugene, 19, 105
McCarthy, Senator Joseph R., 85
McCarthyism, 35, 37, 56, 98
McClellan, Senator John L., 165
McCord, James W., Jr., 69-70
McCormick, Robert R., 54
McGill, William J., 101
McGovern, Senator George, 115, 119
McGrory, Mary, 156
MacIntyre, Prof. Alistair, 72
McKinley, President William, 131, 132
McReynolds, David, 118
Maddox, Robert, 68-69
Madison, Wis., 36, 84, 99
Mafia, 94, 144
Maginot Line, 132
Mailer, Norman, 22, 23, 58, 60, 71, 106-
07, 154, 162
Malcolm X, 167
Male Animal, The, 68
Malthus, Thomas Robert, 44
Manchester Guardian, 16-17, 121-22,
140, 169
Manhattan College, 73
Mao Tse-tung, 93
Maoism, 165
Marcuse, Herbert, 64
Marilyn, 154
Marin, John, 52
Marryat, Captain Frederick, 43
Marshall, Justice Thurgood, 162
Martineau, Harriet, 43
Marx, Karl, 38, 41, 165
Marxism, 80, 105
Mason City, Iowa, 157
Massachusetts, 49, 122, 124; University
of, 76
Massachusetts Institute of Technology,
101, 104, 109
Masters, Edgar Lee, 52
Mathews, Dr. David, 32-33
Mattachine Society of the United States,
60
Mead, Margaret, 30, 33
Meany, George, 124
Meiklejohn, Alexander, 90
Meir, Golda, 172
Memphis, 165

Mencken, H.L., 52, 190
Mendocino, Calif., 135
Metcalf, Senator Lee, 152
Metternich, Prince, 43
Meuse Valley, Belgium, 184
Meyner, Governor Robert B., 61
Michael X, 137
Michener, James, 123
Michigan, 35, 174
Michigan, Lake, 185, 187
Michigan, University of, 66, 70; Survey
Research Center, 174
Michigan Daily, The, 80, 111
Michigan Research Center, 119
Middle America, 99, 152, 156-62, 175, 176
Middle East, 121, 176
Midwestern College, 101
Militant, The (British publication), 133,
167
Millay, Edna St. Vincent, 68
Mills, Kenneth, 93
Milwaukee, 127
Minamata, Japan, 179
Minnesota, 25, 183
Minutemen, 170
Miss America contest, 158
Mississippi River, 179
Missouri, 39; University of, 55, 101
Mr. Sammler's Planet, 72
Modigliani, 49
Montana, 152, 160
Montevideo, 129
Moore, Thomas, 43, 44
Morgan, Robin, 172-73
Morton, Frederic, 82
Mother Earth News (publication), 135-36
Mothers for Peace, 140
Motive (publication), 77, 170, 182
Movement, the, 16-39, 71-86, 89-102
Moynihan, Daniel Patrick, 78, 94, 104,
174
Muller, Herbert, 59-60
Mungo, Frank, 77
Munich, 137
Murrow, Edward R., 68
Muskie, Senator Edmund S., 76, 138
Muste, A.J., 28
My Lai massacre, 17, 74

NAACP, 67, 157
NASA, 109
Nashville, 182
Nashville Breakdown (publication), 133,
139, 167
Nation, The, 47, 52
National Air Pollution Control, 179
National Assessment of Education Pro-
gress, 32

National Committee for a Sane Nuclear Policy, 59
National Experience, The, 19
National Observer, 109, 110, 179, 180, 185
National Sugar Refining Company, 74
NBC, 108-09, 115, 162
Nebraska, 101
Nevins, Allan, 58-59
New Canaan, Conn., 24
New Deal, 52, 53, 54, 74
New Delhi, 86
New Haven, Conn., 79, 92, 93, 150, 151, 155, 168
New Industrial State, The, 89
New Jersey, 175
New Left, 28, 76, 78, 122
New Left and the Origins of the Cold War, The, 68-69
New Left Notes (publication), 74
New Orleans, 115, 144
New School (New York City), 94
New York, 78, 83, 91, 127, 161, 175
New York, City College of, 34, 91
New York, State University of, 102, 128; at Stony Brook, 83
New York City, 18-19, 24, 46, 68, 83, 93, 94, 108, 109, 115, 120, 124, 129, 135, 150, 155, 158, 159, 167, 174-75, 178, 179, 184
New York High School Free Press, 135
New York Post, 152, 153
New York Review of Books, 105, 110
New York Times, 59, 65, 71, 80, 82, 83, 93, 94-95, 96, 99, 110, 111, 112, 113, 114, 116, 118-20, 121, 122, 125, 139, 140, 142, 151-53, 156, 158, 159, 160, 172-73, 174, 175, 178, 180, 185
New York Times Magazine, 30, 116, 117, 124, 188
New York University (NYU), 83
New Yorker, 15, 80, 116, 118, 120
New Zealand, 74
Newark, N.J., 23
Newell, Norman D., 177-78
Newhouse National News Service, 94
Newsday, 152
Newsweek (magazine), 80, 108, 159-60, 177
Newton, Huey, 118, 164
Newton, Isaac, 32
Niebuhr, Reinhold, 58, 59
Nile River, 181, 184
Nine Lies About America, 27, 80, 169
1984, 180
Nisbet, Robert, 91-92
Nixon, President Richard M., 12-13, 16, 17, 19, 20, 21, 56, 62-63, 69, 77, 80, 94, 104, 106-07, 111, 112, 113, 116, 120, 126,

130, 135, 140, 144, 146, 148, 149-54, 155, 156, 160, 161, 165
NLF, 133
Non-Violent Action, Committee for, 28
North Hempstead, N.Y., 175
Northwestern University, 100-101, 134, 162
Notre Dame, University of, 99, 115
Novak, Robert, 98
NOW (National Organization for Women), 172

Oakland, Calif., 116, 164
O'Brian, John Lord, 114
Ochs, Phil, 76
Off Our Backs (publication), 150, 172, 173, 174
Oglesby, Carl, 69-70, 74
Ohio, 141, 153; Highway Patrol, 153; National Guard, 153, 155; State University, 155
O'Keefe, Georgia, 52
Olsen, Theodore, 28
Omaha, 129
O'Neill, Eugene, 52
Oregon, 95, 152, 185, 186
Organization of American States, 74
Orwell, George, 78, 117, 121, 180
Oskaloosa, Iowa, 160
Osward, Lee Harvey, 59, 75
Oughton, Diana, 155
"Out of Place in America," 158
Oxford University, 35, 49

Paine, Tom, 131
Pakistan, 116
Palo Alto, Calif., 155
Paper, The (publication), 135
"Paranoid Style in American Politics, The," 35
Paris, 42, 48-49, 52
Peace and Freedom Party, 140
Peace Corps, 118
Peace News (British publication), 127
Pearl Harbor, 55
Peking, 119
Pennsylvania State University, 29, 68
People's Party, 140
Peoria, Ill., 176
Pericles, 72
Perry, Ga., 138
Philadelphia, 129
Philby, Kim, 117
Picasso, Pablo, 49
Pittsburgh, 130, 179, 184
Pitzer, Kenneth, 99
Pocket History of the Second World War, 72

Podhoretz, Norman, 78
Poland, 54
Ponsonby, Arthur, 51
Portland, Ore., 129
Potter, David, 16
Potter, Norman, 148
Pound, Ezra, 49, 52
Powell, Adam Clayton, 158
Pravda, 140
Prendergast, Maurice B., 52
Prensa Latina, 126
Presidential Commission on Campus Unrest, 65
President's Commission on Student Violence, 153
Princeton, N.J., 32
Princeton University, 46, 76, 176
Progressive (publication), 106
Progressive Era, 177
Progressive Labor Party, 71
Proxmire, Senator William, 63
Puerto Rico, 128, 132
Pusey, Nathan M., 98

Queens College, 93
Quicksilver Times (publication), 136-37

Rabi, Dr. Isador, 95-96
Rag, The (publication), 130, 134, 168, 182
Rand, Ayn, 122
Rand Corporation, 94
Readers' Digest, 30
Real Majority, The, 160
Reasoner, Harry, 75
Red Eye (publication), 84, 111, 132, 134, 138-39, 140, 147, 150, 181, 183
Red Guard, 78
Red Mole (British publication), 80
Red Notes (British publication), 169
"Reflections on Election Day in New York," 121
Reich, Charles, 118, 121-22
Reichstag, 150
Remarque, Erich Maria, 49
Repression News Service, 130
Requiem for a City, 83
Resist (publication), 77
Reston, James, 82, 114, 116, 121, 152, 161, 162
Resurrection (publication), 128, 134, 142-43, 153-54, 156, 168-69, 169-70, 171, 172, 174
Revel, Jean-Francois, 23, 45, 123, 190
Revolutionary Union, 140
Rhodes, Joseph, 153
Rice University, 141, 171
Richmond Times-Dispatch, 85
Rio Grande, 179

Ripon College, 101
Rising Up Angry (publication), 132-33, 149, 150, 168, 169
Roberts, Wallace, 158
Roche, John, 156
Rockefeller, Nelson A., 77
Rockford College, 32
Rockhurst College, 185
Rolling Stone (publication), 154-55, 156
Romanoffs, 73
Romney, George, 77
Roosevelt, President Franklin D., 52, 107, 131
Roosevelt, President Theodore, 48, 131
Roosevelt Torch, The (publication), 79, 96, 97, 152, 153, 181, 182
Roosevelt University, 79, 82, 85, 97, 155
Rosenberg, Julius and Ethel, 55, 117
Rostow, Walt W., 104
ROTC, 84, 91, 95, 135, 150, 152, 155
Rovere, Richard, 118
Rubin, Jerry, 138, 141, 155, 167
Ruby, Jack, 75
Rudd, Mark, 171
Rudolph, Prof. Frederick, 118
Rush to Judgment, 74-75, 143
Russell, Bertrand, 35
Russell, Francis, 68
Russia, 15, 22, 47, 54, 55, 57, 58, 61, 65, 68, 73, 88, 123, 132, 156, 178, 184
Russo-Nazi Pact of 1940, 54
Rutgers University, 83, 93

Sacco, Nicola, 68, 117, 132-33
Sacco-Vanzetti case, 49-50, 68
Sahl, Mort, 60
Saint Joan, 172
St. John, Jeffrey, 91
St. Lawrence River, 178
St. Louis, 160, 184
St. Norbert College, 150
Saint-Saens, Charles Camille, 45
Salinas, Kan., 159
San Francisco, 20, 27, 59, 90, 148, 155, 165
San Francisco State University, 66, 71, 91, 92, 95
San Jose, Calif., 183
San Jose Liberation Front, 140
San Jose State College, 81, 84, 111, 132, 147, 181
San Quentin (prison), 168
Sandburg, Carl, 11, 52
Sanity (Canadian publication), 27-29, 73-74, 127, 146
Santa Barbara, Calif., 155, 178, 185
Santayana, George, 34, 64, 154
Saturday Review, 109, 120-21, 157-58, 179

Savio, Mario, 30
Scammon, Richard M., 159, 160
Scapegoat, Prof. Sacher V., 117
Schanche, Don A., 165
Schlesinger, Arthur M., Jr., 19, 22, 55
Scholastic Aptitude Test (S.A.T.), 32
Schrag, Peter, 157, 158
Scientific American, 177-78, 184
SCUM (Society for Cutting Up Men), 172
SDS. *See* Students for a Democratic Society
Seale, Bobby, 93, 118, 150, 155, 164, 169
Shaw, Clay, 144
Sheridan, Richard Brinsley, 44
Sherwood, Robert, 54-55
Shirer, William L., 49
Shockley, ___, 174
"60 Years of Quiet at Kent State are Shattered in Era of Protest," 113
Skylab, 122
Smith, Howard K., 75
Smith, M. Brewster, 92
Smith, Senator Margaret Chase, 85, 110, 112
Smith, Sidney, 43-44
SNCC, 164
Socony Mobil Oil Company, 155
Soledad Brothers, 169
Solzhenitsyn, Aleksandr I., 120
Sons and Daughters, 147
Sons of Liberty, 135
South Africa, 127
South Bend, Ind., 115
Southern Illinois University, 26, 66, 84, 85
Space City (publication), 79-80, 112, 116, 134, 135, 139, 141, 142, 149, 171, 181-82
Spark (publication), 127
Spectrum (program), 119-20
Spock, Dr. Benjamin, 71, 110, 111, 168
Sputnik, 57
Stag at Sharkey's, 52
Standard Oil Company, 155
Stanford University, 83, 99, 150, 155
Staten Island Advance, 94
Steffens, Lincoln, 50
Stein, Andrew, 123
Steinbeck, John, 49, 64
Steinzor, Rena, 140
Stevens Point, Wis., 127
Stevenson, Adlai, 23, 56
Stone, I.F., 71, 76, 82
Strickland, William, 168
Student Peace Union, 59
Student Society for Travel to Cuba, 70
Students for a Democratic Society, 28, 70, 76, 181
Suburbia, expansion of, 21, 22, 24-25
Sucrest Company, 74

Sugar Bowl, 115
Sullivan, Mark, 47, 157
Sulzberger, C.L., 178
Supreme Court, United States, 81, 162, 177
Sweden, 87, 88
Switzerland, 74, 88

Taft, Lorado, 52
Tamerlaine, 165
Taoism, 38
Tarbell, Ida, 50
Tennessee, 79
Texas, 180; University of, 91
Third World, 135, 168, 169, 170, 171, 180
Thomas, Dylan, 131
Thomas, Norman, 60
Thoreau, Henry David, 15, 82
Thurber, James, 68
Thurmond, Senator Strom, 97
Tibet, 128
Tibetan Book of the Dead, The, 131
Time (magazine), 24, 80, 108, 109, 159, 177, 179
"To a Louse," 97
Tocqueville, Alexis de, 43
"Today" show, 115
Todd, Richard, 92
Tokyo, 129
Tonkin Gulf Resolution, 76
Toronto, 83; University of, 161
Tralee, Ireland, 43
Trinity College, 75
Trow, Prof. Martin, 33-34
Truman, President Harry S., 55-56, 131, 132
Trumbo, Dalton, 60
Trumpet, The (publication), 72-73, 153
Tubman, Harriet, 173
Tuchmann, Barbara, 145
Tucson, Ariz., 134, 142, 153-54, 156
Tufts University, 75, 76
Tugwell, Rexford G., 53
Tule Lake, Calif., 148
Twain, Mark, 113

Un-American Activities Committee, House, 90
Underground Press Syndicate, 126
United Farm Workers, 140
United Irishman, The (publication), 127
United Kingdom. *See* Great Britain
United Nations, 23
United Native Americans Liberation News Service, 126
U.S. News and World Report, 59, 146, 177
United States Student Press Association, 126
UNS, 167

222